1985 Supplement

to

Finding Birds in Mexico (1968)

by

ERNEST PRESTON EDWARDS

and guest authors:
Robert A. Behrstock
T. Ben Feltner
Barbara MacKinnon de Montes
Jerry Strickling
Nancy Strickling
and major contributors:
George Cobb, Janet Cobb, Aldegundo Garza de León

Published and distributed
by
Ernest P. Edwards
Box AQ
Sweet Briar, VA 24595

Library of Congress Catalog Card Number: 84-81944
ISBN 911882-08-1

Composed and printed at Amherst, Va., U.S.A.
by Central Virginia Printing, Inc.

TABLE OF CONTENTS AND LIST OF MAPS

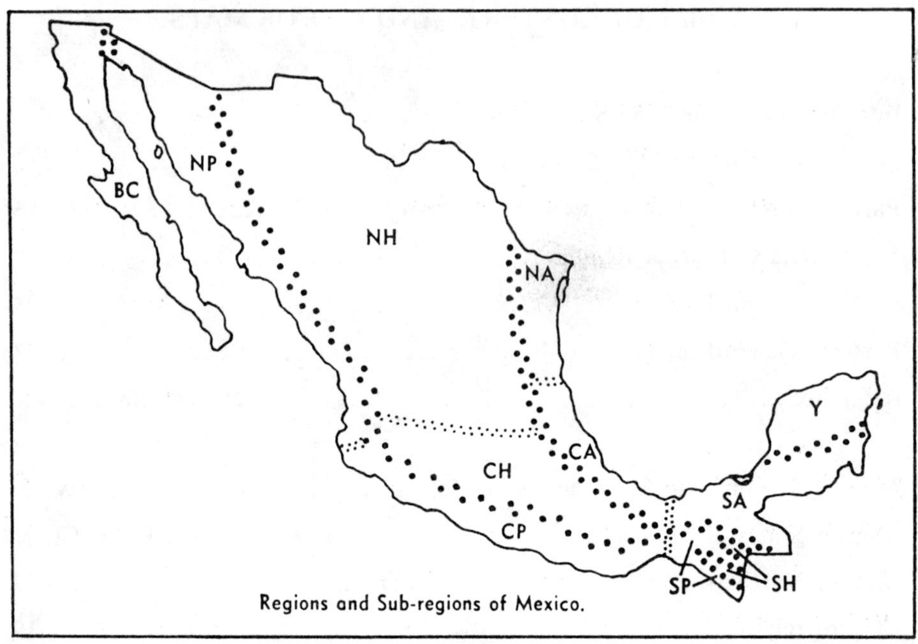

Regions and Sub-regions of Mexico.

States of Mexico

Introduction to the 1985 Supplement

This *1985 Supplement* includes information about more than 90 localities in Mexico, including detailed reports on about a dozen of these for the first time. There are completely re-written reports on many localities, and a considerable amount of new information on most localities. The book includes almost all of the material which was in the *1976 Supplement,* and builds upon it, adding at least an equal amount of new information. Both supplements, of course, have built upon, and added much new or up-dated material to, the 1968 edition of *Finding Birds in Mexico.*

This *1985 Supplement* has been even more of a joint effort than was the *1976 Supplement.* Besides the guest authors and major contributors listed on the title page, to whom I wish to express my deep appreciation, several other persons have been very helpful. Miguel Alvarez del Toro, of Tuxtla Gutiérrez, Chiapas, has informed me of changes which have taken place in the vicinity of that city. Catherine and Charles Truman also sent information about Tuxtla Gutiérrez, and about the Pacific coastal area of the state of Oaxaca. Charles R. Smith, of the Cornell Laboratory of Ornithology, was extremely helpful in providing field data and logistical support on expeditions to Mexico in the late 1970s and early 1980s. His help was indispensable in connection with material on northwestern Mexico, Baja California, northeastern Chiapas, and the Yucatan Peninsula, including Cozumel Island. Many other persons have been helpful in various ways, and to all of these I express my gratitude.

In this *1985 Supplement* you will find a fully alphabetic sequence of localities, following the reprints of the two regional or sub-regional write-ups (NA and Y) which were revised and printed in the *1976 Supplement.* (See FBM, 1968, for all other regional and sub-regional write-ups.) Each locality is separated from the next by a black line in the center of the page. In case a 1984 new account or a 1984 up-date has been written for a particular locality, it is printed first, with the city or town in bold-face capital letters. Next comes the 1976 up-date or 1976 new account for that locality, reprinted verbatim or nearly so from the *1976 Suppl. to FBM.* The heading of such 1976 account is bold-face but not in capital letters, and is indented. In case there is no 1984 new account or 1984 up-date the 1976 new account or 1976 up-date is reprinted and the heading is bold-face but not in capital letters and not indented.

This *1985 Supplement* includes many more maps than did the *1976 Supplement* or the original *Finding Birds in Mexico.* I prepared all the maps, with the help of Winniefred Ferreiro on some of the locality maps, based mostly on sketch maps by Robert Behrstock, George and Janet Cobb, Ben Feltner, Barbara MacKinnon de Montes, Jerry and Nancy Strickling, and Fred Webster, Jr.

Special note about maps - The primary purpose of the maps is to assist you to visualize the situation. Most of them are not drawn to scale, and many do not show all major details, much less the minor ones. Directions are generally only approximate, and curves in the road or trail may not be as shown. Remember that trails, roads, woodland, fields, fences, houses, road signs, and anything else may no longer be as shown. Particularly remember that fences may have been built or taken away; new trails or roads opened up, or old ones blocked off or abandoned; road signs removed or installed; woodlots cut down; marshes drained; dams or housing developments or hotels built; etc.

How to Use this Book

I recommend that anyone planning to travel to Mexico for birding should first read the Introduction in *Finding Birds in Mexico,* 1968, and then the two Introductions in this 1985 Supplement. Then locate the different regions and sub-regions on the map of Mexico, and read all of the sub-regional accounts in *FBM,* 1968 (and the two up-dates, reprinted here from the *1976 Supplement,* and the 1984 Baja California up-date). Then look at the individual maps of the regions in order to familiarize yourself with the names of the localities within each region or sub-region. (Some new localities not shown on the regional maps are: NP - La Capilla del Taxte, Los Mochis, Puerto Vallarta, Topolobampo. CP - Autlán. NH - Cerocahui, Rancho La Estancia.) With this background of information you could determine which regions or sub-regions you would like to (or plan to) visit, and then could pick localities in those regions or sub-regions which would be most appropriate for the type of trip you wish to take and the types of birds you wish to see. Then finally all birders should read about each locality which he or she might plan to visit, beginning, if possible, with the 1968 account, next the 1976 account, and finally the 1984 account. Keep in mind always that there are no guarantees; conditions may change dramatically within a week or a month or a year after a particular account is written, or (in some cases) the situtation may be much like what it was in 1968.

Distances are generally quoted here in kilometers, because more and more travelers are driving rented cars or riding with a driver whose car has an odometer reading in kilometers. To convert to miles, however, is very simple - just multiply kilometers by 0.6 for a very close approximation of miles. For example: 10 km. x 0.6 = about 6 mi; 28 km. x 0.6 = about 17 mi. Note also that many Mexican highways are marked with a numbered post at one-kilometer intervals, showing the distance from some zero point. In some cases you can keep track of distances by checking these posts as you go along, but remember that these could be removed or that distances could change as new roads are constructed.

Precautions

A good rule is to be more cautious about anything and everything than you would be in the United States. Re-read the notes and suggestions in the Introduction to *FBM,* 1968, and in the *1976 Supplement* (partly reprinted in this book), and precautionary notes in *FBM,* 1968, Introduction.

There have always been numerous instances of pocket-picking, and of thefts from vehicles or rooms or camps, and more recently actual assults have become more of a problem. For example, an armed robbery by bandits in the vicinity of Rancho Liebre Barranca was reported (see footnote under La Capilla del Taxte). In some recent years western Mexico has been more dangerous in this regard than other areas, perhaps in relation to the drug trade. The U.S. government *may* put out a travelers' advisory when conditions become particularly serious, therefore be alert for any such advisories, but don't assume the absence of such an advisory means that nothing could happen.* Since the *1976 Supplement* was written I have heard of arrest and official harassment of travelers, ostensibly for smuggling or use of drugs. This can happen without any evidence or proof. (It could happen in the U.S. as well, but our judicial system is much different than that of Mexico.) It's my impression that such things are most likely to happen to young people, and particularly to persons of any age who might appear to be more or less "vagabonding" - that is, camping, riding buses, driving 4-wheel-drive vehicles, hitch-hiking, going into areas where drug plants may be grown, or generally not associated with the more conventional tourist activities and facilities.

There is no guarantee that you can avoid harassment, or even arrest or assault, or accidents, or getting lost, but there are some things you can do to minimize the risk. For one thing, particularly if you have never been to Mexico before, you might consider going on an organized birding tour. Try to pick a reputable group, of course, with experienced and knowledgeable leaders. For several years past the November-December issue of *American Birds* has included a listing of many such tours to all parts of the world. Tour operators also advertise in *Audubon, American Birds,* and *Birding,* and other magazines. Try to find someone who has first-hand knowledge as to the reliability of the operators and leaders.

Whether you choose a tour group or not, we recommend a group of three persons as a minimum for travel in rough terrain or very far from the "beaten path", and can think of almost *no* circumstances in which a person should go out alone. (Even three persons or more would not have prevented the armed robbery at Rancho Liebre, presumably.) We recommend telling a reliable person - the hotel manager, for example - where you are going and approximately when you expect to be back. We recommend hiring a car with *reliable driver,* in many instances, rather than driving your own car or a rented car, but do keep in mind that some drivers take risks which most of us would not. If you drive your own car, put valuables in the trunk before you start the drive, lock the car completely when you leave it (and even while you're in it), and ordinarily park it in a conspicuous place. We recommend asking a reliable person about the possibility of encountering trouble in the vicinity, and at the same time remembering that sometimes persons will say what they think you want to hear. Avoid areas where you think drug plants might be grown.

Of the precautions suggested in the introductions to *FBM*, 1968, and to the *1976 Supplement,* several deserve re-emphasis here:

Overlooks or lookout points: Be *very* careful at *any overlook*. Many are

---

*An article in the *New York Times,* date-lined "Mexico City, Oct. 4" (1984), indicated that the U.S. Embassy in Mexico City was considering whether to recommend the issuance of travel advisories in reference to Highways 2, 15, 57, and an unspecified road in Oaxaca, after "more than three dozen violent incidents involving American tourists here since 1980."

undercut and/or could crumble without warning; you may slip or stumble on stones or loose gravel; do *not trust guard rails or railings,* even if they seem strong and secure - they may be beyond a safe point, may be rotten, may not be firmly set into the ground, and may give way without warning.

Boat trips: Insist on life preservers - "salvavidas". Inspect the boat to be sure it is "seaworthy", and rides high enough in the water so that it will not be swamped in choppy waters; preferably stay out of small "dug-out" canoes, or similar craft, entirely; do not go in a boat that is overcrowded or overloaded - boatmen may take unacceptable risks in this regard; know where the exits are and where the life preservers are and how you get one, on larger boats.

Winding roads: On many mountain roads visibility is poor and traffic moves rapidly, be very careful about turning across traffic, park only where you can pull completely off the road and still have a few feet extra clearance; if you try to bird from the road shoulder stay far from the edge of the traffic lanes, and *don't* try to bird from an ordinary shoulder on a winding mountain road, or on a raised or ditched highway in the flatland, fast-moving trucks often pull out *onto the shoulder* when meeting other vehicles.

Poisonous snakes: Stories of snakes in the tropics are often exaggerated, but the less often you walk on narrow trails through jungle, desert, or rocky mountains, and the more you confine your birding to cleared dirt roads and other wide tracks, the better. The less often you walk at night without good visibility, the better.

Getting lost: Avoid getting out of sight of readily recognizable check points, especially in forest or scrubby desert. Even when walking out in relatively familiar territory, think about how the trail will look as you come back. Be especially careful to watch for side trails (on the way out) which might make confusing Y-forks on the way back; stop and look back at such points to see how the trail will look as you return. Particularly, remember that any map or set of instructions can quickly become outdated.

Other Notes

In some of the accounts you will note that hotels are mentioned, in connection with finding birds. This does not imply one way or another whether the hotel would be suitable for meals or lodging, or even whether it is still in business or not by the time you read this.

With the publication of this *1985 Supplement* I have changed a few names to agree with the 6th Edition of the *AOU Checklist* (and the Checklist has changed a few names back to what I have been using all along). This refers only to the 1984 accounts, not the reprinted 1976 accounts.

1985 Supplement	*1976 Supplement*
Tricolored Heron	Louisiana Heron
Tiger Heron	Tiger Bittern
Greater Pewee	Coues' Flycatcher
Red-legged Honeycreeper	Blue Honeycreeper
Blue-gray Tanager	Blue Tanager

I have also adopted the spelling "Saberwing" instead of "Sabrewing" (contrary to the AOU and to my *Coded Workbook of Birds of the World)* for hummingbirds of the genus *Campylopterus.*

Ernest P. Edwards
November, 1984

Short version of the
Introduction to the *1976 Supplement to Finding Birds in Mexico*

Some of the information contained in the 1968 edition of *Finding Birds in Mexico* has been out-dated by the continuing changes in the landscape of Mexico. These changes have been particularly noticeable in regard to the building of new highways and the improvement and paving of already existing roads, the establishment of many new motels and hotels providing comfortable accommodations, and the clearing of vast tracts of land for farming or cattle-ranching. In addition there have been thousands of relatively small but cumulative encroachments upon the natural environment. But the 1968 edition of *Finding Birds in Mexico* (hereinafter cited as Edwards, 1968, or just 1968) also contains a great amount of information which is still correct and relevant, both the basic material about the geography and ecology of the various regions of the country, and much of the more detailed information about the localities covered. Therefore we have not written a completely revised edition, but instead have prepared a 1976 supplement, an up-to-date appendix to the basic book. This supplement is intended to pin-point the material which is still applicable, and that which is not; and to present additional up-to-date information. This supplement, too, will inevitably, though gradually, become outdated, but both it and Edwards (1968) will be useful for years to come, if used judiciously together.

This supplement has been more of a joint effort than Edwards (1968) in several ways. We have treated two Christmas Count localities in eastern Mexico in great detail, with the help of two "guest co-authors" as follows: El Naranjo (with T. Ben Feltner), and Gómez Farías (with Fred S. Webster, Jr.).

Allan R. Phillips, who has worked carefully and perceptively with Mexican birds in the field and in the museum for many years, has contributed much information and has checked the rough drafts of Parts I, II, and III. Mr. and Mrs. George Cobb have helped with information about western Mexico as well as contributing in a major way to the section on Yucatan, where they have studied birds throughout several years. Ben B. Coffey, Jr., who knows the distribution and vocalizations of Mexican nightjars in detail, has been particularly helpful in regard to the night birds of Mexico. To sum up, I am especially indebted to John C. Arvin, Mr. and Mrs. George Cobb, Mr. and Mrs. Ben B. Coffey, Jr., Victor Emanuel, T. Ben Feltner, Kenneth Kertell, Allan R. Phillips, Peter Scott, and Mr. and Mrs. Fred S. Webster, Jr., for providing information and for checking portions of the manuscript. They are not to be held responsible for any possible errors in this supplement, however, because I have analyzed, summarized, and re-worked their material. Neither can the fact that they helped with the work be construed automatically as an endorsement of the finished supplement. To achieve uniformity I have used bird names which in some cases the above-named persons would not use in their own writings.

We have up-dated the References Section also, and the new material reflects some important developments in the field of periodical literature related to Mexican birds. Firstly, *American Birds* (National Audubon Society) now includes a number of Christmas Bird Counts from Mexico (more than just the two counts which we emphasize in this supplement), effectively indicating much about the occurrence and abundance of species in winter at the localities covered, along with mention of habitats and climatic conditions. This same journal has occasionally included a "Site Guide", a detailed article about bird-finding around a particularly interesting locality, which on at least one occasion has been a Mexican locality.

Secondly, *Birding,* published as a bi-monthly journal by the American Birding Association, frequently contains articles about bird watching in Mexico. These may be in the form of special inserts dealing with a particular area or with a particular species of bird, or in the form of articles dealing with birds of Mexico in some other way.

How To Use This Supplement Along With *Finding Birds In Mexico, 1968*.

The first step is to read this introduction from beginning to end. Then the introduction to Edwards (1968) should be read from beginning to end. All the while the reader should have an up-to-date road map of Mexico at hand, remembering that most of the maps in this supplement and in Edwards (1968) are for general orientation, and that changes will inevitably occur (and remembering also that any map may include inaccuracies). An up-to-date general tourist guidebook is virtually essential as well, both because such a book provides information about accommodations and general procedures not given in this book, and because it might provide information about changes which will have taken place after the writing of this supplement. Travel agencies, publishers of road atlases, bookstores, airlines, oil companies, automobile clubs or the Mexican Government Ministry of Tourism (1976 address: Juárez 92, México 1, D.F.) may be able to provide, or help the prospective traveler to obtain, guidebooks, maps, or other informational material.

The first general statement which follows applies to all of the situations covered in this supplement, while the next two general statements apply to virtually all regions and sub-regions, and virtually all localities, respectively. These statements can be assumed to be part of each locality write-up or each regional or sub-regional write-up, and are not repeated each time.

1. Information presented here should be checked against up-to-date maps, books, pamphlets, recent issues of appropriate journals, and other sources, and verified whenever possible by discussion with persons knowledgeable about the current situation in the locality or area in question.

2. (Regions or sub-regions) Many miles of new major highways and other paved roads have been constructed within this area, greatly increasing the size and coverage of the road network. Many new paved roads now connect various localities which were previously relatively isolated from each other and from the major population centers. Conversion of large tracts of land to agricultural purposes has proceeded relentlessly and has even accelerated recently, along with large lumbering operations in most regions or sub-regions. Smaller disturbances have occurred also, and it is now more difficult than before to find undisturbed patches of woodland or other natural vegetation and easier to find cattle ranches or cornfields or other farmlands.

3. (Most localities) The town or city has grown considerably since 1968 in both population and in area covered by commercial and residential areas with the result that the visitor can expect to have to go farther from the center of town to find favorable bird-watching areas. More congestion can be expected in the business section of town, and more crowded conditions can be expected in sections which once were relatively open residential areas or parks. Specific bird-watching areas mentioned in the discussions in Edwards (1968) may no longer be accessible or even in existence as such, and directions for reaching them may no longer be applicable. Local inquiry is strongly recommended, but information obtained in that way must be judiciously evaluated. In most cases, however, if suitable habitat can be found the appropriate bird lists should still be more or less applicable unless otherwise indicated.

Abbreviations used in the bird lists are as follows: summer (s.), this usually means late spring and early fall as well; winter (w.), this usually means fall and spring as well; transient (t.), generally only a short while in fall and spring; nocturnal (n.).

Spanish accents have generally not been used in a word coupled with an English word, as Yucatan Peninsula, or otherwise used in an English context.

Precautions and General Information

Most of the notes (Edwards, 1968) dealing with possible discomforts and inconveniences of travel in Mexico were contained in the Introduction, while most of those concerning possible hazards were in the various locality write-ups. In working up the present supplement we have deleted most of the cautionary notes from the locality write-ups, expecting the traveler to be alert and perceptive in evaluating each particular situation with the help of the notes below, and to make his or her own judgment as to reasonable and prudent actions, allowing for unforeseen circumstances. Check the Introduction and the locality write-ups (Edwards, 1968) in addition to the notes below.

Outside of the United States much more of the responsibility for safety is placed on the individual. There are fewer institutional procedures to protect the individual from danger or to warn against danger, or to mitigate the effects of untoward occurrences. Although the traveler need not be continually apprehensive or suspicious, it cannot be assumed that customary (in the U.S.A.)

safety measures are being applied. Don't expect warning signs, for example. Local residents, probably because they are accustomed to a situation, will often underestimate, or fail to mention, hazards.

The following list is just as applicable to travel in parts of the United States as in Mexico, but it would be advisable to be more concerned in the latter country about: boat trips (our mention of boat trips is not a recommendation that you take a boat trip); cliffs, precipices, high banks with loose dirt, crumbly river banks, loose rock on steep slopes, weak or broken (or non-existent) guard rails or fences; swimming (or wading, in some cases) especially in unfamiliar waters (well-known resorts *not* excepted, don't take chances); bites of dogs, bats, or other mammals, or of poisonous snakes or spiders (or ticks, fleas, mosquitoes, or centipedes); stings of scorpions (including some kinds of small ones) wasps, bees, or hornets; driving at night or in low visibility; not seeing livestock or people in the road (they may be sitting or lying in the road, or may suddenly come onto the road); unmarked slides or washouts; road shoulders narrow or concealed by vegetation, or both; real flash-floods, especially in desert or semi-desert; deep mud or deep soupy wet sand (in such places as swamps, marshes, stream valleys, or tidal flats); hostile or antagonistic local residents, in some situations, including some celebrations; food additives and other materials, sprays and room vaporizers, of types banned in the U.S.A.; hurricanes; earthquakes; precipitous stairways at archaeological sites; stinging plants; transportation facilities; unsanitary food and water and food service; getting lost; etc.

Some recommended procedures are: Consult a physician about advance immunizations, what to do about bites or stings or other exposure to toxins or disease, and about food, water, and sanitation in general; learn to read signs in Spanish and heed them, but don't assume that everything is normal in the absence of signs; get permission before going on private property, and always close gates, put back barriers, and leave things as they were; check road conditions in advance, particularly dirt or rock roads, and evaluate information judiciously; travel and do field work in a large group of two or more persons. We recommend again that you have an up-to-date, authoritative, general guidebook, and an up-to-date road map.

A further note about pull-offs is in order because we frequently state that the observer should "find a place to pull off and park". The car should be completely off the pavement, a minimum of 8 to 10 feet from the edge of the pavement on the nearest side because huge trucks and buses often meet on very narrow roads and run onto the shoulder somewhat, even in normal traffic on straight roads. Walking along the shoulder is risky - somewhat less so if you are 8 or 10 feet from the pavement. Often there will be much broken glass and sharp metal at wide pull-offs.

Since the 1968 edition was written we have noted that many trailer courts and camp grounds are being advertised. Anyone interested could obtain information from guidebooks which evaluate tourist accomodations. We have not seen any of these facilities. We are not aware of any public camping or trailer facilities comparable to the ones in state parks or national parks in the U.S.A.

Please note we do not attempt to recommend any tourist facilities, and our mention of a hotel or resort or restaurant cannot be construed as a recommendation. In fact, we are not even in the business of *recommending* bird-watching areas - we try to show what the bird-watching potentialities are, and how to find the birds, and what birds to expect.

Changes in Names or Status of Mexican Birds, and Comparisons of Usage of Common Names

The following species have been added to Edwards' list of regularly occurring Mexican birds, since 1968:

Short-tailed Shearwater (name change and status change)	Rock Sandpiper
	Pomarine Jaeger
Laysan Albatross	Long-tailed Jaeger
Cook's Petrel	Ancient Murrelet
Audubon's Shearwater	**Cuvier's Hummingbird**
Mottled Duck	Blue Jay
Rough-legged Hawk	Winter Wren
Chukar	Brown Thrasher
Ring-necked Pheasant	Pine Warbler
Piping Plover	

The following species have been added to the list of accidentals in Mexico, since 1968:

Yellow-billed Loon	Connecticut Warbler
Cape Petrel	Common Grackle
New Zealand Shearwater	**Lineated Heron**
Harcourt's Petrel	(from regular list)
Glaucous Gull	Common Murre
Northern Wheatear	

Some names have been changed in my books from 1968 to 1976 as follows:

Finding Birds in Mexico Edwards, 1968	**Bird-finding Supplement** Edwards, 1976
(Slender-billed Shearwater)	Short-tailed Shearwater
Galapagos Storm Petrel	**Galapagos Petrel**
Great Blue Heron } Great White Heron }	Great Blue Heron
Common Egret	Great Egret
Wood Ibis	Wood Stork
Jabiru	**Jabiru**
Snow Goose } Blue Goose }	Snow Goose
Common Scoter	Black Scoter
Collared Forest Hawk	**Collared Micrastur**
Barred Forest Hawk	**Barred Micrastur**
Pigeon Hawk	Merlin

Sparrow Hawk	American Kestrel
Rufous-bellied Chachalaca } Plain Chachalaca (part)	**West Mexican Chachalaca**
Plain Chachalaca (part)	Plain Chachalaca
Plain Chachalaca (part)	**White-bellied Chachalaca**
Harlequin Quail	Montezuma Quail
Sora Rail	Sora
Oystercatcher	{ Common Oystercatcher { Black Oystercatcher
Thick-billed Plover	Wilson's Plover
Upland Plover	Upland Sandpiper
Cabot's Tern	Sandwich Tern
Noddy Tern	Brown Noddy
Fairy Tern	**White Tern**
Orange-chinned Parakeet	**Tovi Parakeet**
Yellow-cheeked Parrot	**Red-lored Parrot**
Whiskered Owl	Whiskered Screech-Owl
Potoo	**Common Potoo**
Spot-tailed Poor-will	**Pit-sweet**
Jacobin Hummingbird	**White-necked Jacobin**
Red-shafted Flicker } Gilded Flicker } (Yellow-shafted Flicker) }	Common Flicker
Thin-billed Creeper	**Souleyet's Creeper**
Mountain Ovenbird	**Mountain Leaf-gleaner**
Ruddy Ovenbird	**Ruddy Leaf-gleaner**
Buff-throated Ovenbird	**Buff-throated Leaf-gleaner**
Least Ovenbird	**Plain Xenops**
Tawny-throated Ovenbird	**Tawny-throated Leafscraper**
Scaly-throated Ovenbird	**Scaly-throated Leafscraper**
Streaked Cotinga	**Streaked Attila**
Speckled Cotinga	**Speckled Mourner**
Rufous Cotinga	**Rufous Mourner**
Whistling Cotinga	**Rufous Piha**

(The preceding four species have been moved from the Cotinga family to the Flycatcher family.)

Rose-throated Cotinga	Rose-throated Becard
Black-capped Tityra	**Black-crowned Tityra**
Tropical Kingbird	{ Tropical Kingbird { Couch's Kingbird
Kiskadee Flycatcher	Great Kiskadee
Northern Tody-Flycatcher	**Common Tody-Flycatcher**
Traill's Flycatcher	{ Alder Flycatcher { Willow Flycatcher
Ridgway's Swallow } Rough-winged Swallow }	Rough-winged Swallow

Collie's Magpie-Jay **White-throated Magpie-Jay** }	**Magpie-Jay**
Northern Brown Jay **White-tipped Brown Jay** }	**Brown Jay**
Common Bushtit Black-eared Bushtit }	Bushtit
Northern House Wren Brown-throated Wren }	Northern House-Wren
Northern Catbird	Gray Catbird
White Wagtail	White Wagtail
Parula Warbler	Northern Parula
Olive-backed Warbler **Socorro Warbler** }	Tropical Parula
Myrtle Warbler Audubon's Warbler }	Yellow-rumped Warbler
Ovenbird	Ovenbird
Northern Yellowthroat **Chapala Yellowthroat** }	Common Yellowthroat
Red-breasted Warbler	**Red-breasted Chat**
Gray-throated Warbler	**Gray-throated Chat**
Boat-tailed Grackle (part)	Great-tailed Grackle
Baltimore Oriole Bullock's Oriole }	Northern Oriole
Olive-backed Towhee Spotted Towhee **Socorro Towhee** }	Rufous-sided Towhee
Slate-colored Junco Oregon Junco **Guadalupe Junco** Gray-headed Junco }	Dark-eyed Junco
Baird's Junco Mexican Junco **Guatemala Junco** }	Yellow-eyed Junco

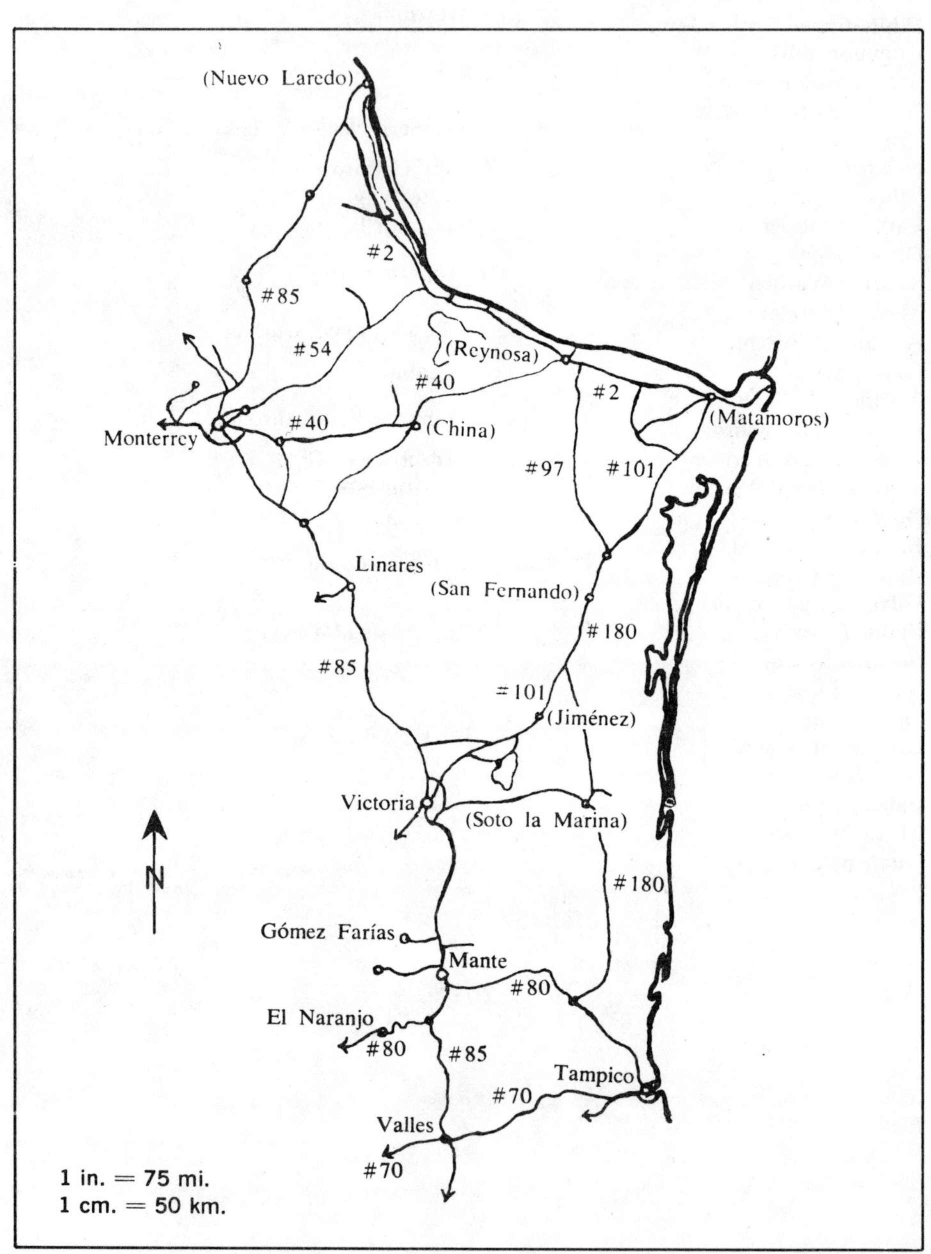
(Nuevo Laredo)
#2
#85
#54
(Reynosa)
#40
#2
#40
(China)
(Matamoros)
Monterrey
#97
#101
Linares
(San Fernando)
#180
#85
#101
(Jiménez)
Victoria
(Soto la Marina)
#180
N
Gómez Farías
Mante
#80
El Naranjo
#80
#85
Tampico
#70
Valles
#70
1 in. = 75 mi.
1 cm. = 50 km.

PART I

NORTHERN ATLANTIC LOWLANDS SUB-REGION

Full revision — 1976

This is a rather small sub-region which is not sharply set apart in its northern half from the Northern Highlands Sub-region. It extends from the United States border (southern Texas) south to the Rio Pánuco (which flows roughly on a line between Valles and Tampico) where it merges with the Central Atlantic Lowlands Sub-region. As a specific, though arbitrary, southern boundary of the NA sub-region we designate highway #70, from Tampico to Valles and on to the western boundary of the region. As noted above it merges very broadly with the Northern Highlands Sub-region in the west and northwest. It extends to the Gulf of Mexico on the east. Its straight-line dimensions are about 250-350 miles north-south, and 100-200 miles east-west, the lengths of its southern and eastern borders being considerably less than those of the northern and western, respectively.

Several paved highways (including a relatively new one from Falcon Dam to Monterrey) lead into the sub-region, mostly in a generally southwesterly direction. These lead into two major highways (#85 and #101) which extend generally southeastward and southwestward respectively, and converge into what was once the only major north-south highway (#85, the Pan-American Highway) at about the center of the sub-region. However, many miles of paved roads have been constructed within this sub-region recently, greatly increasing the size and coverage of the highway network. It is now possible to drive on major roads from Matamoros or Reynosa in the northeast to Tampico in the southeast without going as far west as highway #85. The eastern portion of the sub-region is thus open to vehicular traffic. There are several paved roads leading out of the NA sub-region into the Highlands Region to the west, and at least three of these have been constructed rather recently. A major highway now runs parallel to the Río Grande from Nuevo Laredo to Matamoros and on out to the Gulf Coast, and there are three east-west highways farther south. There are many new paved roads connecting various localities which had been relatively isolated from each other.

The Northern Atlantic Lowlands Sub-region is much the driest of the three Atlantic Lowlands Sub-regions, with some vast semi-desert areas of flatlands or gently rolling terrain in the northern portion, and arid lower mountain slopes at least as far south as Linares. There are extensive areas of mesquite-grassland, with the mesquite or other small trees fairly dense in places, but only a little more moist than the semi-deserts which are covered by low, scrubby, thorny vegetation. There may be pockets of moist habitat, however, where bands of large trees grow along river valleys in otherwise dry country. South of the Río Guayalejo (about 40 miles south of Victoria) luxuriant vegetation (including bald cypress) grows along the river valleys, large areas of rather dense woodland of small to medium-sized trees occur on the plains, and dense forests of tall, broad-leafed, evergreen or semi-evergreen trees grow along the mountain slopes. There are a few pine woodlands. There are a few, small, isolated patches of true cloud forest (luxuriant broad-leafed evergreen forest on cloudy, rainy mountain slopes between 3000 and 4500 feet above sea level). Some extensive palm forests remain in broad valleys, and scattered small palm groves and individual palm trees are numerous in the southeast. Near the coast there are large swamps and marshes, large lagoons, and transitory ponds. Along the coast and the barrier islands are sandy beaches, still relatively difficult to reach. Cattle and horses graze over great expanses of the mesquite-grassland, and goats graze and browse on the vegetation of the semi-desert.

The construction of huge dams and water impoundments, and the extension of irrigation to many thousands of square kilometers of land has transformed agricultural practices in the northern part of this sub-region, with major consequences for people and birds. Vast tracts of mixed grass and shrubs and small trees and low desert or semi-desert vegetation have been cleared for cropland. Whereas cotton and henequen were formerly important crops in this area, much of the recently cleared land in the Mexican portion of the Rio Grande Delta is now devoted to small grains, mostly grain sorghum. Grainfields extend about 70 miles south of the border, from Matamoros to the hill country a few miles north of San Fernando, and in early June this part of highway #101 is crowded with grain trucks and harvesting machinery. In winter the waste grain in flooded fields attracts multitudes of geese, ducks, cranes and other waterbirds and shore birds. At almost any time of year there is enough water in ditches, canals, ponds or flooded fields to attract many species formerly seldom seen in that area. Some very large areas are still devoted to cattle-ranching. On some of these areas imported grass has been planted after removal of native trees, shrubs and grass as noted above.

Farther south corn, sugar cane, and tropical fruits are grown while cattle graze on cleared and planted areas as well as existing mesquite-grassland.

In much of the sub-region the spring weather is dry and increasingly hot until the advent of the rainy season in May when it becomes *slightly* cooler and much more humid. Near the 5000-foot level, which constitutes the boundary line between this sub-region and the Northern Highlands Sub-Region, it is much cooler with much local variation in amount of rainfall. Vegetation in the drier areas is notably greener after the rains. Birds are active and conspicuous in the rainy season. This activity is at a peak in the early morning hours, particularly in the northern portions of the sub-region.

In early autumn the rains slacken and the temperatures gradually drop, until in winter there may be an occasional frost in the north or in the mountains. In very unusual years, there may be a freeze or frost which will denude or even kill some of the broad-leafed evergreen trees in the south. Trees and shrubs in the northern portion of the sub-region lose their leaves seasonally in response to lower temperatures and decreased soil moisture. During the winter months there may be occasional storms called *nortes,* characterized by cold, cloudy, windy weather and usually rain, sometimes lasting several days.

Large numbers of transient birds from the United States and Canada move into the NA sub-region in early autumn, many of them going farther south, but many remaining here throughout the winter. Winter visitant ducks, shore birds and water birds in general are found in the marshes and lagoons along the coast and in the flooded fields of the northeast. Small land birds are common. Many species of warblers and sparrows move about with the local resident species particularly in brushy fields, hedgerows, woodland edge, or open woodland. Only a very few species of breeding birds move out of the sub-region, but there is a considerable amount of short-range movement from higher to lower elevations. A number of species gather into large winter flocks.

Approximately 420 species of birds are known to occur regularly in the Northern Atlantic Lowlands Sub-region, and about two-thirds of these are breeding birds in the sub-region. About sixty percent of these breeding birds are also found in the United States. Some of the breeding birds shared with the United States are principally northern birds breeding only a short distance into Mexico, while many others are predominantly tropical, breeding only a short distance into Texas. Even the Texan, however, and more so the bird watcher from farther north, will find a host of unusual birds in the southern portion of the NA sub-region. As a whole, Mexico has 16 *families* of birds which do *not* occur in the United States, and almost half of these are found in the NA sub-region. The arrival of approximately 140 species of North American birds as transients or winter visitants assures an interesting mixture of arctic, temperate, and tropical birds in winter.

The most frequently observed birds of the Northern Atlantic Lowlands Sub-region, listed here by habitat, are as follows:

Sandy shores, beaches, or nearby ocean:

Black-bellied Plover (w.)	Lesser Yellowlegs (w.)
Spotted Sandpiper (w.)	Dunlin (w.)
Willet	Sanderling (w.)

Ring-billed Gull (w.)	Royal Tern
Laughing Gull	Black Skimmer
Least Tern (s.)	

Lagoons, shallow ponds, mud or sand flats, marshy meadows, marshes, swamps, irrigation canals, ditches and flooded fields:

Least Grebe	Lesser Scaup (w.)
Pied-billed Grebe	Ruddy Duck (w.)
White Pelican (w.)	Sandhill Crane (w.)
Olivaceous Cormorant	Common Gallinule
Anhinga	American Coot
Green Heron	Jacana
Little Blue Heron	Wilson's Plover (w.)
Reddish Egret	Long-billed Curlew (w.)
Great Egret	Lesser Yellowlegs (w.)
Snowy Egret	Long-billed Dowitcher (w.)
Cattle Egret	Common Snipe (w.)
Louisiana Heron	Least Sandpiper (w.)
Wood Stork	Black-necked Stilt
White-faced Ibis	American Avocet
White Ibis	Wilson's Phalarope (w.)
Roseate Spoonbill	Ring-billed Gull (w.)
Canada Goose (w.)	Laughing Gull
White-fronted Goose (w.)	Black Tern (t.)
Snow Goose (w.)	Gull-billed Tern
Black-bellied Tree Duck	Forster's Tern (w.)
Pintail (w.)	Black Skimmer
Gadwall (w.)	Ringed Kingfisher
Green-winged Teal (w.)	Belted Kingfisher (w.)
Blue-winged Teal (w.)	Green Kingfisher
American Wigeon (w.)	Eastern Phoebe (w.)
Shoveler (w.)	Red-winged Blackbird

Partially open country, cultivated fields with nearby hedgerows, grazing land with scattered trees, farmyards, outskirts of villages, and scrubby, dry woodland or shrubland:

Turkey Vulture	Common Bobwhite
Black Vulture	Red-billed Pigeon
White-tailed Kite	Mourning Dove
Harris's Hawk	White-winged Dove
Marsh Hawk (w.)	Inca Dove
Crested Caracara	Common Ground-Dove
American Kestrel (w.)	Yellow-billed Cuckoo

Groove billed Ani	Blue-gray Gnatcatcher
Greater Roadrunner	Loggerhead Shrike (w.)
Pauraque (n.)	White-eyed Vireo
Chip-willow (n.)	Orange-crowned Warbler (w.)
Golden-fronted Woodpecker	Yellow-rumped Warbler (w.)
Eastern Phoebe (w.)	House Sparrow
Vermilion Flycatcher	Red-eyed Cowbird
Scissor-tailed Flycatcher	Great-tailed Grackle
Couch's Kingbird	Brewer's Blackbird (w.)
Tropical Kingbird	Altamira Oriole
Great Kiskadee	Hooded Oriole
White-necked Raven	Eastern Meadowlark
Mexican Crow	Cardinal
Black-crested Titmouse	Collared Seedeater
Cactus Wren	Olive Sparrow
Northern House-Wren (w.)	Lark Bunting (w.)
Long-billed Thrasher	Lark Sparrow (w.)
Curve-billed Thrasher	Lincoln's Sparrow (w.)
Northern Mockingbird	

River-edge woodland, humid forest edge, and scattered remnants of humid forest:

Rufescent Tinamou	**Blue-crowned Motmot**
Olivaceous Cormorant	**Barred Antshrike**
Tiger Bittern	**Masked Tityra**
Muscovy Duck	**Boat-billed Flycatcher**
Roadside Hawk	**Social Flycatcher**
Bat Falcon	Great Kiskadee
Red-billed Pigeon	**Brown Jay**
Green Parakeet	**Spotted-breasted Wren**
Red-crowned Parrot	**Clay-colored Robin**
Red-lored Parrot	Red-eyed Vireo
Squirrel Cuckoo	Red-eyed Cowbird
Ferruginous Pygmy-Owl	**Singing Blackbird**
Buff-bellied Hummingbird	**Yellow-throated Euphonia**
Elegant Trogon	**Black-headed Saltator**
Ringed Kingfisher	Olive Sparrow
Green Kingfisher	

Dense woodland of medium-sized trees, and dense, broad-leafed, ever-green or semi-evergreen forest:

Rufescent Tinamou	Red-billed Pigeon
Singing Quail	White-fronted Dove

Squirrel Cuckoo   **Brown Jay**
Ferruginous Pygmy-Owl   Green Jay
Green Woodpecker   **Spotted-breasted Wren**
Lineated Woodpecker   **Clay-colored Robin**
Flint-billed Woodpecker   **Golden-crowned Warbler**
Laughing Creeper   **Red-crowned Tanager**
Sulphur-bellied Flycatcher (s.) **Jungle Tanager**

Cloud forest:

Rufescent Tinamou   **Spotted-breasted Wren**
Singing Quail   **Blue Mockingbird**
Red-billed Pigeon   **White-throated Robin**
White-fronted Dove   **Clay-colored Robin**
Vaux's Swift   **Brown-backed Solitaire**
Azure-crowned Hummingbird   **Black-headed Thrush**
Cazique Hummingbird   **Peppershrike**
Mexican Trogon   **Spot-breasted Warbler**
Laughing Creeper   Tropical Parula
Spotted-crowned Creeper   Black-headed Oriole
Mexican Cotinga   **Striped Tanager**
Olivaceous Flycatcher   **Hooded Grosbeak**
Coues' Flycatcher   **Rufous-capped Finch**
Green Jay   Olive Sparrow

Winter visitants (w.) in river-edge woodland, lowland forest, and cloud forest:

Spotted Sandpiper   Black-and-white Warbler
Eastern Phoebe   Orange-crowned Warbler
Empidonax sp.   Nashville Warbler
Northern House-Wren   Yellow-rumped Warbler
American Robin   Black-throated Green Warbler
Ruby-crowned Kinglet   Wilson's Warbler
Cedar Waxwing   Lincoln's Sparrow
Solitary Vireo

For information about precautions, and general information, generally omitted in revising these write-ups, refer to the Introduction in this supplement (1976), and the Introduction and locality write-ups in Edwards (1968).

BAJA CALIFORNIA REGION
(1968, p. 1)

1984 up-date

Highway 1, which reached only a few dozens of miles south of Ensenada in 1968, has now been extended all the way to the southern end of the peninsula, where it has joined a road network already in place, reaching the southernmost point in Baja California, Cabo San Lucas. There are numerous branch roads, most of them unpaved, leading away from this main north-south highway.

Although there is a considerable extent of near-coastal grassland and other moderately moist situations in the lower elevations of the northern portion of the peninsula, and some moderately humid woodland in the mountains in the north, most of Highway 1 traverses hundreds of miles of desert or semi-desert. The vegetation in such semi-desert areas is generally low and dense, characterized by several kinds of cactus, ocotillo, *Agave,* and other thorny, shrubby plants, and a few scattered, small thorny trees. There is typically very little grass or other herbaceous ground cover. In some of the occasionally-flooded, usually-dry, stream valleys, and in other slightly moist "pockets", trees and vines are more numerous, and grow to heights of 20 to 30 feet in places. Some hillsides are very rocky, while some flatlands are covered with deep sand. Although average annual rainfall is not great, some individual rainstorms can be torrential, causing flash-floods in valleys and other low-lying areas, sometimes miles from the area where the rain is falling.

Many of the offshore islands, and even some of the peninsula's rocky headlands provide nesting sites for numerous sea birds.

Most of the birds listed for "Semi-desert lowlands and low hillsides" (FBM, 1968, p.3) are to be expected in such areas throughout the peninsula, but some of these are more common in the north, while a few not listed are to be expected in the south. Among these latter are the White-winged Dove, Xantus's Hummingbird, and Pyrrhuloxia. See also new locality accounts for Cabo San Lucas, La Paz, Rancho Buena Vista, and San José del Cabo, in addition to the 1968 account for Ensenada.

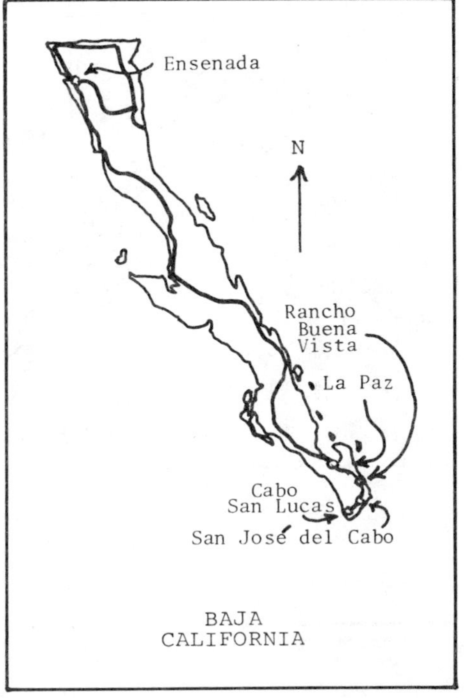

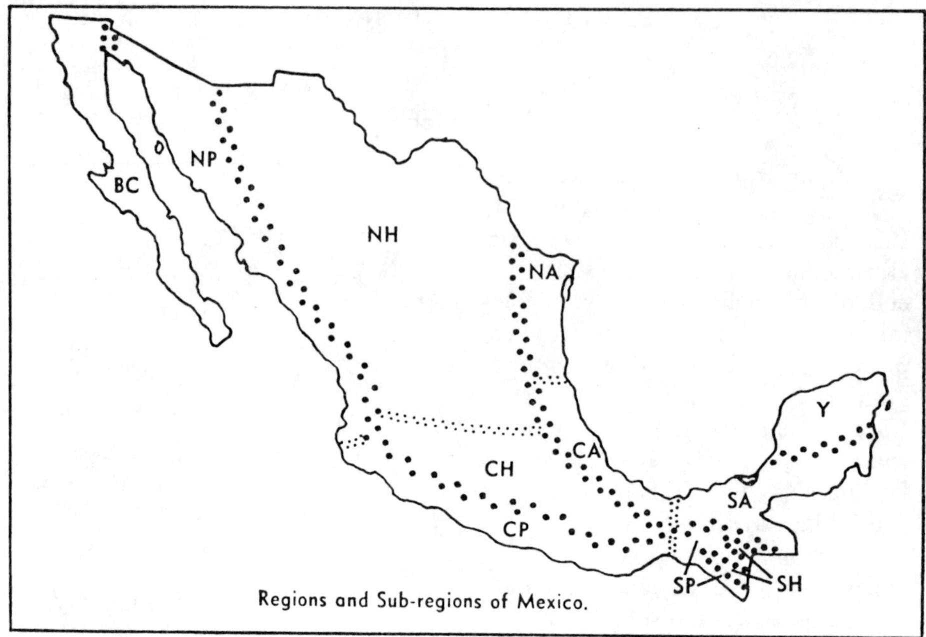

BC
O
NP
NH
NA
CH
CA
CP
SA
Y
SP
SH
Regions and Sub-regions of Mexico.

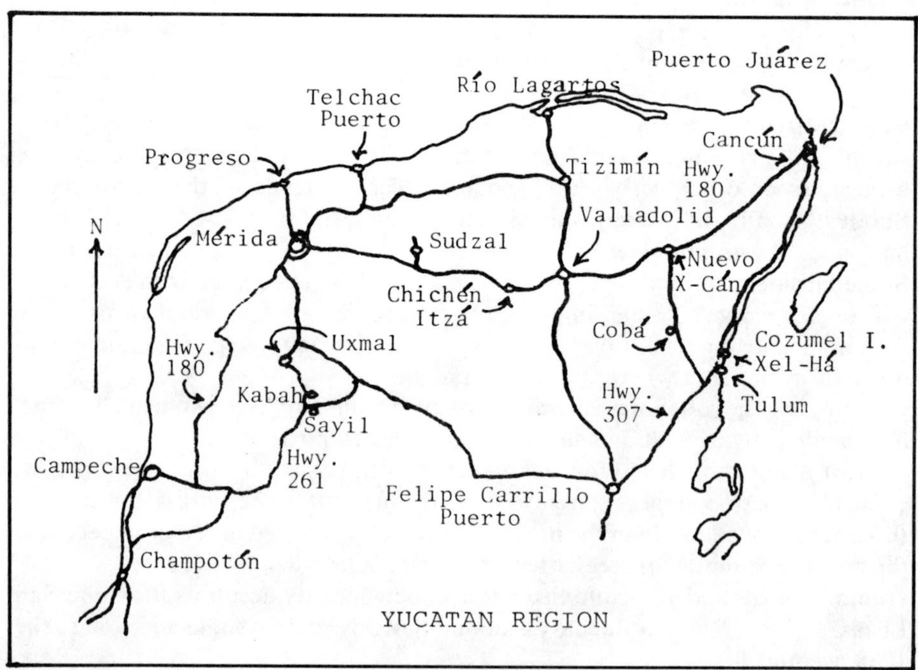

Puerto Juárez
Río Lagartos
Telchac
Puerto
Cancún
Progreso
Tizimín
Hwy.
180
N
Valladolid
Mérida
Sudzal
Nuevo
X-Can
Chichén
Itzá
Coba
Cozumel I.
Hwy.
180
Uxmal
Xel-Ha
Kabah
Hwy.
307
Tulum
Sayil
Hwy.
261
Campeche
Felipe Carrillo
Puerto
Champotón
YUCATAN REGION

YUCATAN REGION

Full revision — 1976

This is the smallest of Mexico's ornithological regions, and is relatively uniform in climate and topography as compared with the other regions. It is not divided into sub-regions. A checklist of the birds which regularly occur in the Yucatan Region as delineated here includes about 370 species, fewer species than one would find in any one of the *sub-regions* of the Atlantic Lowlands Region, for example. This is due not only to the small size of the region, and the uniformity of climate and topography mentioned above, but also to the relative aridity of most parts of the region. Although its southern limits must be arbitrarily set, the region is fairly well defined in terms of its bird life because it is bounded on three sides by ocean waters and on the other side by large tracts of more humid forest. The birds of these humid areas to the south do not penetrate to a great extent into the relatively dry country which is characteristic of the Yucatan Region. Conversely, some species which are the same as, or closely related to, birds of the West Indies are common, particularly in the eastern portion of the region, but have not spread far south into the much more humid environment of the SA sub-region.

The Yucatan Region includes all of the Yucatan Peninsula north of the northern limit of the Southern Atlantic Lowlands Sub-region, merging with that adjacent sub-region along a line or belt extending roughly from Champotón on the southwest to Felipe Carrillo Puerto and on out to the east coast of the peninsula. The zone of overlap with the SA sub-region broadens considerably as one moves from west to east into more humid terrain and heavier forests. In order to mark a specific southern boundary for the Y region, however, we draw a straight line from the Gulf of Mexico through a point five miles south of Champotón (on the west) through a point five miles south of Felipe Carrillo Puerto (farther east) and on out to the coast of the Caribbean Sea at the Bahía de la Ascensión. Thus it is bounded on the west and north by the Gulf of Mexico, on the east by the Caribbean Sea, and on the south by the forests and savannas and swamps of the SA sub-region.

The Yucatan Region, thus delineated, is approximately 220 miles airline distance from west to east, and approximately 150 miles airline distance from north to south, and includes the northern portion of Campeche, all of Yucatán, and the northern portion of Quintana Roo. (Note that some maps show the southern tip of the V-shaped state of Yucatán extending somewhat south of the above-designated line, while others show the southmost point of the state as being north of our line. If the former maps are correct our arbitrary line should be adjusted southward in the interior of the peninsula to the extent necessary to take in *all* of the state of Yucatán.) The region, of course, includes the adjacent offshore islands, notably Isla Holbox, Isla Contoy, Isla Blanca, Isla Mujeres, Isla Cancún, and Isla Cozumel.

Less than two decades have elapsed since the construction of the first paved highway link between the Yucatan Region and the rest of Mexico, but now two principal paved highways lead into the region at Champotón from Ciudad del Carmen and Escárcega, respectively, and a paved highway comes into the region at Felipe Carrillo Puerto from Chetumal. The principal paved highways within the Yucatan Region run roughly north-south on the west coast and east coast, and west-east and northwest-southeast across the interior of the peninsula. There are numerous paved roads now connecting small towns in the vicinity of Mérida, including paved roads to Sisal and Celestún, respectively, from Hunucmá.

The paved highways of most potential importance to the visitor are: highway #180 which comes into the region from the southwest, goes through Champotón and Campeche to Mérida and then eastward to Puerto Juárez via Chichén Itzá and Valladolid; highway #261 which is the same as #180 from Champotón to Campeche and to a point about 20 miles east of that city, where highway #180 branches off and #261 continues past Uxmal and through Muna to Mérida and on to Progreso; highway #184, extending southeastward from Mérida to Felipe Carrillo Puerto via Ticul; highway #295 extending southward from Valladolid to Felipe Carrillo Puerto; and highway #307 extending from near Puerto Juárez to Felipe Carrillo Puerto, via Cancún and Tulum. Also there is an all-weather road from near the site of Tulum to the site of Cobá. This may be paved soon and perhaps extended to highway #180 somewhere east of Valladolid.

There is little variety in type of terrain and natural vegetation. Most of the region is extremely rocky and flat, with a few scattered small hills or very low ridges. The western portion of the region was once covered with a rather low and scrubby but very dense, thorny, deciduous woodland. Toward the east, particularly the southeast, there is a gradual trend toward larger and larger trees in a more luxuriant growth approaching the aspect of tropical rain forest. There are almost no surface streams or lakes in the western or central portions of the region, although there are numerous *cenotes* or large pools of standing water in caverns or in limestone sinks where the roof of a cavern has collapsed. In these limestone sinks the water may be seen from the surface in the form of a small pond, usually considerably below the general ground level. These *cenotes* have traditionally provided water for the inhabitants of the region, and water is still brought up manually from the open limestone sinks or pumped up from underground reservoirs. In most portions of the region the layer of soil is very thin, and the ample rains of the summer drain quickly through the surface, leaving little moisture to maintain plant life the rest of the year. In the eastern part of the region, however, there are some lakes, and the soil is deeper, not so porous, and not so completely underlain by very porous rock, which largely explains the existence of a much taller and more luxuriant forest, or lush grass and more vigorous corn plants. Along all coasts of the region there are numerous lagoons and extensive mangrove swamps and a few marshy areas. Some of the marshes and swamps are dry or nearly dry during parts of the year, and water levels in the lagoons may fluctuate considerably, but along the east coast this sort of habitat tends to remain more nearly constant throughout the year. Sandy beaches extend for miles along the coasts of Yucatán, especially in the west and north, and many of them can now be reached with little difficulty. Coral reefs and low, rocky shores are to be found along some parts of the east coast particularly, perhaps the best known ones being on Cozumel Island and on the adjacent mainland at Xel-Há.

Even though the climate and soil of the western and central portions of the Yucatan Region are not favorable for most types of agriculture, the original vegetation has been removed over extensive areas to permit the cultivation of *henequén,* from which a tough fiber is produced. In these same areas there are many fields of corn, the plants often not very robust, and sometimes maintained with the aid of irrigation, and a few citrus orchards, particularly near towns. Cattle and horses graze in small clearings in the scrubby woodland, but the destruction of the original habitat in order to provide pastures has not been extensive in the west. Farther east, in contrast, cattle-ranching on lush pastures is an important agricultural enterprise now, and corn fields are more extensive and the plants grow more luxuriantly, following the cutting and clearing of vast tracts of the more humid forest. At this writing there is still a large amount of low to medium-sized, moderately humid forest along the west-east highway between X-cán and Puerto Juárez, and even larger trees in dense woodlands along the coast road from Puerto Juárez to Tulum and on south to Felipe Carrillo Puerto, but there has been much clearing also. One can expect more cornfields and cattle ranches, and fewer woodlands, in the near future.

In summer the weather is hot, and there are frequent rains, often in the form of rather sudden storms of wind and heavy rain. At this time the vegetation seems green and luxuriant, even in what we call the scrubby woodland of the western portions of the Yucatan Region. Butterflies are very abundant. Birds are active and conspicuous, especially in the early morning and immediately after a rain.

The changes to be expected with the advent of late autumn are not as dramatic as in more northern latitudes generally, but the weather does become noticeably milder, with warm days and not so much rain. Occasionally a hurricane or tropical storm will sweep across the peninsula from the Caribbean Sea, mostly from early spring to late autumn. As winter approaches the woodland plants lose many of their leaves, particularly in the western parts of the region, and the woodlands appear drier and more open. Occasional storms interrupt the otherwise rather idyllic climate of winter. Most of these storms move in from a westerly or northerly direction mainly, in the form of *nortes*, which bring chilly, windy weather and rain, and may persist several days. Nesting activities and singing of birds virtually cease in winter, although almost all of the breeding birds remain in the vicinity throughout the year. Many become much less conspicuous, and a few others move locally from relatively open areas to dense woodland after the breeding season. One can expect an influx of migratory birds in autumn, many of them coming in to spend the winter, and others going farther south, to reappear briefly in spring. Along the beaches and shores many sandpipers and plovers, terns and gulls, and larger numbers of herons and other waterbirds will generally be in evidence. Also, in coastal areas there will be flocks of swallows, particularly Purple Martins, **Gray-breasted Martins,** and Barn Swallows, for short periods in the autumn and spring. In the upland areas and in the vegetation along the coast numerous kinds of flycatchers and warblers, and some grosbeaks, buntings and sparrows appear in autumn, to remain throughout the winter, or to move south and then pass through again on the way north in spring. The fall migration commences by late August or early September, and some of the transients or winter visitants from the north regularly remain into May. Occasional stragglers stay into late June or even all summer.

Of the approximately 370 species of birds known to occur regularly in the Yucatan Region, about two-thirds are resident birds. Of these resident species, about half do not occur in the United States, so the avifauna does appear definitely tropical. The variety of distinctively tropical species is not as great, however, as in the Atlantic Lowlands Region to the south and west, and the presence of nearly 100 species of North American birds as transients or winter visitants assures an interesting mixture of familiar and exotic birds in winter. The aridity of much of the Yucatan Region appears to have prevented some of the birds of the humid tropical forests on the south from extending their breeding ranges northward to the tip of the peninsula, even though there is no water barrier or mountain barrier. Those which have ranged northward seem to have done so mostly in the eastern portions of the region.

Among the most frequently observed birds of the Yucatan Region, by habitat or situation, are the following:

Sandy shores and beaches and adjacent ocean:

Brown Pelican
Magnificent Frigatebird
Black Vulture
Black-bellied Plover (w.)
Snowy Plover
Wilson's Plover (w.)
Spotted Sandpiper (w.)
Willet (w.)

Ruddy Turnstone (w.)
Sanderling (w.)
Laughing Gull
Black Tern (t.)
Least Tern (s.)
Royal Tern
Sandwich Tern (w.)
Great-tailed Grackle

Lagoons, tidal flats, shallow estuaries, or mangrove swamps:

Magnificent Frigatebird
Great Blue Heron
Little Blue Heron
Reddish Egret
Great Egret
Snowy Egret
Louisiana Heron
Pintail (w.)
American Wigeon (w.)
Black Vulture
American Coot
Jacana
Killdeer (w.)
Lesser Yellowlegs (w.)
Greater Yellowlegs (w.)

Spotted Sandpiper (w.)
Western Sandpiper (w.)
Black-necked Stilt
Laughing Gull
Royal Tern
Belted Kingfisher (w.)
Great Kiskadee
Tree Swallow (w.)
Mangrove Swallow
Mangrove Warbler
Yellow-rumped Warbler (w.)
Common Yellowthroat (w.)
Great-tailed Grackle
Red-winged Blackbird
Savannah Sparrow (w.)

Villages and suburban areas with scattered overgrown vacant lots:

Black Vulture
Common Ground-Dove
Ruddy Ground-Dove
Groove-billed Ani
Vaux's Swift

Tropical House-Wren
Tropical Mockingbird
Great-tailed Grackle
Gray Saltator

Partially cleared archaeological sites, overgrown fields, woodland edge, or dense, scrubby, deciduous woodland:

Turkey Vulture
American Kestrel (w.)
Plain Chachalaca
Yucatan Bobwhite
Common Ground-Dove

Ruddy Ground-Dove
White-fronted Dove
Aztec Parakeet
Groove-billed Ani
Lesser Roadrunner

Ferruginous Pygmy-Owl
Lesser Nighthawk
Pauraque (n.)
Vaux's Swift
Cinnamon Hummingbird
Turquoise-browed Motmot
Golden-fronted Woodpecker
Yucatan Woodpecker
Laughing Creeper
Rose-throated Becard
Masked Tityra
Couch's Kingbird
Great Kiskadee
Social Flycatcher
Olivaceous Flycatcher
Empidonax sp. (w.)
Cave Swallow (s.)
Rough-winged Swallow
Yucatan Jay

White-bellied Wren
Tropical Mockingbird
Blue-gray Gnatcatcher
White-lored Gnatcatcher
Peppershrike
Mangrove Vireo
Northern Parula (w.)
Magnolia Warbler (w.)
Yellow-rumped Warbler (w.)
Black-throated Green Warbler (w.)
Red-eyed Cowbird
Altamira Oriole
Hooded Oriole
Black-headed Saltator
Gray Saltator
Cardinal
Rose-breasted Grosbeak (w.)
Blue Grosbeak (w.)
Blue-black Grassquit

Moderately tall, humid, tropical evergreen or semi-evergreen forest (also expect many of the species from the preceding list):

Scaled Pigeon
Yucatan Parrot
Wedge-tailed Sabrewing
White-bellied Emerald
Flint-billed Woodpecker
Barred Antshrike
Brown Jay

Green Jay
Gray Catbird (w.)
American Redstart (w.)
Black-cowled Oriole
Orchard Oriole (w.)
Scrub Euphonia
Jungle Tanager

There are numerous readily accessible localities near which one or more of the various types of habitat may be conveniently studied. See the locality write-ups in alphabetical order in the remaining portions of Part II: Campeche, Cancún, Champotón, Chichén Itzá, Chunyaxché, Cobá, Cozumel Island, Felipe Carrillo Puerto, Kabah, Mérida, Progreso, Puerto Juárez, Sudzal, Telchac Puerto, Tizimín, Tulum, Uxmal, Valladolid, Xel-Há.

Note that although this Part II of this supplement is a full revision some information about precautions and about seasonal changes has been dropped from the locality write-ups, so the reader should refer to the introduction in this supplement, and to the introduction and locality write-ups in Edwards (1968) for that information.

GENERAL REVIEW OF ALL LOCALITIES

Acaponeta, Nayarit - 1976 up-date, based on library studies. See FBM, 1968, p. 45.

The population is reported to be about 8500. It may be easier now to reach coastal lagoons and mangrove swamps where water birds and shore birds are numerous (abundant in winter), either southwest or almost due west of Acaponeta. It is not likely that the same large borrow-pit (1968,p.46) is to be found in the same condition, and almost certainly the kilometer marks have been changed. The characteristic land birds of the low woodland or partially cleared areas (1968,p.45) may be seen by pulling off the highway and working through nearby overgrown fields, hedgerows, and woodland edge.

Acapulco, Guerrero - 1976 up-date, based on library studies and a brief stop at the airport, in January, 1976. See FBM, 1968, p. 46.

The population is reported to be about 175,000. Highway number 200, along the coast, passes through Acapulco approximately at right angles to highway number 95.

Many new homes and hotels have been constructed recently northwest of town, toward Pie de la Cuesta, and southeast along the Costera Miguel Aleman, and it is now much more difficult to find open country along those roads. Expect great changes and development, and consequently fewer water birds, in the vicinity of Pie de la Cuesta. To see land birds in that direction it probably will be necessary to drive farther in the direction of Zihuatanejo than before, and road configurations may be different. If you proceed in a southeasterly direction expect major changes also. The branch road to the right at a point 2.9 miles southeast of the statue of Diana (1968,p.47) will be harder to find, and development may well have reduced drastically the number and variety of birds there.

Farther southeast, around Puerto Marquez and on the road to the airport, houses and hotels and other tourist facilities have doubtless replaced much of the natural habitat. The environs of the bridge over a mangrove-lined estuary about 100 yards beyond the traffic circle (1968,p.48) may have been changed radically. The grounds of the country club a short distance beyond the bridge, toward Playa Revolcadero, should still be good for bird watching, however, if you are permitted to enter. Also near Playa Revolcadero you can find numerous birds in the low growth along dirt roads or tracks leading toward the beach.

If you drive along the main highway from the traffic circle to the airport, you can expect bird watching opportunities to be as good as before. For water birds and land birds you can park at or near the airport and walk more or less northeastward on a dirt road to the shores of the Laguna (de) Papagayo (or Tres Palos). I did not see Acapulco from the ground in 1976, but while flying into and out of the airport I was able to see a dirt road approximately opposite the airport entrance, and another a short distance east of the airport. These dirt roads lead through woodland several hundred meters, then through a marshy area, to the shores of the Laguna. As implied in 1968 (p.51) there is a much greater variety of ducks, other water birds, and shore birds than actually named in the lists. Land birds should be numerous also in the moderately tall woodland which extends along the left side of the highway beyond the airport.

Remember the words of caution (1968,pp.47,48,50,51;1976, Introduction) especially about swimming or wading, and boat trips.

Acatlán, Puebla - 1976 up-date, based on library studies. See FBM, 1968, p. 52.

The population is reported to be about 7300. The elevation is now indicated as about 4000 feet. This is one of the very few Mexican towns where our introductory statement (1976, pp. 54, 55) about increased congestion, and spread of residential areas, does not seem to apply. Avoid stream valleys, especially during the rainy season, because of possible flash floods.

Aguascalientes, Aguascalientes - See FBM, 1968, p. 53.

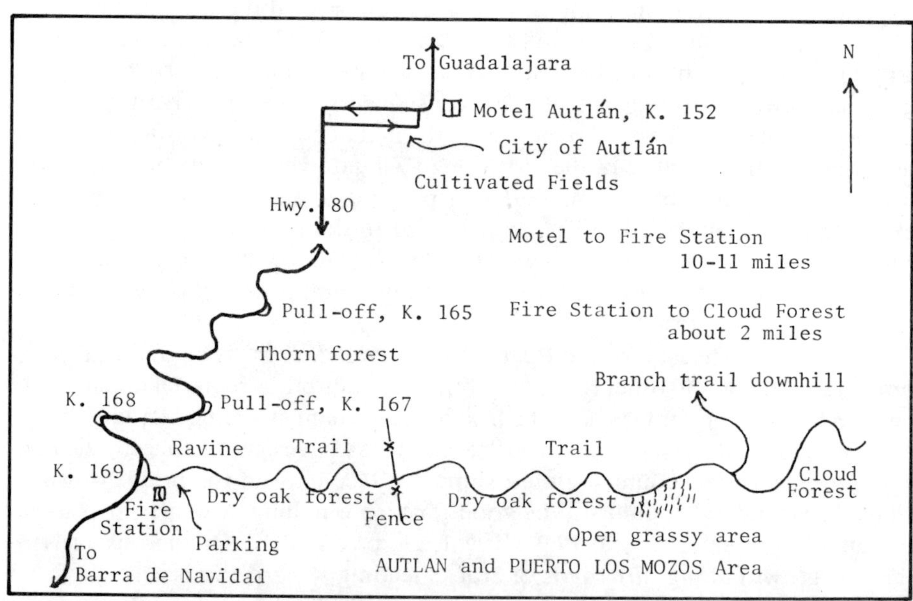

AUTLAN, Jalisco - New account, 1984, by Jerry and Nancy Strickling, on the basis of field studies made in November, 1982.

Autlán is situated in an area where the flatlands and valleys are in the Central Pacific Lowlands sub-region, while the nearby hills and mountains are in the Central Highlands sub-region. The city itself lies in a broad valley at an elevation of about 3950 feet. It is about 840 km. west of Mexico City and about 190 km. southwest of Guadalajara on National Highway 80. The population is about 50,000 (local inquiry and estimate). Official figures for average annual rainfall and monthly mean temperature are not available to us, but local information indicates that there are about 50 inches of rain from May through September, and about 10 inches from October through April. The same sources indicate that the monthly mean temperature varies from a low of 60 degrees F. in January to a high of 80 degrees F. in July. It was quite hot at mid-day when we were there in November.

Autlán is located in the rather broad, flat and agriculturally rich valley of the Río San Pedro, and is surrounded by vast fields of tomatoes. There are packing and processing plants and truck terminals at both the north and south entrances to the city. The city itself is rather colonial in appearance. At the north entrance to the city on the east side of Highway 80, there is a large modern hotel (Motel Autlán), which we have used as a bench mark for distances to birding areas.

The city itself, the motel grounds, and the cultivated fields around the city did not seem rewarding for birding. However, there is access to some interesting birding locations, including cloud forest, within a few miles south of the city on highway 80. To reach those areas from the Motel Autlán (which is at kilometer marker K-152) follow highway 80 generally westward on a one-way street, then make a left turn and proceed southward to emerge from the city on its south side. (A truck route around the city on the east side, not shown on our map, is not recommended for passenger vehicles.)

The road leads about 6 or 7 miles (10-12 km. from the Motel) through relatively flat tomato fields, then begins to wind upward through scrubby thorn forest, to a mountain pass - Puerto Los Mozos - at an elevation of about 6000 feet. Meanwhile, after you begin to climb out of the valley, and before you reach the pass, you should be able to find pull-offs where you may park your car clear of the pavement, and explore the thorn and scrub forests. We particularly noted pull-offs near K-165, K-167, and K-168 (see sketch). Caution should be observed as the highway is somewhat winding and traffic is rather heavy at times. Be particularly careful when pulling off to the left, and any time when you can't see far ahead and behind.

Some fairly common birds to be seen along the highway and in the scrubby woodland are:

***Wagler's Chachalaca**	**Lesser Roadrunner**
Banded Quail	**Berylline Hummingbird**
White-winged Dove	**Social Flycatcher**
Mourning Dove	Tropical Kingbird
White-fronted Dove	**San Blas Jay**
Blue-rumped Parrotlet	**Streaked-backed Oriole**

*(Sometimes called West Mexican Chachalaca. The *rufous*-bellied race of this species occurs in the Autlán area.)

Once you reach Puerto Los Mozos, at K-169, about 11 miles from the Motel Autlán, you should see a blue-green Forestal fire-station building on the east side of the highway (on your left as you drive south from Autlán). There is ample parking space here, and usually someone is on duty at the fire-station. You should obtain permission here to enter the fenced area if you wish to walk the trail from the fire-station through an oak forest to the cloud forest. This is a distance of about 2 miles along a fairly good, well-defined trail that was apparently graded out for a fire road. It was not passable for vehicles, however, when we were there in 1982.

As you follow this trail from an elevation of abut 6000 feet at Puerto Los Mozos, you climb approximately 1000 feet in a distance of about 1½ miles through rather dry oak forest mixed with a few pines (avoid over-exertion). This oak forest gives way to cloud forest at about 7000 feet elevation. Sweet Gum trees are a prominent feature of the cloud forest, and other moisture-loving plants abound. Arboreal ferns and mosses and other epiphytes are numerous there.

Before leaving the vicinity of the fire-station you may want to search for the **Rusty-crowned Sparrow,** not a rare bird in some parts of western Mexico, but often hard to find because of its habit of lurking on the ground in dense, brushy undergrowth. We found several on three successive days, in the ravine adjacent to, and just north of, the fire-station.

Among the dry oaks and pines along the lower part of the trail the following species of birds occur fairly regularly:

Black Vulture	Green Jay
Turkey Vulture	**White-throated Robin**
Rufous Hummingbird (w)	Warbling Vireo
Calliope Hummingbird (w)	Painted Redstart
Broad-billed Hummingbird	**Slate-throated Redstart**
Gray-crowned Woodpecker	**Golden-crowned Warbler**
Strickland's Woodpecker	**Rufous-capped Warbler**
Tufted Flycatcher	Black-headed Grosbeak
Olivaceous Flycatcher	Lesser Goldfinch
Greater Pewee	Chipping Sparrow
Rough-winged Swallow	

Many of the birds expected in the dry oak forest may be found also in the cloud forest. In addition to those, you should expect to find many of the following in the cloud forest:

Vaux's Swift	**Brown-backed Solitaire**
Plain-capped Starthroat	**Orange-billed Thrush**
Berylline Hummingbird	**Highland Thrush**
White-striped Creeper	**Gray Silky-Flycatcher**
Olivaceous Creeper	**Blue-hooded Euphonia**
Mexican Becard	**White-winged Tanager**
Blue Mockingbird	**Red-headed Tanager**

Several species of warblers which nest in the United States spend the winter in this area, and may be found in mixed flocks feeding along the trail in the oaks and in the cloud forest. These include:

Black-and-white Warbler	Tennessee Warbler

Orange-crowned Warbler	Black-throated Gray Warbler
Lucy's Warbler	Townsend's Warbler
Yellow-rumped Warbler	Hermit Warbler

A few unusual species, *not* in our regular lists because they are particularly rare and "elusive", have been reported from this vicinity, as follows:

The **Eared Poorwill,** along the main highway near the fire-station in the month of March; the **Slaty Vireo,** in the dry oak woodland above the fire-station; the rare and difficult-to-find **Highland Shrike-Vireo,** within the cloud forest 200-300 yards up-trail from the dry oak woodland. The shrike-vireo usually perches quietly, high in the trees, often is extremely wary, and may fly far when disturbed.

Another cloud forest species, although not as rare as the other three species mentioned here, is the **Striped Finch**, not on our regular list because it so often remains concealed among the tangled vegetation on the forest floor.

Travelers driving south along highway 80 from Puerto Los Mozos toward Barra de Navidad on the Pacific Ocean descend rapidly into the main Central Pacific Lowlands sub-region. Near the village of La Huerta (about 30 miles from our original base-point, the Motel Autlán) the highway passes through wetlands where the traveler may stop at pull-outs and see numerous water birds, especially in winter, including most of the following:

Black-bellied Tree-Duck	Purple Gallinule
Ruddy Duck	Common Gallinule
Masked Duck	Northern Jacana

BARRANCA DEL COBRE - See Copper Canyon and Cerocahui.

BARRANCA RANCHO LIEBRE - See La Capilla del Taxte.

BUENA VISTA - See Rancho Buena Vista.

CABO SAN LUCAS, Baja California Sur - New account, 1984, based on field studies made in May, 1983.

See also San José del Cabo.

Cabo San Lucas is situated on the coast at the southern end of the Baja California Region. It is the southern terminus of National Highway 1, and is about 1200 km. straight-line distance northwest of Mexico City, and about 1700 km. by highway south-southwest of Tijuana, BCN, and about 220 km. (by Highway 1) south of La Paz, BCS. Its population is reported to be about 1000, but this is probably a very low estimate since the town has been growing rapidly in recent years; also many tourists visit the area. The average annual rainfall is probably about the same as that of La Paz, which is about 7 inches per year,

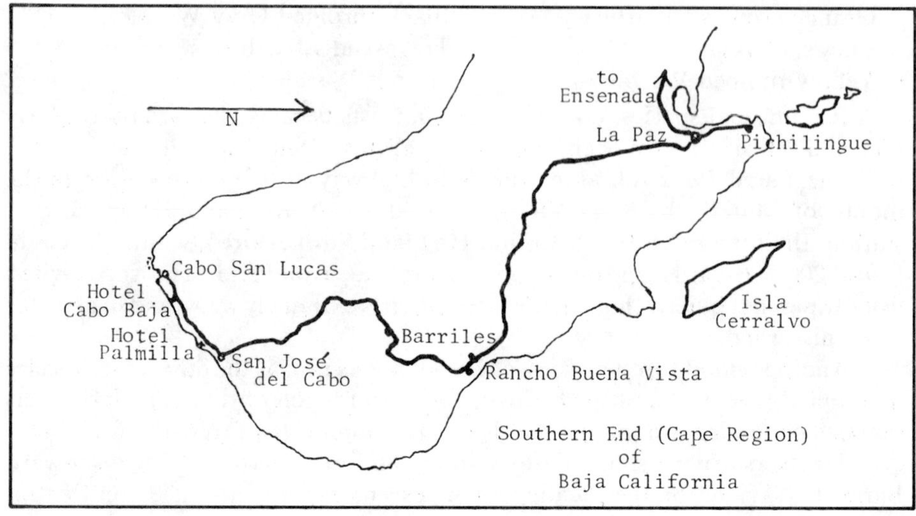

almost all of it falling from July through February, and only about 0.05 inches from March through June. Temperatures are probably somewhat similar to those of Mazatlán, which vary from a monthly mean of about 67 degrees F. (January-March) to about 82 degrees F. (July-September). Daylight hours extended generally from about 5:30 a.m. to about 6:45 p.m., local time, in May.

This is a small resort town mostly situated around Cabo San Lucas Bay, but expanding rather rapidly eastward along the ocean front. The small business section of small stores, souvenir shops, offices, and restaurants is situated mostly a short distance off (north of) the main drive which circles the inland side of the bay. It is now expanding eastward, particularly along the highway to San José del Cabo. Most hotels and motels are located somewhat away from the main business section, along the ocean front. Usually there are numerous visiting pleasure boats at anchor or moving about in the bay, and there are some docks there for light commercial use, and a ferry terminal for the ocean-going, vehicle-and-passenger ferry to Puerto Vallarta. (Birding on the ferry trip to Puerto Vallarta is described at the end of this Cabo San Lucas write-up.)

There is a rather abrupt transition between the town and the surrounding countryside, as the crowded business area and somewhat more open residential areas give way to a low but rather dense growth of mesquite-like small trees, cactus, and other thorny shrubs and trees. This type of vegetation extends for miles northward and eastward, and is typical particularly of the terrain along the 30-35 km. of highway between Cabo San Lucas and San José del Cabo. Some major hotels are situated along this highway, not really being a part of either Cabo San Lucas or San José del Cabo. They are interesting birding "localities" in their own right, being surrounded partly by the typical scrubby, thorny vegetation (and usually a few dwellings) and partly by the rocky coastline and sandy beaches. Numerous palm trees and ornamental shrubs, planted around these hotels and around some others in town, add to the variety of habitat, attracting some birds which would probably not be there otherwise. One of these hotels, the Hotel Cabo Baja, will be treated here under Cabo San Lucas, while another, the Hotel Palmilla, will be treated under San José del Cabo.

Arrangements can be made for boat trips to the rocky promontories and isolated, small, rocky islets at the very tip of the Baja California peninsula. Some of the boats departed from, and returned to, the beach a short distance east of the Hotel Hacienda beach. It was necessary for us to wade a few feet in the surf to a rowboat, transfer to a small power boat 50 to 100 yards off the beach, then go in the power boat (some are glass-bottomed boats for viewing undersea life) along the coastline to the cliffs and rocky islets. Our boat then circled and cruised back and forth in the churning, tossing waves, close to (sometimes only 10 to 20 feet from) the huge rocks. (See cautionary notes about boat trips, in the Introduction.) The duration of the boat trip was about 1½ to 2 hours.

A major attraction of this boat trip was the sight of sea lions in small groups on the rocks. Our list of birds for the trip to the rocks and back included:

Magnificent Frigatebird	Bonaparte's Gull
Brown Pelican	Least Tern
Brown Booby	Wandering Tattler (w)
Heermann's Gull	

We saw most of those species at other times along the beaches and in the bay as well, plus the Double-crested Cormorant, California Gull, and Western Gull. Doubtless at other seasons (fall, early spring, and to some extent winter) you would be able to find several to many species of shorebirds along the beaches, on rocky headlands, and around the rim of the bay.

Almost any time of day, over the gardens and patios of the Hotel Hacienda we saw Turkey Vulture, House Sparrow, Hooded Oriole, and House Finch. At twilight several Lesser Nighthawks came to the swimming pool to drink. They flew gracefully and buoyantly over the pool and then swooped down and fluttered along close to the water, their short legs dangling, and their tiny feet touching the water, to scoop up some water in the partly-open mouth. Soon the nighthawks disappeared and bats came to drink in somewhat similar fashion.

In some of the vacant lots in the eastern borders of the town, and in the scrubby, thorny vegetation just beyond the developed areas, you can expect to find most of the following species, as long as numerous shrubs and scattered trees remain:

Turkey Vulture	Cactus Wren
Crested Caracara	Verdin
White-winged Dove	Hooded Oriole
Common Ground-Dove	Cardinal
Gila Woodpecker	House Finch
Cassin's Kingbird	House Sparrow
Phainopepla	

A more representative sample of native birds of the thorny desert scrub can be found near the Hotel Cabo Baja. To reach this area drive about 4 to 6 kilometers from the center of Cabo San Lucas toward San José del Cabo until you see a large sign for the Hotel Cabo Baja on your right, and a paved side road immediately followed (20 to 50 feet) by a dirt road, both leading to your right. The paved road leads to the hotel, and the dirt road leads about a half-mile to a sandy bluff overlooking the ocean. We walked down the dirt road and back and saw the following species (doubtless the same species could be seen along the paved road to the hotel):

California Quail	**Gray Thrasher**
White-winged Dove	Black-tailed Gnatcatcher
Common Ground-Dove	Verdin
Xantus's Hummingbird	Scott's Oriole
Gila Woodpecker	Hooded Oriole
Ash-throated Flycatcher	Cardinal
Scrub Jay	Black-throated Sparrow
Cactus Wren	

Ferry trip from Cabo San Lucas to Puerto Vallarta:

This is an overnight trip of approximately 18 to 20 hours, on a large vehicle-and-passenger ferry. Bedrooms could be reserved, and there was a restaurant on the particular ferry which we took. We traveled in what seemed to be very calm weather (although a slight rain fell during part of the trip) and noticed a considerable amount of pitching in the motion of the ship, but not much rolling and almost no yawing. Presumably the motion could be considerably worse or perhaps somewhat less severe in different weather. If the ferry should leave on schedule and arrive on schedule, persons traveling in May would have about 2 to 3 hours of daylight after the afternoon departure, and about 4 to 6 hours of daylight the next morning before arrival in Puerto Vallarta.

Soon after we cleared Cabo San Lucas Bay we began to see Manx Shearwater and Black Petrel. Throughout the remainder of the afternoon many of the shearwaters went past but almost always far from the ship, banking steeply and gliding, mostly seeming to follow a straight course toward the north or northwest. A dozen or more of the petrels followed close behind the ferry, coursing from side to side over the churning wake, silhouetted against the late afternoon sun and the reflected glare from the water. Farther out we saw 2 Red-billed Tropicbirds, a Sooty Shearwater, and two other birds not certainly identified.

The next morning the sky was overcast, and in late morning some light rain fell. Manx Shearwaters were again in evidence, but they were flapping much more than were the individuals seen the afternoon before. A single Blue-footed Booby soared along with the ferry for a time, mostly directly over it. The Black Petrels did not show up in the wake of the ship until about 8:30 a.m.; they too flapped more than did the ones we had seen the afternoon before. A few Parasitic Jaegers flew close to the stern of the ship. As we moved through the vicinity of the Tres Marías Islands, particularly, more Blue-footed Boobies were in evidence, and many small groups of up to 8 or 10 Brown Boobies flew past, close to the surface of the water.

The big surprise of that morning, when we were still about 100 to 150 miles off (northwest of) Puerto Vallarta, and about 30 to 50 miles from the nearest land, the Tres Marías Islands, was the presence of several small land birds following the ship as it proceeded southeastward. A Lesser Nighthawk, a Sulphur-bellied Flycatcher, and one of the yellow-bellied kingbirds, probably the Tropical Kingbird, were to be seen following the ship. The kingbirds seemed to be in some difficulty, and occasionally we saw one very close to the surface of th water, but when one overtook the ship and flew alongside it did not attempt to land on the ship. We assumed that these sightings were exceptional, perhaps related to the approach of the hurricane, the fringes of which struck Puerto Vallarta about 16 to 20 hours later. By the time we came within 20 to 30 miles of Puerto Vallarta the land birds had been lost from view. Brown Boobies and Black Petrels were still in sight as the ship approached to within two or three miles of the harbor. (See cautionary notes about boat trips, in the Introduction.)

CAMPECHE, Campeche - 1984 up-date based on a brief visit in June, 1978. See 1976 Suppl. to FBM, p. S63 (or 1976 up-date below), and FBM, 1968, p. 54.

The population is reported to be about 100,000.

The city seems to be growing rapidly and particularly "sprawling" toward the south along the coast with some light and medium industry and other commercial development, and railroad yards along congested streets. A bypass swings south of the city, from a point about 9 km. east to a point about 12 km. southwest of the center of the city, and possibly is considered to be Alternate 180. Another way of bypassing the city is much farther east and south, and possibly is now considered to be Highway 261, which formerly went through Campeche, along with Highway 180.

The visitor should expect fewer individual birds now, although perhaps much the same assortment of species, in the parks and open residential areas, and along the waterfront and in the port area. Similarly, one should expect to have to go farther from the city center, perhaps along one of the alternate routes south of the city to find areas where the typical land birds of the dry western part of the Yucatan Peninsula are common.

Campeche, Campeche - 1976 up-date, based on library studies and reports from contributors.

Campeche is situated approximately at sea level. It is about 1300 km. east of Mexico City by road, and about 190 km. southwest of Merida. The highway which goes through the town is numbered both 180 and 261. Campeche's population is reported to be about 70,000. The average annual rainfall is about 35 inches; 29 inches from June through October and 6 inches from November through May. Monthly mean temperatures vary from 73 degrees F. in January to 82 degrees F. in May.

This is a small seaport city on the west coast of the Yucatan Peninsula. Along the waterfront in the main part of the city there is little access to beach or shore, and little to be expected there in terms of bird-watching opportunities. The commercial portion of the city extends back several blocks from the waterfront and is surrounded on three sides by residential areas interspersed with a few small business establishments. There are some gardens and parks fairly close to the center of town, but open areas, vacant lots, and small patches of scrubby woodland are more numerous farther out, beyond the principal residential areas. There the town gradually merges into scattered small farms and cultivated fields, which in turn give way to extensive tracts of low woodland and more fields. The terrain is generally flat or very slightly rolling, with a few scattered limestone sinks containing a little water in the bottom, but there are no surface streams or extensive marshy areas near the city. A considerable distance south of the city, along the coastal highway to Champotón, one encounters mud flats, lagoons, mangrove swamps, and some marshy areas, but most of the natural vegetation remaining within a few miles of the city is the typical scrubby, deciduous woodland.

In the commercial port area and nearby along the waterfront, the traveler may expect to see mainly the following:

Brown Pelican	Purple Martin (t.)
Magnificent Frigatebird	**Gray-breasted Martin (s.)**
Black Vulture	Barn Swallow (t.)
Laughing Gull	Great-tailed Grackle

In some of the more extensive city parks, and among gardens and vacant lots in open residential areas, the observer should be able to find most of the following:

Black Vulture	**Tropical House-Wren**
Common Ground-Dove	**Tropical Mockingbird**
Groove-billed Ani	Great-tailed Grackle
Vaux's Swift	**Gray Saltator**

In order to study a larger and more interesting sample of the characteristic birds of this area the observer may drive out along the highway toward Mérida, or in the opposite direction toward Champotón. Many of the common water birds listed for the Yucatan Region can be seen as one approaches Champotón, while the common land birds may be expected both toward Champotón and along either of the branches of the highway toward Mérida. The westmost of the two branches, number 180, is a shorter way to reach Mérida, while the eastmost and longer, number 261, passes close to the two well-known archaeological sites of Uxmal and Kabah, both discussed in this supplement. Within a few miles of Campeche along any of the highways leading out of the city the observer should be able to find a good place to leave a vehicle parked off the road near patches of woodland and hedgerows and perhaps cultivated fields, and walk along trails nearby. There one should be able to find many of the species of common land birds of the region, specifically most of the following:

Turkey Vulture	Golden-fronted Woodpecker
Yucatan Bobwhite	Tropical Kingbird
White-fronted Dove	**Social Flycatcher**
Lesser Nighthawk	Cave Swallow (s.)
Pauraque	Rough-winged Swallow
Turquoise-browed Motmot	Green Jay

Yucatan Jay   Altamira Oriole
White-bellied Wren   Hooded Oriole
Peppershrike   Cardinal
Mangrove Vireo   Blue Grosbeak (w.)
Northern Parula (w.)   **Blue-black Grassquit**
Yellow-rumped Warbler (w.)   Olive Sparrow
Red-eyed Cowbird

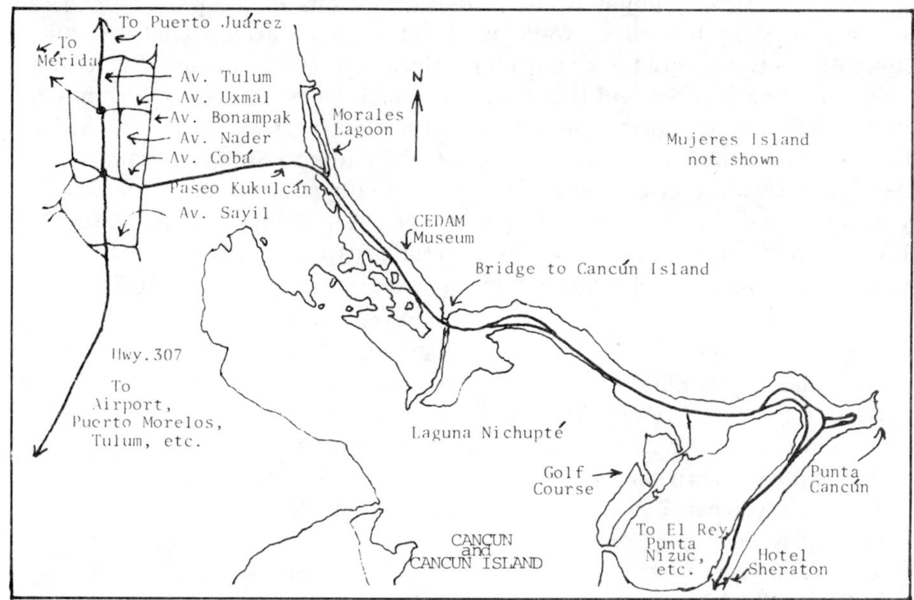

CANCUN, Quintana Roo - New account, 1984, by Barbara MacKinnon de Montes, based on continuing field studies as a permanent resident of Cancún. This account replaces that of the 1976 Suppl. to FBM, pp. S64-S66.

Cancún is in the northeastern portion of the Yucatan Region, approximately at sea level. It is about 320 km. east of Mérida, Yucatán, and about 7 km. south of Puerto Juárez, on National Highways 180 (barely) and 307. Its population has grown to more than 60,000 since the city was founded in 1979. Temperature and rainfall data have been recorded for only a few years, but annual rainfall seems to average about 40 inches (most of it from June through October) and temperatures probably vary from a monthly mean of about 72-73 degrees F. (January) to a monthly mean of about 81 degrees F. (July-August).

This island resort and adjacent mainland urban area is still growing rapidly, and one must expect to have to go progressively farther from the center of the city to find undisturbed forests, swamps, marshes, and beaches, and even overgrown fields, as the years go by. Meanwhile, however, such areas as golf courses, partially-wooded parks and residential areas, and experimental farms and gardens will continue to provide favorable habitat for a great variety of interesting birds which do not require large tracts of undisturbed forest.

The commercial section of the mainland city extends principally in a narrow belt north and south along the main street called Avenida Tulum, while residential areas spread east and west from Avenida Tulum. Most of the resort hotels are situated on the northern and northeastern portions of Cancun Island.

The residential areas referred to as Supermanzana 3 and 4, east of Avenida Tulum, provide opportunities for observing numerous species of birds resident in the natural humid woodlands, as well as transients (especially during the *fall* migration). You could expect to see more birds on a quiet Sunday morning than at other times. You might begin your observations in the park behind the **Fonatur** offices, then either walk out front to Av. Carlos Nader, or follow footpaths between buildings, and go northward to the Municipal Palace, and investigate the park behind that building, which faces Av. Nader. From there you could continue north to Av. Uxmal, then turn east to Bonampak, and go back south on the latter and across Av. Cobá and into Supermanzana 4. You need not follow a specific routine, however. If you concentrate on areas where you find numerous trees and shrubs between Av. Tulum (on the west), Av. Uxmal (on the north), Av. Bonampak (on the east), and Av. Sayil (on the south) you should find most of the following species:

Vaux's Swift	Red-eyed Vireo (s)
Prevost's Mango	Black-and-white Warbler (w)
Cinnamon Hummingbird	Prothonotary Warbler (t)
Golden-fronted Woodpecker	Tennessee Warbler (t)
Sulphur-bellied Flycatcher (s)	Parula Warbler (w)
Boat-billed Flycatcher	Cape May Warbler (w)
Social Flycatcher	Yellow Warbler (w)
Great Kiskadee	Orange Oriole
Tropical Pewee	Altamira Oriole
Yellow-bellied Elaenia	Hooded Oriole
Purple Martin (t)	**Blue Honeycreeper**
Barn Swallow (t)	**Yellow-throated Euphonia**
Tropical House-Wren	**Yellow-winged Tanager**
Gray Catbird (w)	**Gray Saltator**
Clay-colored Robin	

To proceed from this area to Cancun Island and some of the major hotels and some favorable areas for shore birds and water birds especially, you would follow Paseo Kukulcán generally eastward and onto a causeway which leads to the *short* bridge which connects the mainland to Cancun Island across Nichupte Canal. Mangrove swamps extend along the causeway, with ornamental plantings lining the boulevard itself. A sidewalk and separate bicycle path extend beside the boulevard on the north side. Parking is not permitted anywhere between Av. Bonampak and the **Cedam** Museum (on the causeway), a distance of 3.1 km., nor do public buses stop to pick up or discharge passengers anywhere between those two points.

For some interesting birding in this vicinity you could drive along Paseo Kukulcán to the Hotel Carrousel on your left where you can swing around the median strip to the other side of the boulevard and drive a short distance back to the **Cedam** Museum (or you could go to the **Cedam** Museum by bus) which is about 1.3 km. before you reach the bridge to the island. From the Museum you could walk back (west) about a half-mile to the Morales Lagoon (on your right as you go back) at the bend in the boulevard. Or, beginning at Avenida Bonampak you could walk to Morales Lagoon, and on to the **Cedam** Museum or back to town. Or you could walk along the south side of the causeway to the bridge, birding between the boulevard and Nichupte Lagoon. Observing birds along the boulevard and overhead, and in the swamps and lagoons beside the causeway (watch out for mopeds, runners, and bicycles), you should find many of the following species:

Double-crested Cormorant	Tropical Kingbird
Olivaceous Cormorant	**Tropical Pewee**
Anhinga	**Northern Tody-Flycatcher**
Magnificent Frigatebird	**Caribbean Elaenia**
Turkey Vulture	**Black Catbird**
Black Vulture	**Mangrove Warbler**
White-winged Dove	Prairie Warbler (t)
Ruddy Ground-Dove	Palm Warbler (w)
Aztec Parakeet	Common Yellowthroat (w)
Lesser Nighthawk	Great-tailed Grackle
Belted Kingfisher (w)	Hooded Oriole
Golden-fronted Woodpecker	Collared Seedeater

If you continue generally eastward along Paseo Kukulcán (presumably by automobile or local bus) you will cross the short bridge over Nichupte Canal and arrive on Cancun Island. From there you could follow the road about 4 to 5 km. (about 3 mi.) eastward to Punta Cancún, then about 12 to 14 km. (about 8 mi.) south to Punta Nizuc (the local bus only goes about 2 to 3 km. south, at present, to the Hotel Sheraton). From Punta Nizuc the road leads westward a kilometer or two to the short bridge connecting to the mainland, and then about 6 km. farther to intersect Highway 307 just north of the branch road to the airport. From here you can turn right and complete a circle tour back to Cancún, or turn left toward Puerto Morelos, Xel-Há, and Tulum.

Areas often favorable for birding on Cancun Island include the Golf Course, the rocks off (south of) Punta Cancún, the marshes across from the Hotel Sheraton, any undeveloped areas south of that hotel, and the vicinity of the El Rey ruins.

To reach the Golf Course, assuming you have just come from mainland Cancún *onto* the northwest tip of Cancun Island, continue eastward on Paseo Kukulcán about 2 to 3 km. to a large peninsula projecting to your right (south) before you reach the Hotel El Presidente on your left. When you come to the entrance to the Golf Course Clubhouse, turn right and drive on past the Clubhouse and up over a bridge. From this point you can drive to the tip of the peninsula, stopping to look for birds at suitable places along the way (beware of flying golf balls). Particularly during fall migration, and especially if the drainage system for the golf course is *not* working well, you may be able to find many of the following species, in areas of wet grass, or among the trees and shrubs, or along the shore:

Cattle Egret	Laughing Gull
American Kestrel (w)	Royal Tern
Black-bellied Plover (w)	Sandwich Tern
Semipalmated Plover (w)	**Zenaida Dove**
Killdeer (w)	**Cinnamon Hummingbird**
Greater Yellowlegs (w)	Tropical Kingbird
Spotted Sandpiper (w)	**Tropical Mockingbird**
Ruddy Turnstone (w)	Yellow Warbler (w)
Short-billed Dowitcher (t)	Yellow-rumped Warbler (w)
Common Snipe (t)	Palm Warbler (w)
Sanderling (t)	Red-eyed Cowbird (s)
Least Sandpiper (w)	Savannah Sparrow (w)
Pectoral Sandpiper (t)	

Returning to the boulevard, a right turn will lead you toward Punta Cancún. The maze of roads as you approach the Convention Center can be confusing, but if you swing around the Convention Center and continue to a point east of, not south of, the Convention Center, and reach the grounds of the new Hyatt Regency or Camino Real hotels you should be able to look seaward to the rocks south of Punta Cancún. There you may be able to find Sooty Terns and Brown Noddies (April to August) on the rocks; Brown Pelicans and Double-crested and Olivaceous Cormorants may fly past; and Magnificent Frigatebirds frequently soar overhead.

From Punta Cancún you can circle back around the Convention center and head southward about 2 to 3 km. until you see the Hotel Sheraton on your left, while on your right a marshy peninsula projects far out and almost touches the tip of the Golf Course peninsula. The peninsula across the road from the Sheraton is slated for development in the near future, but in the meantime if you park at the Sheraton, and walk across the road to look out over the marsh at low tide you should be able to find many of the species listed for the Golf Course, and many of the following:

Great Blue Heron (blue phase)	White Ibis
Great Blue Heron (white phase)	Black-bellied Tree-Duck
Green Heron	Blue-winged Teal (w)
Little Blue Heron	Wilson's Plover (w)
Reddish Egret	Black-necked Stilt
Great Egret	Least Tern (s)
Snowy Egret	Western Sandpiper (w)
Tricolored Heron	

To see the common land birds of the area you could proceed southward from the Hotel Sheraton, stopping occasionally where you can find a place to pull off and park clear of the road, and bird in the brushy dune vegetation and the coconut groves. If you drive to the El Rey ruins, about 4 to 7 km. south of the Sheraton, and on your right, you can drive into the archaeological site, where there is space to park away from the highway. Around the borders of this small site you should be able to see some of the typical birds of the scrubby vegetation of the island. (Remember you may not use tripods or 16 mm. movie cameras in the archaeological site.) Birds to be expected near El Rey and along the highway include:

Plain Chachalaca	**Social Flycatcher**
Red-billed Pigeon	Great Kiskadee
Common Ground-Dove	Wied's Flycatcher (s)
White-fronted Dove	**Spotted-breasted Wren**
Caribbean Dove	**Mangrove Vireo**
White-fronted Parrot	**Yucatan Vireo**
Ferruginous Pygmy-Owl	Yellow-throated Warbler (w)
Lineated Woodpecker	**Singing Blackbird**
Yucatan Woodpecker	**Black-cowled Oriole**

As you proceed all the way to the southern end of Cancun Island you continue to see dry scrubby woodland, and then mangrove swamps as you near the bridge back to the mainland. Once across this bridge you should pass through mostly marshy areas, as you go westward toward the main highway. You should be able to find places where you can park clear of the highway and look for the characteristic birds of these marshes. (See the lists for the Golf Course and the marsh across from the Hotel Sheraton). Also you may hear the loud chattering "whinny" of the **Red Rail,** among marsh vegetation.

Once you reach the main highway you could turn left and drive southward about 20 km. (about 12 mi.) (to a point 1.2 km. north of Puerto Morelos) and turn into the entrance of the Centro de Investigaciones de Quintana Roo, which is on the west side of the highway (to your right as you drive south). If you drive directly from the city of Cancún down Highway 307, without going on the island, you should reach the Centro de Investigaciones just 33 km. (20 mi.) south of the fountain monument on Avenida Tulum in Cancún.

You should be able to find space to park just outside the entrance, pulling clear of the highway *and* of the entrance road, and walk along the narrow dirt entrance road, looking for birds in the humid forest and open fields beyond. This will probably continue to be a favorable area to find some of the more "exotic" birds of the vicinity of Cancún, as more and more of the woodlands closer to the city are cleared and developed. Among the species to be expected here are:

Groove-billed Ani	**Brown Jay**
Ferruginous Pygmy-Owl	Green Jay
Wedge-tailed Saberwing	**Yucatan Jay**
Fork-tailed Emerald	Hooded Warbler (w)
Citreoline Trogon	American Redstart (w)
Violaceous Trogon	**Jungle Tanager**
Collared Toucan	**Black-headed Saltator**
Rose-throated Becard	Cardinal
Masked Tityra	Blue Grosbeak (w)
Black-crowned Tityra	**Blue Bunting**
Rough-winged Swallow	Indigo Bunting (w)

See also the next list for some of the hawks and falcons which you may see along the highway between Cancún and the Centro de Investigaciones.

A similar assemblage of birds is to be expected along the unpaved road to the *chicle* camp called "Vallarta". This road leads to the right (west) from a point about 2 km. south of the above-mentioned Centro de Investigaciones.

Another area of relatively moist woodland is west of Cancún, on Highway 180 toward Chichén Itzá and Mérida. To reach this area drive west on Highway 180 from Cancún, measuring 28 km. (about 17 mi.) from the last traffic circle as you leave Cancún. Then turn to the right (north) onto a dirt road where there is a sign indicating "Agropecuaria". If you park well off the tracks of the road (there are some quarries along the road which would be suitable) so vehicles can pass, you can walk alongside the dirt road through humid woodland, cultivated fields and brushy areas. Along this dirt road (and in some cases along the main highway) you can expect to see many of the species listed for the Centro de Investigaciones de Quintana Roo, south of the city, and many of the following:

Rufescent Tinamou	**White-bellied Emerald**
Cayenne Kite	**Keel-billed Toucan**
Gray Hawk	**White-throated Spadebill**
Great Black Hawk	White-eyed Vireo (w)
Black Crane-Hawk	**Gray-headed Vireo**
Laughing Falcon	Worm-eating Warbler (w)
Bat Falcon	Black-throated Green Warbler (w)
Plain Chachalaca	Bananaquit
Blue Ground-Dove	**Red-crowned Tanager**
Squirrel Cuckoo	Rose-breasted Grosbeak (w)
Pauraque	

CATEMACO, Veracruz - New account, 1984, by Jerry and Nancy Strickling, based on field studies in December, 1980, and November, 1981, and seven times before that. This account replaces that of the 1976 Suppl. to FBM, pp. S96-S97 (not reprinted here), and that of the Catemaco portion of the San Andrés Tuxtla account in FBM, 1968, pp. 156-159.

Catemaco is in the Central Atlantic Lowlands sub-region at an elevation of about 1100 feet above sea level. It is about 550 km. east of Mexico City, and about 160-170 km. southeast of Veracruz, on National Highway 180. The population is reported to be about 24,000, and apparently has grown very little in the past 20 years. Average annual rainfall at Catemaco is probably about 75 inches, most of it falling from April or May through September or October. There is much local variation, however, and rainfall at Coyame, just a few miles east of Catemaco, is much greater. Monthly mean temperatures vary from a low of about 67 degrees F. in January to a high of about 84 degrees F. in April, May or June.

The area is relatively rich in bird life as shown by the Christmas Counts which were conducted there from 1973 through 1980. The total number of species observed there on a Christmas Count has exceeded 290 on occasion.

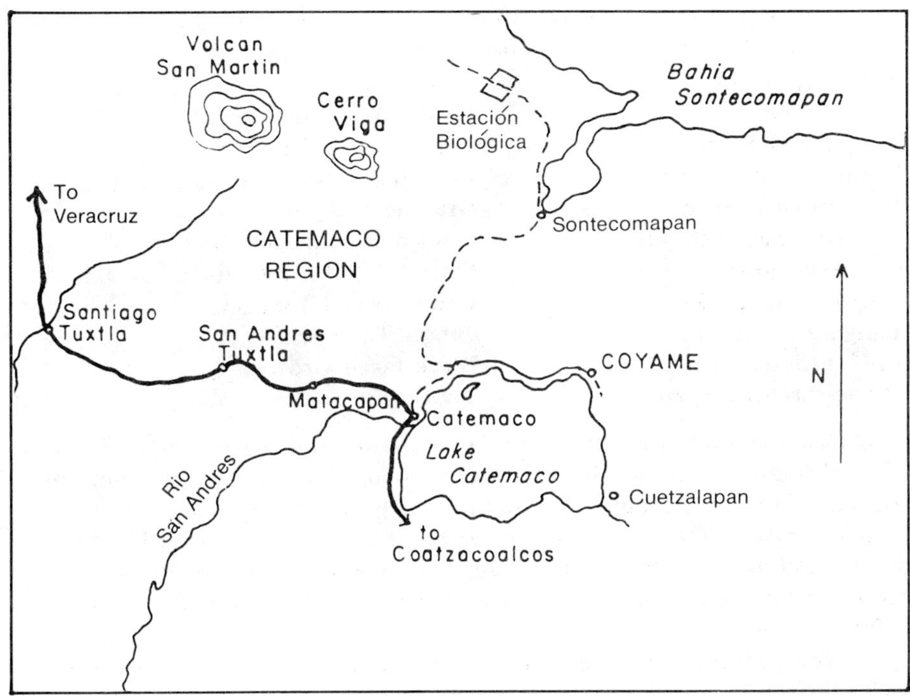

Situated as it is on the northwest shore of Lake Catemaco, the town's principal economic support is derived from fishing and tourism. Highway 180 bypasses (goes west of) most of the town, and goes through areas which are relatively unrewarding for birding. The better areas for birds can be reached by taking a road generally eastward or northeastward into and through Catemaco itself to a road fork a few kilometers northeast of town, and then exploring the two principal branch roads from there, one going around the north through Sontecomapan and the Gulf of Mexico. The road into town from Highway 180 leads about 1 mile to the main plaza of Catemaco. Continuing past the main plaza, and working your way 6 to 8 blocks to the left, you should find the cinder-gravel road which leads toward the principal birding areas.

This road from Catemaco eastward or northeastward forks at a point about 6 km. from town. The left branch leads about 16 km. to or near tropical rain forest and scrubby lowland fields to the village of Sontecomapan, located on a mangrove lagoon. Boats may be rented here for birding the lagoons and waterways to the seashore (see note about boat trips). Continuing past the village about 5 km. the road goes through the relatively undisturbed rain forest of the tropical research station - the Estación Biológica de los Tuxtlas. To visit the station proper you must have permission from the Instituto Biología, Ciudad Universitaria, in Mexico City. It should not be necessary to actually enter the station, however, because birding along the public road *near* the station can be most rewarding, through tropical forest on both sides of the road. There is a good chance that you will be able to see a **White Hawk** there, (or over or near

the Sontecomapan lagoon) as well as many of the birds on the next *three* lists.
Watch, or listen, especially for the following:

Short-billed Pigeon	Green Jay
Wedge-tailed Saberwing	**Lowland Wood-Wren**
Long-tailed Hermit	**White-throated Robin**
White-bellied Emerald	**Long-billed Gnatwren**
Violaceous Trogon	**Gray-headed Vireo**
Blue-crowned Motmot	**Golden-crowned Warbler**
Collared Toucan	**Olive-backed Euphonia**
Brown Woodpecker	**Red-crowned Tanager**
Laughing Creeper	**Jungle Tanager**
Buff-throated Leaf-Gleaner	**Black-faced Grosbeak**
White-throated Spadebill	**Tuxtla Finch**

Back at the road fork 6 km. from Catemaco, if you turn right (instead of left
to Sontecomapan) you will be on a paved road which continues around the
north side of the lake, about 16 km. to the village and bottling plant of Coyame.

If you bird in the vicinity of the road fork (before you proceed eastward
toward Coyame or northward toward Sontecomapan) you may find a **Lovely
Cotinga**. It has been fairly common at times in the hedgerows on the south (lake)
side of the road.

As you proceed from the road fork on the paved road toward Coyame
watch for open fields or dirt roads along hedgerows or into patches of second-
growth woodland. You will see coffee plantations, orchards and small farms that
are fenced but you will also find many open dirt roads and trails which go along
woodland borders where a considerable number of birds may be seen. There are
numerous places to pull off the road and park, although many of these dirt roads
turn to mud in wet weather. Some of the birds generally along the road to
Coyame are:

Cattle Egret	**Golden-olive Woodpecker**
Turkey Vulture	Golden-fronted Woodpecker
Black Vulture	**Rufous-breasted Spinetail**
Roadside Hawk	**Barred Antshrike**
Gray Hawk	**Masked Tityra**
American Kestrel (w)	Tropical Kingbird
Red-billed Pigeon	Sulphur-bellied Flycatcher (s)
Ruddy Ground-Dove	**Boat-billed Flycatcher**
White-fronted Dove	**Social Flycatcher**
Squirrel Cuckoo	Great Kiskadee
Groove-billed Ani	Olivaceous Flycatcher
Ferruginous Pygmy-Owl	*Empidonax* sp. (w)
White-collared Swift	**Yellow-bellied Elaenia**
Vaux's Swift	Brown Jay
Rufous-tailed Hummingbird	**Spotted-breasted Wren**
Collared Toucan	Gray Catbird (w)
Keel-billed Toucan	Clay-colored Robin

Wood Thrush (w)
Cedar Waxwing (w)
Red-eyed Vireo (s)
Black-and-white Warbler (w)
Yellow Warbler (w)
Magnolia Warbler (w)
Black-throated Green Warbler (w)
Wilson's Warbler (w)
Rufous-capped Warbler
Montezuma Oropendola
Yellow-billed Cacique
Great-tailed Grackle
Singing Blackbird

Orchard Oriole (w)
Northern Oriole (w)
Red-legged Honeycreeper
Yellow-throated Euphonia
Blue-gray Tanager
Yellow-winged Tanager
Crimson-collared Tanager
Summer Tanager (w)
Black-headed Saltator
Gray Saltator
Collared Seedeater
Blue-black Grassquit
Olive Sparrow

In addition to the **Rufous-tailed Hummingbird** listed above, several other species of hummingbirds occur in the forests, woodland borders, and hedgerows, and are likely to be concentrated around individual flowering trees, shrubs, and herbs, or groups of such plants. One place in particular to look for a variety of hummingbirds is in the gardens and ornamental plantings of the lakeside Hotel Playa Azul, which is about two to three kilometers from Catemaco on the "north-shore" road before you reach the branches going north and east, respectively. Permission to bird the grounds has been readily obtainable in the past, at the hotel office. You might find the **Rufous-breasted Spinetail** in dense shrubbery there as well, and the **Wood Owl** has been seen and heard there at night. Hummingbirds which you might find there (or occasionally in forests and woodland borders) are:

Long-tailed Hermit
Little Hermit
Wedge-tailed Saberwing
Violet Saberwing

Prevost's Mango
Fork-tailed Emerald
White-bellied Emerald

The Catemaco bottling plant is located about halfway between the "north-shore" road fork and the Coyame bottling plant and village. It is situated near the lake on the Arroyo Agrio (sour gulch), so-called because of the naturally acid carbonated springs in the area. You should be able to obtain permission, at the bottling plant, to bird the grounds. Besides the birds of fields and hedgerows and woodland borders, you should be able to hear the **Red Rail** in the extensive marsh there, and find other marsh birds and other long-legged waders. (See note about marshes.)

A boat trip across the lake from Catemaco to the mouth of the Rio Cuetzalapan, and an exploratory trip in the same boat up this small river may be worthwhile. You should allow about 30-40 minutes each way, plus whatever time you wish to devote to the trip up-river and back. (See note about boat trips in the Introduction; insist on life-jackets - "salvavidas".) You can arrange for a boat and boatman in Catemaco. All five species of Mexican kingfishers have been seen here - the Ringed, Belted (w), **Amazon,** Green, and **Pygmy.** The **Pygmy Kingfisher** is usually the hardest to find, and if you see it at all it may be only in the small tributary streams or backwaters. You might also see the **Yellow-tailed Oriole** and the **Yellow-backed Oriole** there.

The lake itself does not provide much opportunity to see large numbers of water birds, although by working extensively around the shores you should find a few individuals of most of the following kinds, and perhaps some others in even smaller numbers:

Least Grebe	Great Blue Heron
Pied-billed Grebe	Green Heron
Olivaceous Cormorant	Little Blue Heron
Common Egret	Ringed Kingfisher
Snowy Egret	Belted Kingfisher (w)
Lesser Scaup (w)	

Generally more favorable for the study of water birds, marsh birds, and waders, if water levels and other conditions are favorable, are the moist meadows, marshes, and ponds between Alvarado and Santiago Tuxtla along the highway from Veracruz, the marshes and shallow open water between Minatitlán and Coatzacoalcos, and the marshes in the vicinity of Villahermosa and Palenque.

Activity among the resident land birds diminishes in winter, when there is no nesting, and little song, and particularly when occasional cold winter storms, or *nortes,* sweep through the area, but there are other birds moving into the area to spend the winter or moving through on migration. Among these would be flycatchers, swallows, warblers, and some finches and sparrows.

Among the principal night birds of the area are the **Wood Owl** and the Pauraque.

Birds associated with the marine habitat, such as Brown Pelican, Magnificent Frigatebird, and various herons, plovers, sandpipers, gulls and terns are found in the vicinity of the mangrove lagoons and the seashore.

The environs of Lake Catemaco and the Sierra de Tuxtla have been studied intensively by naturalists for many years. Most helpful to the birder of the 1980s would probably be the Christmas Counts in *American Birds* magazine, April or July issues, 1974 through 1981.

CEROCAHUI, Chihuahua - New account, 1984, based on field studies made in May, 1983.

Cerocahui is in the Northern Highlands sub-region at an elevation of about 5400 feet above sea level. It is about 1300 km. straight-line distance northwest of Mexico City, and about 260 km. straight-line distance southwest of Chihuahua. The dirt and gravel road from Bahuichivo to Cerocahui, and from Cerocahui to Urique does not connect directly to the main Mexican highway network. Most tourists visiting Cerocahui reach there by riding the Chihuahua-Pacific Railroad as far as Bahuichivo, then riding a special (Hotel Misión) bus about 13 km. (about a 30-45 minute ride) over a rough, twisty, dirt and gravel, mountain road to Cerocahui. Possibly a taxi could be found instead (in Bahuichivo) (if you haven't arranged for the bus to meet you) but it's not advisable to attempt the trip without making advance arrangements in Chihuahua or Los Mochis.

The population of Cerocahui was reported to be about 600 in 1978, and probably has not changed greatly since then. Temperature and rainfall figures are not available, but annual rainfall is probably about 25 to 35 inches, most of it probably falling from June through September. Temperatures probably vary from a monthly mean in the 50s or slightly below in December and January to a monthly mean in the high 60's or low 70's in June and July. Daylight birding hours in May - about 6:30 or 7:00 a.m. to about 7:00 or 7:30 p.m.

The central portion of this village consists of a large church, with a colonial-ranch-style hotel and a few small stores and houses. Other houses and yards and small farm plots are on the outskirts of the village, and other houses and orchards and larger croplands are farther out, on both sides of a small river which flows through the valley in which Cerocahui is situated. In the vicinity of the large church and the hotel you could expect to find the Cliff Swallow, Barn Swallow, Violet-green Swallow, House Sparrow, and House Finch.

During a short walk to and along the river which flows within 200 to 300 meters (east) of the center of town we found the village birds mentioned above and the following:

Turkey Vulture	Vermilion Flycatcher
Killdeer	Rough-winged Swallow
Acorn Woodpecker	American Robin
Black Phoebe	Eastern Bluebird
Cassin's Kingbird	Red-eyed Cowbird

(Note that this river, lined with Bald Cypress on one side, is very shallow and rocky in the dry season, with no bridge, only rather hazardous stepping-stone crossings. Flash-floods are possible in the rainy season.)

A dirt road leading eastward from the river, more or less an extension of the road leading from the village center *to* the river, goes between orchards and fields toward the narrow deep ravine where the waterfall "La Cascada" is located. If you cross the river from the village and follow this road away from the river, and then leave the road and go more or less straight ahead up and over a rocky hill when the road swings to the right, you can see numerous birds and eventually reach the narrow ravine. Large areas of the surface of the hill are exposed solid rock, but there are some scattered areas of heavily-grazed grass and some pines and cedars.

Within the deep, steep-sided ravine there was a dense woodland of true cypress trees (*Cupressus*), leathery-leaved oaks, and madrone. We saw the American Dipper at the mouth of the ravine, and had we gone farther up the ravine we might have expected some of the typical birds of the humid woodlands of the Northern Highlands sub-region (1968, p. 20).

Species which we saw or heard on the rocky hill, or near the mouth of the ravine, or along the dirt road en route were:

Red-tailed Hawk	Band-tailed Pigeon
Rock Dove	Acorn Woodpecker

Vermilion Flycatcher	Canyon Wren
Cassin's Kingbird	Curve-billed Thrasher
Greater Pewee	Hutton's Vireo
Barn Swallow	House Sparrow
Violet-green Swallow	Red-eyed Cowbird
American Dipper	Hepatic Tanager
Rock Wren	House Finch

The Hotel Misión operated a bus tour on a gravel road (not the road to Bahuichivo) up to a high ridge about 18-20 km. from Cerocahui and then part way down the other side. (Alternatively, a taxi could probably be engaged for this trip.) Beyond the ridge top there are some dramatic views of the tremendous Urique Canyon. The road continues to the village of Urique on the floor of the canyon, but we turned back (toward Cerocahui) after a final leisurely look at the Urique Canyon from a natural look-out point high on a shoulder of the mountain (see precautionary note about overlooks in the Introduction).

Birding from a taxi or tour bus, and during short walks along the road and around the grounds of the Urique Canyon Cabins (on the ridge top) one could expect to find most of the following species, and possibly others from the lists of common birds of the Northern Highlands sub-region (1968, pp. 19-20):

Turkey Vulture	Mexican Jay
Black Vulture	Steller's Jay
Inca Dove	Rock Wren
White-throated Swift	Canyon Wren
Acorn Woodpecker	Hutton's Vireo
Cassin's Kingbird	Painted Redstart
Rough-winged Swallow	Yellow-eyed Junco
Violet-green Swallow	

Most of the above-mentioned species could probably be found also in wooded areas along the road from Cerocahui to the railroad station at Bahuichivo.

CHAMPOTON, Campeche - 1984 up-date, based on very brief visits in June, 1978, and April, 1981. See 1976 Suppl. to FBM, p. S66 (or 1976 up-date below) and FBM, 1968, p. 56.

Champotón has obviously grown considerably since 1968, and the presence of a big new bridge across the Río Champotón, and a paved viaduct along the south bank of the river has made the river banks much less favorable for birding. You still might be able to see wading birds as you look toward the north bank of the river in town, but you could probably see more water birds, as well as typical land birds, along the coastal highway north of Champotón.

Watch for lagoons or mud-flats on your left as you go north, where there is a sand road leading off, or where the road-shoulders are wide enough so that you can park clear of the highway. (Be careful of loose sand where a vehicle could get stuck.) One such side road to the left a few km. north of Champotón led almost parallel to the highway past a dense tract of low woodland, to the beach. There were a few herons and shorebirds along the beach (possibly mud flats and more birds might be visible at a different tide), and a surprising variety of plants, from prickly-pear cactus to colorful orchids, in the woodland (early April).

Champoton, Campeche - 1976 up-date, based on library studies and reports from contributors.

Champotón is situated approximately at sea level. It is about 1240 km. east of Mexico City by road, and about 260 km. southwest of Mérida, where highways 180 and 261 come in from the south and join and proceed northward as one highway. Its population is reported to be about 5000. The average annual rainfall is 47 inches; 37 inches from June through October, and 10 inches from November through May. Monthly mean temperatures vary from a low of 74 degrees F. in January to a high of 84 degrees F. in May.

The upland areas in the vicinity of this town provide suitable habitat for many of the characteristic bird species of the rather dry, scrubby portions of the Yucatan Region. In addition, the presence of a river opening into the ocean at Champotón, with swampy areas, fresh, brackish, and salt water, and open mud flats at times, usually assures the observer an opportunity to see a considerable variety of water birds.

The aspect of Champotón is that of a small coastal town with a very small congested section giving way close by to more open residential areas with yards, gardens, and vacant lots interspersed. The Gulf of Mexico and its beaches are on the west side, the Río Champotón and its mangrove lagoons and tidal flats are on the north, while low woodlands, cultivated fields and overgrown fields extend inland from the successively more scattered human habitations at the edge of town. Coconut plantations are to be found along the coast, particularly along the highways leading north and southwest.

Any part of the waterfront in Champotón should be reasonably productive of aquatic birds, but the observer should be able to see much more (if the town hasn't become much more congested in the last few years) by going to the portion of town which lies in the corner where the river opens into the gulf. There, without missing the characteristically coastal salt water species, he should also be able to see a pleasing variety of water birds which are attracted to the fresh water and brackish water and the mangrove lagoons and tidal flats. In this situation, or else by separate visits to a waterfront area and then to a favorable portion of the riverbank near its mouth, the observer should be able to see most of the following:

Brown Pelican	Yellow-crowned Night-Heron
Olivaceous Cormorant	White Ibis
Magnificent Frigatebird	Roseate Spoonbill
Great Blue Heron	Black Vulture
Little Blue Heron	Jacana
Reddish Egret	Lesser Yellowlegs (w.)
Snowy Egret	Greater Yellowlegs (w.)
Louisiana Heron	Spotted Sandpiper (w.)

Willet (w.)	Eastern Kingbird (t.)
Ruddy Turnstone (w.)	Purple Martin (t.)
Sanderling (w.)	**Gray-breasted Martin**
Black-necked Stilt	Cave Swallow (s.)
Laughing Gull	Barn Swallow (t.)
Black Tern (t.)	Great-tailed Grackle
Royal Tern	

If tidal conditions are not right or if the birds have been disturbed at the above-mentioned area, or if there are just too many people or buildings in the area now, the observer may drive north on the road to Campeche not more than five or ten miles and encounter other mangrove lagoons and tidal flats. Some of these are easily visible from the highway, off to the left as you drive north. In these places the chances of finding the birds mentioned above should be just as good as at the mouth of the Río Champotón, and the chances of seeing the following would be even better:

Belted Kingfisher (w.)	Yellow-rumped Warbler (w.)
Mangrove Swallow	Northern Waterthrush
Mangrove Warbler	Common Yellowthroat (w.)

The highway which leads past the lagoons north of Champotón also passes through upland areas, of course and the observer may want to watch for a dirt road or good trail beside cultivated fields and scrubby woodland, in order to study the characteristic land birds of the area. The field trips for aquatic birds and land birds may easily be combined because the scrubby, deciduous woodland commences near the beach and extends for many miles inland, broken only by coconut plantations first, then cultivated fields. Some dirt banks north of Champotón may be used by the **Turquoise-browed Motmot,** which has been known to nest there in almost a semi-colonial manner. If you can find a suitable place to pull off of the road near there, you might be able to observe such nesting in early summer. Among the land birds to be expected in the general vicinity discussed here are:

Black Vulture	**Yucatan Jay**
Turkey Vulture	**White-bellied Wren**
Yucatan Bobwhite	**Tropical Mockingbird**
Ruddy Ground-Dove	**Mangrove Vireo**
White-fronted Dove	Northern Parula (w.)
Groove-billed Ani	Yellow-rumped Warbler (w.)
Lesser Nighthawk	Red-eyed Cowbird
Pauraque (n.)	Great-tailed Grackle
Turquoise-browed Motmot	**Singing Blackbird**
Golden-fronted Woodpecker	Altamira Oriole
Tropical Kingbird	Cardinal
Social Flycatcher	**Blue-black Grassquit**
Great Kiskadee	Olive Sparrow
Empidonax sp. (w.)	

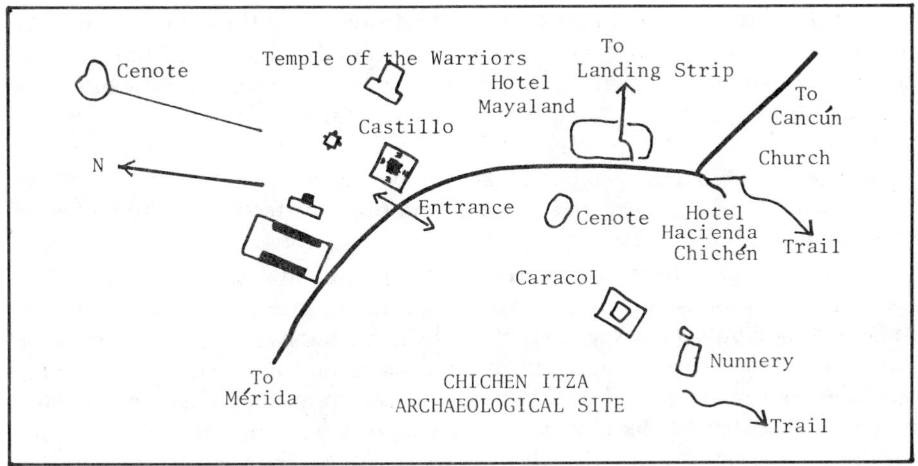

CHICHEN ITZA, Yucatán - 1984 up-date, based on field studies made in June, 1978, March, 1979, and April, 1981. See also 1976 Suppl. to FBM, p. S68 (or 1976 up-date below), and FBM, 1968, p. 59.

A bypass has now diverted heavy trucks and other through traffic moving between Mérida and Cancún, so that walking along the paved road between the entrance to the archaeological site and hotels to the south is safer than before. Nevertheless, one still encounters private cars, taxis, and tour buses along this road, so should be cautious about extensive birding there. Easily accessible partially overgrown dirt roads and trails provide favorable birding areas away from vehicular traffic.

One which we have found rewarding for both day and night birding branches off the paved road immediately adjacent to the south end of the main Hotel Mayaland building. It leads as a well-used dirt road behind the building and for some distance through the hotel gardens, and then dwindles into a more or less overgrown road through low woodland to a landing strip for light planes. Along this road, in the gardens and low woodlands, you should be able to find many of the species in the first and second 1976 lists.

On a night walk along this road in spring or early summer you should be able to hear, and possibly see with a strong spotlight, the Ferruginous Pygmy-Owl and the Pauraque. On a moonlight night in March we saw and heard those, and also heard the relatively little-known **Guatemalan Screech-Owl** and **Yucatan Poorwill.**

We have continued to find the main grounds of the Hotel Hacienda Chichén (mentioned in 1976) favorable for birding. **The Social Flycatcher** and Clay-colored Robin seem always to be active there, and transient or wintering warblers and grosbeaks are numerous in the proper season (add Black-and-white Warbler, Yellow-throated Warbler, and Rose-breasted Grosbeak to the 1976 list). If you walk southward from the hacienda gate toward the Catholic Church, and swing to your right shortly before reaching the church, then proceed around some old hacienda buildings, you should come to a partly overgrown dirt road leading generally southwestward through low, brushy woodland. Along this track you should have a good chance of finding some of the more elusive species, such as the Plain Chachalaca, **Yucatan Bobwhite,** and **Yucatan Jay** (in summer watch for mostly-white juvenal jays, with blue wings and tail, along with the black-and-blue adults). The track leads to a seldom-visited group of old Maya buildings, whence another trail leads generally northward to the Nunnery and Caracol and other better-known buildings of Chichén Itzá.

Beginning near the Caracol, and following the path (mentioned in 1976) leading into the woodland beyond (south of) the Nunnery, on a hot mid-day in June we found only a few species such as the Ferruginous Pygmy-Owl, **Yucatan Jay,** and Alta Mira Oriole, but on an early morning walk you should see many more. At the end of this trail we came upon a small group of small, partially reconstructed buildings in a clearing (the buildings mentioned in the previous paragraph). From this clearing we could then retrace our steps to the Nunnery and the Caracol, or proceed generally northeastward on an overgrown dirt road to the Hotel Hacienda Chichén.

Chichén Itzá, Yucatán - 1976 up-date, based on field studies in January, 1976, and reports from contributors.

Chichén Itzá is in the central part of the Yucatan Region at an elevation of about 60 feet above sea level. It is about 120 km. east of Mérida, on highway #180. The village of Chichén Itzá, which is adjacent to the archaeological site of the same name, has grown considerably in the last few years and now probably has a population of several hundred persons. Climatic data are not readily available but the situation is undoubtedly much the same as in Valladolid, which is about 40 km. (25 mi.) to the east. There the average annual rainfall is about 47 inches; 35 inches from May through October, and 12 inches from November through April; and monthly mean temperatures vary from 72 degrees F. (January) to 81 degrees F. (May).

In the woodlands and park-like fields of the archaeological site at Chichén Itzá and in the easily accessible surrounding countryside many of the characteristic birds of the Yucatan Region are prominent and easy to find. One will find here loose clusters of old ruined buildings, some well restored, others partially restored or completely untouched. There are two major groups of buildings, those in Old Chichen, south of the highway, and a more recently constructed group including the Castillo and the Temple of the Warriors north of the highway. In both of these areas there are open, grassy spaces which are usually kept cleared, and these are surrounded mostly by woodland of moderately large trees and thorny tangled undergrowth, and hedgerows, thickets, and overgrown fields. The unrestored portions of the original city extend for hundreds of yards away from the principal buildings, and there, where foot trails and dirt roads lead past mounds which were once Maya temples but which now are covered with dirt and a tangle of vines and trees, the observer should be able to study the bird life of the characteristic habitat of the rather arid portions of the Yucatan Region.

Many species of birds of the area live in the immediate vicinity of the major reconstructed buildings, while others visit there at one time or another. The birds most likely to be noted frequently during the observer's walk around the Castillo, the Temple of the Warriors, the Ball Court, and the other most publicized buildings, and nearby woodland edge and thickets, are as follows:

Black Vulture	Cave Swallow (s.)
Turkey Vulture	Rough-winged Swallow
Common Ground-Dove	**Yucatan Jay**
Ruddy Ground-Dove	**Clay-colored Robin**
White-fronted Dove	**Peppershrike**
Groove-billed Ani	Northern Parula (w.)
Vaux's Swift	Yellow-rumped Warbler
Turquoise-browed Motmot	Great-tailed Grackle
Golden-fronted Woodpecker	**Singing Blackbird**
Social Flycatcher	Altamira Oriole
Yucatan Flycatcher	**Gray Saltator**
Olivaceous Flycatcher	Cardinal
Gray-breasted Martin	

The observer might then wish to go farther afield, to the Nunnery and the Caracol and other parts of Old Chichen, on the south side of the highway. From the outskirts of the ruins, particularly in Old Chichen, it should be rewarding to follow small paths or dirt roads into uncleared portions or cultivated fields. One such path, which should be noticeable going beyond the Nunnery on the right as you approach from the Caracol leads to a gateway and beyond for a kilometer or more through woodlands and semi-open areas where there has been less extensive restoration of the old Maya buildings. Prior inquiry should be made at the main ticket office as to whether the path is still usable, and whether one is allowed to go through the gate (may be identified as providing access to the Temple of the Lintel and the Date Group). There may be cattle in this area, and the gate may be locked. In such places one should be able to find most of the species on the preceding list, and most of the following:

Plain Chachalaca	**Yellow-bellied Elaenia**
Yucatan Bobwhite	**Brown Jay**
Aztec Parakeet	**White-browed Wren**
Barn Owl (n.)	**Spotted-breasted Wren**
Ferruginous Pygmy-Owl	**White-bellied Wren**
Lesser Nighthawk	Blue-gray Gnatcatcher
Pauraque (n.)	Red-eyed Vireo (s.)
Chip-willow (n.)	Magnolia Warbler (w.)
Lineated Woodpecker	Red-eyed Cowbird
Laughing Creeper	**Yellow-throated Euphonia**
Barred Antshrike	**Black-headed Saltator**
Rose-throated Becard	**Blue Bunting**
Masked Tityra	**Blue-black Grassquit**
Boat-billed Flycatcher	Olive Sparrow
White-eyed Flycatcher	

The gardens and grounds and immediate environs of at least two of the hotels at Chichén Itzá, the Hotel Mayaland on the left and the Hotel Hacienda Chichén on the right, a few hundred meters beyond the main entrance to the archaeological site (as you come from Mérida and go toward Valladolid), provide very good opportunities for bird watching. Many of the common resident birds of the area and a large number of winter visitants, in season, should be found at either of these places. My list for an early morning walk on the grounds of the Hotel Hacienda Chichén in January, 1976 included:

Black Vulture	Blue-gray Gnatcatcher
Gray Hawk	**Peppershrike**
Plain Chachalaca	White-eyed Vireo (w.)
Ruddy Ground-Dove	Northern Parula (w.)
White-fronted Dove	Magnolia Warbler (w.)
Ferruginous Pygmy-Owl	Yellow-rumped Warbler (w.)
Cinnamon Hummingbird	Black-throated Green Warbler (w.)
Golden-fronted Woodpecker	Great-tailed Grackle
Masked Tityra	Altamira Oriole
Couch's Kingbird	Hooded Oriole
Great Kiskadee	**Singing Blackbird**
Social Flycatcher	**Scrub Euphonia**
Empidonax sp. (w.)	Summer Tanager (w.)
Green Jay	**Black-headed Saltator**
Clay-colored Robin	**Gray Saltator**

CHIHUAHUA, Chihuahua - 1984 up-date, based on a visit in May, 1983. See also FBM, 1968, p. 61.

See also Cerocahui and Rancho La Estancia.

Chihuahua is about 375 km. south of El Paso, Texas on National Highways 45 and 16. The population is reported to be nearly 400,000.

(Although not technically the eastern terminus of the Chihuahua-Pacific Railroad, this city is the eastmost and traditional boarding point for tourists riding the passenger trains westbound through the spectacular canyons and mountains of western Chihuahua and eastern Sinaloa. There are some places along, or accessible from, the railroad where tourists may be accommodated overnight, including Cerocahui, Creel, and Divisadero. We have included details about Cerocahui in this Supplement. Anyone wishing to make this trip should consult travel agencies in the U.S.A. and/or Chihuahua, or in Los Mochis which is the west-most passenger terminus.

Although we did see two species of birds (near the airport) which were not on the 1968 lists, the Rock Dove and Red-winged Blackbird, birding opportunities in or near the city seem to be more limited than before. Chihuahua, however, can serve as a "staging area" for studies of the land birds of the rugged hills and low mountains about 150 km. (road distance) west of the city, or the wintering waterfowl in the shallow lakes or flooded fields in the general vicinity of the town of Cuauhtémoc.

While traveling from Chihuahua to one such place (Rancho La Estancia) via Highway 16 westward we found some additional places where the birds of the 1968 Chihuahua lists could be expected. One of these was about 40 km. out of the city, where the road descended after winding through some low hills. Another was about 10 km. beyond (generally west of) the first, where a small river lined with cottonwoods bordered the town of General Trías. We found that (a pale race of) the Horned Lark was relatively common on the heavily-grazed short-grass high plains west of General Trías. As we neared the town of Cuauhtémoc we noticed large nets in the apple orchards, similar to ones I had surmised might be for protecting the fruit from birds, near San Antonio de las Alazanas (which is near Saltillo). These proved instead to be steel-mesh nets to be deployed over the trees in case of violent storms, to protect against hail.

CHIHUAHUA-PACIFIC RAILROAD - See Cerocahui, Chihuahua, and Los Mochis.

Chunyaxché, Quintana Roo - New account, 1976, based on field studies made in January, 1976.

Chunyaxché is in the southeastern part of the Yucatan Region, just a few feet above sea level. It is about 370-410 km. southeast of Mérida by road, and about 20 km. south of the village of Tulum, on highway number 307. At this writing only a few people live at the site, in perhaps a half-dozen houses. Temperatures are probably slightly higher than, and rainfall probably about the same as, at Cozumel Island (1976, p. S73).

There is a considerable variety of situations for bird watching within a few hundred meters of what appears to be the main building of the ruins. To reach the ruins turn left (as you approach from Tulum) off highway number 307 onto a dirt road which leads about 100 meters or so to the east to the area of the houses and the partly restored buildings. If this road is very muddy or rough, one could probably park at a large wooden building (which may be a restaurant or store) on the east side of the highway, just south of the other turn-off, and walk back to the side. (There may be a good gravel road at the building, leading to a lagoon, but not to the archaeological site). There has been some clearing around the houses (of the caretakers?) and the principal old Maya building, and from there a path leads through moist forest to the remnants of various other buildings where there has been very little excavation or restoration. This forest looks like a smaller version of the humid tropical evergreen forest which occurs farther south in parts of the SA sub-region. The birds of the humid forest at Chunyaxché were elusive and quiet at the time of our visit, but when they are active you should find most of the species which are on the list for the humid forest of the southeastern portion of the Yucatan Region.

In another direction (generally toward the Caribbean Sea) a path and a road lead through partially cleared areas, low woodland, and mangrove swamp, to the edge of a vast lagoon (which was almost devoid of birds when we were there). Our list of species seen during a short visit to these partly cleared woodlands and to the edges of the mangrove swamp, in late afternoon in January, 1976, included the following:

Great Egret	**Clay-colored Robin**
Turkey Vulture	Black-and-white Warbler (w.)
Gray Hawk	American Redstart (w.)
Aztec Parakeet	Hooded Oriole
Empidonax sp. (w.)	Summer Tanager (w.)
Yucatan Jay	**Jungle Tanager**

CIUDAD LAS CASAS - See San Cristóbal de las Casas.

CIUDAD MANTE - See Mante.

CIUDAD MEXICO - See Mexico City.

CIUDAD (DE) VALLES - See Valles.

CIUDAD VICTORIA - See Victoria.

CIUDAD XICOTEPEC DE JUAREZ - See Xicótepec.

CIUDAD DEL CARMEN, Campeche - 1984 up-date, based on library studies. See also FBM, 1968, p. 63 - the 1968 account was based on field studies around the ferry terminal a few km. from the island, and on detailed reports from contributors.

Ciudad del Carmen is situated on the southwest end of the narrow, approximately 40 km. long island called Isla del Carmen. It is about 170 km. by road and ferry northeast of Villahermosa, and about 215 km. by road and ferry southwest of Campeche. The population is reported to be about 80,000.

Probably there is much more evidence now of petroleum-related commercial enterprises in the town, and it may be more difficult now to find suitable areas for field work on the island.

Coatzacoalcos, Veracruz - 1976 up-date, based on library studies and contributor's reports. See also FBM, 1968, p.65.

It is about 680-750 km. east of Mexico City by road.

The population is reported to be about 70,000. The area near the old ferry to Nanchital may no longer be rewarding. There is increasing industrialization, pollution, and congestion on the east side of the river along Highway #180 and along side roads up and down the river. In the vicinity of the roads to Nanchital and Allende expect a confusing array of roads and refineries and other industrial enterprises, and fewer areas suitable for birds. It may be difficult or unrewarding to make the suggested circuit through Nanchital and Chapo, or the trip to Allende (FBM, 1968, p.68), because of industrial development.

COBA, Quintana Roo - 1984 up-date, based on field studies in April 1981. See also 1976 Suppl. to FBM, p. S72 (or 1976 up-date below).

The actual road distance from Mérida, Yucatán east to Cobá is now only about 275 km., since a paved road from Nuevo X-Cán to Cobá and Tulum has been built. Cobá is about 150 km. shortest road distance southwest of Cancún, and about 47 km. northwest of the Highway 307 road junction near Tulum. In 1981 it was still a small village (along with the archaeological site).

The lake shore (Lago Cobá) was considerably more disturbed in 1981 than it was in 1976, but we were nevertheless able to find a greater number of shorebirds and waders and other waterbirds in April, 1981, than we found in January, 1976. Beginning from the Villa Arqueológica one could walk along the lake shore to the "main street" of the village and then on to the end of the lake near the gate to the archaeological site, or one could walk from the Villa Arqueológica in a direction away from the village and the archaeological site, to the opposite end of the lake. Birds to be expected (in addition to those on the first 1976 list) along these shores are:

Least Grebe	Snowy Egret
Double-crested Cormorant	Solitary Sandpiper (w.)
Olivaceous Cormorant	Common Snipe (w)
Green Heron	Pectoral Sandpiper (w)
Great Egret	Green Kingfisher

The low woodland, woodland borders, and weedy fields within the archaeological site are still favorable places for finding numerous birds. Another favorable area is the grassy lake borders and nearby woodland at the upper end of the lake. To reach the latter area walk from the Villa Arqueológica along the lake shore away from the village and the archaeological site, and then continue on the path into the woods beyond the end of the lake. In both of the above-mentioned areas you should expect most of the birds in the second 1976 list, and many of the following as well:

Rufescent Tinamou	**Cinnamon Hummingbird**
Black Vulture	**Citreoline Trogon**
Plain Chachalaca	Golden-fronted Woodpecker
Yucatan Bobwhite	**Yellow-bellied Elaenia**
White-fronted Parrot	**Yucatan Jay**
Groove-billed Ani	Clay-colored Robin

Peppershrike	Alta Mira Oriole
Yellow-green Vireo	**Yellow-faced Grassquit**
Great-tailed Grackle	Lesser Goldfinch
Hooded Oriole	

Cobá, Quintana Roo - 1976 account, based on field studies in January, 1976.

Cobá is in the eastern portion of the Yucatan Region, not far above sea level (probably 50 to 100 feet). It is approximately 250 km. straight-line distance east of Mérida, but at this writing it is much farther by round-about distance. It is approximately 30-40 km. (Ed. note, 1984: 45-50 km.) in a northerly direction from the village of Tulum by all-weather gravel road. This road will probably soon be paved and extended northward to join highway number 180 near Chemax or X-cán, which would reduce the road distance between Mérida and Cobá to perhaps less than 300 km. or about 160 to 180 mi., and would open up a shorter route from Mérida to Tulum. A very small village is associated with the archaeological site - there are probably only a few dozen people living there at this writing. Temperatures probably average about the same as at Valladolid, and annual rainfall is probably somewhat more than at Valladolid (1976,p.S92).

The vegetation in the vicinity of Cobá, and along the road between Tulum and Cobá, is more luxuriant than farther west, the trees being taller, with more evergreen trees and shrubs, and fewer thorny shrubs. The **Laughing Falcon** is frequently to be seen along the road from Tulum to Cobá. There is a lake at Cobá, with some marshy shores, providing a favorable area for water birds. Some of the principal buildings are a considerable distance apart, with trails or sharp-rock roads, or dirt roads between them. It is possible to see many birds as you go from one building to another, or around any one of the buildings, because the woodland on the site has been opened up considerably but not completely cleared. If time permits it might be rewarding to walk along the roads and trails and around the edges of the clearings which exist, and down along the shores of the lake.

At present the visitor drives in along the shore of the lake, past a place where tickets are sold, and then can drive (or walk) about 200 meters or so, up a dirt and rock road to one of the principal buildings. Most of the birds in the regional list for archaeological sites and scrubby woodlands should be here, as well as many of those in the regional list for humid tropical forest.

Along the lake and its shores you might find a few ducks and the following birds as well:

Pied-billed Grebe	Jacana
Little Blue Heron	Killdeer (w.)
Red Rail	Spotted Sandpiper (w.)
Common Gallinule	Ringed Kingfisher
American Coot	Common Yellowthroat (w.)

During an hour or two of walking on the roads and trails among the old Maya buildings you can expect to see:

Turkey Vulture
Ruddy Ground-Dove
Aztec Parakeet
Squirrel Cuckoo
White-bellied Emerald
Barred Antshrike
Couch's Kingbird
Boat-billed Flycatcher
Social Flycatcher
Great Kiskadee
Olivaceous Flycatcher
White-eyed Flycatcher
Brown Jay

Green Jay
Spotted-breasted Wren
Gray Catbird (w.)
Orange-crowned Warbler (w.)
Northern Parula (w.)
Magnolia Warbler (w.)
Yellow-throated Warbler (w.)
American Redstart (w.)
Orchard Oriole (w.)
Scrub Euphonia
Black-headed Saltator
Collared Seedeater

Colima, Colima - See FBM, 1968, p. 70. For more detailed information on birding near the city of Colima, and in other parts of the state of Colima, see the section (by Warren D. Harden) on Birds of Colima in the book *Colima A Guide to Fiesta Country* by Juan Oseguera Velasquez (translated by Richard H. Hancock), published by International Training Programs, The University of Oklahoma, Norman, Oklahoma.

COMITAN, Chiapas - 1984 up-date, based on field studies by EPE in March, 1981, and field studies by Robert Behrstock in October, 1983. See also 1976 Suppl. to FBM, p. S99 (or 1976 up-date below), and FBM, 1968, p. 72.

The population is reported to be about 40,000.

The 1968 bird lists are still accurate, but can be supplemented as follows:

Residential and commercial areas: add Rock Dove and House Sparrow.

Cultivated fields, pastures, and grassy plains south and southeast of town: add Cattle Egret, White-tailed Kite, Mourning Dove, Tropical Kingbird, and **Tropical Mockingbird.**

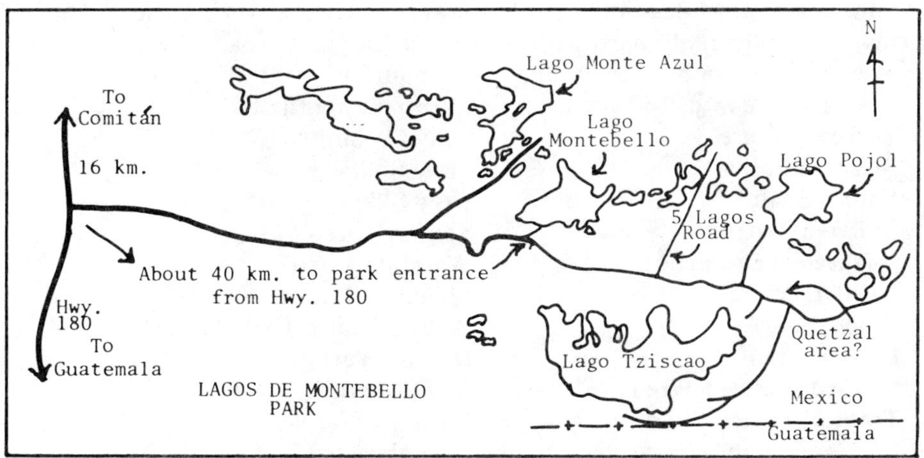

The principal birding attraction in the vicinity of Comitán is the humid forest around a group of lakes known as Lagos de Montebello, or Lagunas de Montebello. To reach the principal birding areas in the forest proceed (basically as indicated in 1976) south from Comitán about 15 km. on Highway 190, then turn left (as you approach Trinitaria) onto a paved road and follow it about 40 km. past open fields, pastures, cropland, and perhaps a few open woodlots. Watch for a large gravel turn-off and gravel road leading to the right. At this point there should be one or two buildings or shelters, and a large sign on your right indicating **Parque Natural Ejidal Tziscao,** and perhaps an arrow indicating that you should go to the right to reach an "Albergue." Turn right and follow the gravel road as it winds upward through the forest. For the principal birding areas do not go to Lago Monte Azul or Lago Montebello; instead continue up the main gravel road about 10 to 12 km., meanwhile passing one or two dirt roads swinging left. You pass one or more overlooks (see note about overlooks in Introduction) where you can see Lago Tziscao on your right, until you come to a prominent side road going to the right toward the Albergue. This junction may be well-marked with signs pointing ahead to other lakes, and a sign pointing to the right toward the Albergue Tziscao. (The Albergue is a combination restaurant-dormitory-picnic area in a relatively flat, broad open space on the southeast shore of Lago Tziscao, in an area of farms, clearings, overgrown fields, and scattered houses.) To find many of the birds of the humid forest you could park near the road junction, clear of traffic, and walk back toward the park entrance or ahead toward the other lakes (**not** to the right toward the Albergue), birding from the road shoulder as you go a kilometer or two in either direction. In this general vicinity some persons have found the **Quetzal** (by birding early in the morning in spring). The park road may be very rough and rutted, dusty or muddy.

It's not necessary to plunge into the forest or even to follow the trails which lead off the road in places. Birding from the gravel road should be productive for all but a few of the most secretive species of the forest interior, as you will have a relatively unimpeded view of the treetops and woodland borders. Alternatively you could drive back toward the park entrance and park and walk down one of the dirt roads which lead off (mostly toward the right as you go back). These roads are considerably narrower than the main gravel road, the vegetation crowds in closer on both sides, and there should be less traffic.

Among the birds to be expected in the park are the following:

Turkey Vulture	Gray Catbird (w.)
Black Vulture	**Slaty Solitaire**
Vaux's Swift	**Gray Silky-Flycatcher**
Collared Trogon	Solitary Vireo
Olivaceous Creeper	Warbling Vireo
Greater Pewee	Magnolia Warbler (w)
Wood Pewee	Black-throated Green Warbler
Barred Wren	Hermit Warbler
Spotted-breasted Wren	MacGillivray's Warbler
Tropical House-Wren	Wilson's Warbler
Highland Wood-Wren	**Slate-throated Redstart**

Golden-crowned Warbler   **Common Bush-Tanager**
Yellow-backed Oriole

Comitán, Chiapas - 1976 up-date, based on library studies.

The new figure for elevation is about 5050 feet. The population is reported to be about 21,000.

A new paved road to the Lagunas de Montebello provides access to an additional area for birding. There are about two dozen lakes in a wooded region, indicated as a National Park on some maps. Whether this is formally a park or not, much of the land may have been cleared, and almost certainly there are no special tourist facilities there. There should be tracks or paths along woodland edge or into patches of woodland or through open areas with scattered trees along lake shores, however. Birds to be expected would be many of those in the lists for savannahs, or other partially open country, and for edge of humid forest, in the southern Atlantic Lowlands Sub-region (1968,pp.39-40).

To reach the Lagunas de Montebello you would go about 15 km. (9 mi.) south of Comitán on highway number 190, then angle left on a paved road, just before reaching La Trinitaria on the main highway. The branch road to the left may not be marked. The lakes are about 44 km. (about 27 mi.) from the highway number 190 junction. Information about the Lagunas de Montebello might be available in Comitán.

COPPER CANYON - This is the name often applied to the large canyon of the Rio Urique, along with subsidiary canyons of the Tararecua, and Cobre and others. See Cerocahui.

Córdoba, Veracruz - 1976 up-date, based on library studies. See also FBM, 1968, p. 74.

The distance from Mexico City to Córdoba is about 290 km. by toll road. The town is on Highway 150D as well as Highway 150. The population is reported to be about 80,000.

For information about the Cañon de Metlac see Fortín de las Flores.

COZUMEL ISLAND, Quintana Roo - 1984 up-date, based on field studies in June 1978, March, 1979, and April, 1981. See also 1976 Suppl. to FBM, p. S74 (or 1976 up-date below) and FBM, 1968, p. 78.

Cozumel can be reached by airplane or ferry. We don't recommend the passenger-only ferry.

Although almost any side road or broad path leading through relatively unpopulated portions of the island is likely to be reasonably good for birds, several particular places can be "pinpointed" here. About 7 km. southwest of the main pier at San Miguel, a stretch of old road has been cut off where the new shore highway swings a few hundred feet inland and then back close to the shore. A right turn (as you drive away from San Miguel) at about the mid-point

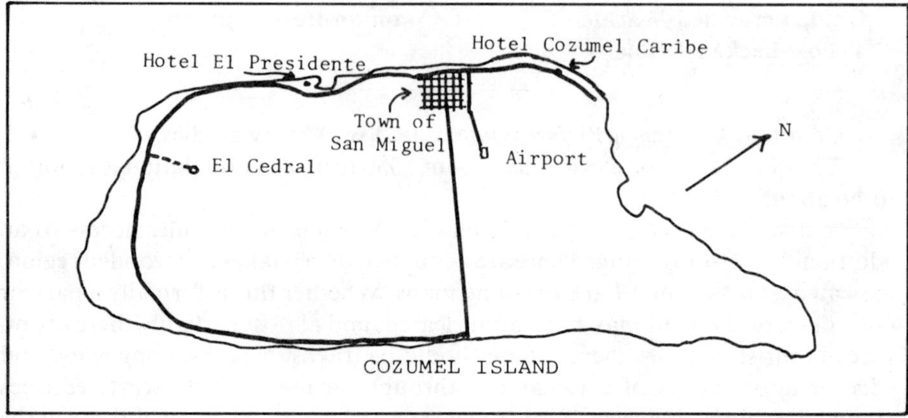

of this inland "bulge" will lead you to and across the old road and into the parking lot of the Hotel El Presidente. If you follow the old road toward the southwest it leads back to the main highway, while toward the northeast it leads past a yacht basin and along the shore.

Birding around the hotel grounds, the parking lot, and along the northeastern segment of the old road, past overgrown vacant lots and low woodland, you should find most of the species in the 1968 lists, and most of the following:

Roadside Hawk	Black-and-white Warbler (w)
Yucatan Parrot	Yellow (Golden) Warbler
White-fronted Parrot	Magnolia Warbler (w)
Prevost's Mango	Black-throated Green Warbler (w)
Fork-tailed Emerald	American Redstart (w)
Streaked Attila	**Rose-throated Tanager**
Olivaceous Flycatcher	Blue Grosbeak (w)

North of San Miguel it is possible to find interesting birding areas in the vicinity of some of the luxury hotels, although we found fewer species and fewer individuals there than around the Hotel El Presidente. One of these is about 3 or 4 km. north of San Miguel as you go north on the main coastal boulevard. To reach it continue past the Puerto de Abrigo, and shortly before you reach the Hotel Cozumel Caribe (on your left) a road goes to the right from the boulevard into low woodland, fields, farmland, and a residential area.

Another area is beyond the Hotel Mayan Plaza where the boulevard ends and becomes a dirt road. You can follow this more or less straight ahead through low woodland, or swing left after a short distance and follow a branch road through the mangroves, and eventually reach the shore if you wish. The birds to be expected in these areas are many of those of the 1968 lists and some of those in the 1984 list above.

The forests of the island's interior are more luxuriant and have more tall trees than the woodlands near the shore. A sample of somewhat larger forest can be studied relatively easily on the road to El Cedral. To find this area drive southwest from San Miguel on the coastal highway past the Hotel Presidente, past the Laguna Chancanab, and past some public beaches on your right. After the highway swings southward and then southeastward watch for a dirt road leading left - it may be marked by a sign for El Cedral. This road goes several kilometers to the village of El Cedral and a small Maya building.

For best birding results you could drive a kilometer or two in from the highway, find a wide place to park, and walk as far as you like on the dirt road. The road was easily passable in March, 1979, but you should check as you go along (and when you try to park) for possible deep sand, or mud-holes in the rainy season.

It's not advisable to bird along the main paved roads because they are narrow, the shoulders are mostly narrow (and may be soft sand or mud), and traffic is sometimes heavy and almost always fast-moving.

(See also **The Living Bird Quarterly,** Winter/1984, pp. 22-26; published by the Laboratory of Ornithology, Cornell University.)

Cozumel Island, Quintana Roo - 1976 up-date, based on library studies and reports from contributors.

Cozumel Island is in the extreme eastern part of the Yucatan Region not far above sea level. It is approximately 280-290 km. straight-line distance east of Mérida. The population of the small town of San Miguel on the west coast of the island, is still reported to be about 3000, but it is the center of an extensive resort complex extending up and down the coast, and numbering perhaps as many as 15,000 to 30,000 inhabitants, or more. The average rainfall is 59 inches; 47 inches from May through November, and 12 inches from December through April. Monthly mean temperatures vary from a low of 73 degrees F. (January) to a high of 81 degrees F. (July-August). It is accessible by ferry from the mainland.

The partly overgrown fields, pastures, scrubby woodlands, and open residential or resort areas are favorable places for the observation of many typical species of the Yucatan Region, as well as a few species which are restricted to Cozumel Island and are fairly common there. The aspect is that of a small resort town on the shore of an island, with a crowded business section and dock area at the water's edge giving way rather abruptly to residential areas and many hotels and other resort facilities which extend several miles north and south, principally close to the shore. The populated area is thus rather narrow, with typical residential areas a short distance away from the beach, and then a rather abrupt transition to a few pastures and cultivated fields, and the scrubby woodland characteristic of most of the island. The main road on the island leads north and south along the west coast from San Miguel, while foot-paths and dirt roads and tracks lead inland from this road and from the outskirts of San Miguel.

Along the borders of quiet pools, in marshes (particularly near the north end of the island), or at secluded beaches, there are wading birds of several kinds, the most frequently seen being:

Green Heron	Great Egret
Little Blue Heron	Yellow-crowned Night-Heron

Cuernavaca, Morelos - 1976 up-date, based on library studies and reports from contributors. See FBM, 1968, p. 76.

It is still on highway 95, but highway 95D now technically by-passes it, swinging around the eastern edge of town. The population is reported to be about 135,000. Some outlying areas may now be included in the population figures.

There may be an increased number of tourist facilities and housing developments along the road from Curenavaca to the Cañon de Lobos, along with further encroachment on habitat near, or within, the Cañon de Lobos. The grounds of resort-type hotels and the gardens and intervening fields or vacant lots of low-density residential areas along this road should be suitable for a number of species of small birds, especially wintering warblers and finches.

Yellow-headed Blackbirds (w.) and Red-winged Blackbirds frequent moist or flooded fields mostly south or east of Cuernavaca.

The Tucuchillo (n.), **Happy Wren** and **Blue Mockingbird** can be added to the Cañon de Lobos list.

At higher elevations, on the old road to Mexico City, the situation should be somewhat as noted earlier (1968,pp.80-82) with some alteration of specific areas by further development and more restrictions by property owners.

Culiacán, Sinaloa - 1976 up-date, based on library studies. See FBM, 1968, p. 83.

The population is reported to be about 168,000.

The grounds of the suburban motels should still attract numerous birds, but probably there will be fewer favorable places along the river near the north edge of town (1968,p84). South of the city the places mentioned (1968,p.84) may have been altered, but if so, other places nearby should be satisfactory. Expect the **Mexican Parrotlet** in parks and residential areas, especially in winter.

Durango, Durango - 1976 up-date, based on library studies. See FBM, 1968, p. 85.

The population is reported to be about 150,000.

It may be difficult now to find patches of pine woodland and vegetation other than grassland within 30 or 40 miles of the city. See Mazatlán (1976, p. S104) for notes on highway 40 between Durango and Mazatlán. Add White-crowned Sparrow (w.), and some other wintering finches and warblers to the mesquite-grassland list (1968,p.86).

EL NARANJO, San Luis Potosí - New account, by T. Ben Feltner, based on field studies in December, 1983, and many times before that. This account replaces that of 1976 Suppl. to FBM, pp. S23-S28 (not reprinted here), and the very brief write-up of El Salto, FBM, 1968, p. 87.

El Naranjo is in the southwestern portion of the NA sub-region, at an

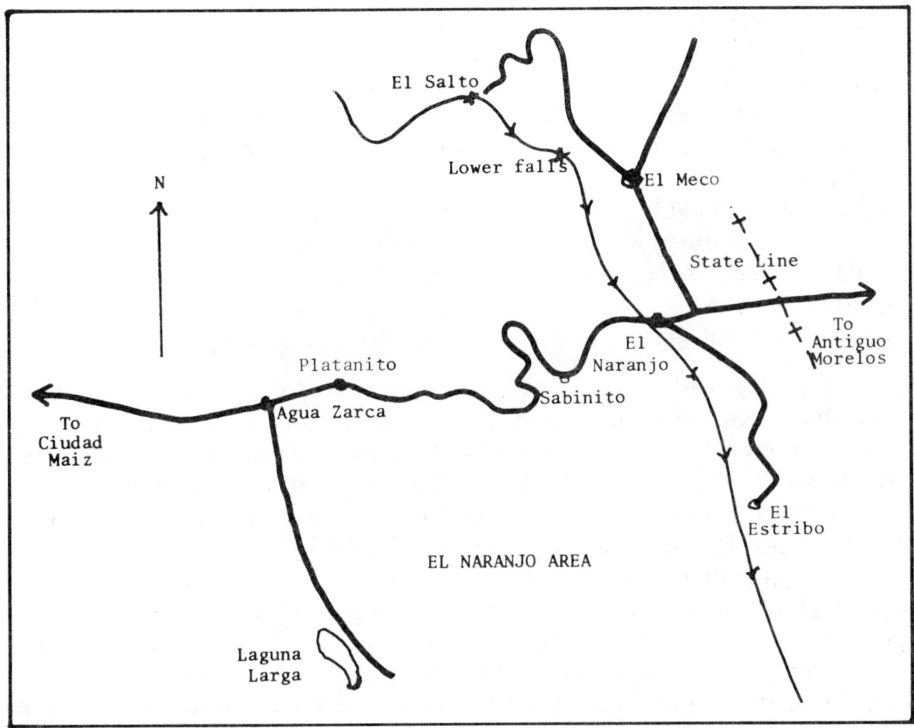

elevation (estimated) of about 600 feet. By road distance it is about 560 km. north of Mexico City, about 500 km. south-southwest of Brownsville, Texas, and about 60 km. southwest of Mante, on Highway 80. The population (estimated) is several thousands. Average annual rainfall and monthly mean temperatures are probably similar to those in Tampico, although rainfall may be somewhat greater.

The El Naranjo Christmas Count Circle is situated in one of the richest birding areas in northeastern Mexico. This richness, and variety, is mostly attributable to the great amount, and varied nature, of largely undisturbed habitat still remaining in this broad valley bordered by hills and mountains. Humid oak-sweetgum forest, river and river-edge woodland, semi-arid brushland, arid upland-grassland, dry oak-savannah, tropical deciduous forest, tropical evergreen forest, lake and marsh, villages, towns, and croplands, all are present in the circle. Access to the locality is by way of Highway 80 coming eastward from Ciudad del Maiz, or coming westward from Antiquo Morelos. For uniformity and clarity we refer to the latter route in giving directions to birding areas.

Coming from Antiguo Morelos you will find an interesting area a few hundred yards past the sign-posted border between the states of Tamaulipas and San Luis Potosí. Here there are several pull-offs on the right, where you may park and look for birds in the semi-arid hillside brushland and nearby wooded ravines. The following species may be found here:

Rufescent Tinamou	Brown Jay
Red-billed Pigeon	Carolina Wren
Green Parakeet	Clay-colored Robin
Red-crowned Parrot	Blue-gray Gnatcatcher
Squirrel Cuckoo	Orange-crowned Warbler (w)
Ferruginous Pygmy-Owl	Nashville Warbler (w)
Fork-tailed Emerald	Wilson's Warbler (w)
Buff-bellied Hummingbird	Hooded Oriole
Ladder-backed Woodpecker	Alta Mira Oriole
Couch's Kingbird	Olive Sparrow
Least Flycatcher (w)	Lincoln's Sparrow (w)

Proceeding westward you will come to the paved branch road to El Salto Falls, about 1 km. before the main part of the town of El Naranjo (which is at the bridge). To go to the falls turn right (north) from Highway 80, and follow the road 10 km. to the village of El Meco; then swing left and continue.

Watch for parrots and raptors in or over the sabal palm forest which flanks the branch road, and on the power lines and pylons.

Among the flowering Hibiscus shrubs in El Meco you may find orioles and hummingbirds, including, in summer, the **Prevost's Mango.** Swing left at the fork in the road in El Meco and continue generally parallel to the Río Naranjo.

As you proceed a few miles past El Meco you will reach an overlook for a waterfall on the left (not El Salto) where you may park. (See note in Introduction about overlooks, railings, etc.) Hundreds of **White-collared Swifts** roost there, in crevices in the cliff behind the falling water. (The birds fly through the waterfall to roost under its veil.) Each evening the flock congregates at about dusk, and makes a series of spectacular passes at the waterfall leaving a small "break-off" group at each pass. The process continues until all the swifts are "bedded down".

Continuing toward the main El Salto falls, you finally reach the gate of a permanent National Guard encampment surrounded by a high chain-link fence. *Do not try to pass this point.* There is a pull-off to the left where there is adequate parking space. Also a small dirt road (not suitable for driving) leads left to the bank of the river and the base of the falls.

El Salto, situated on the Río Naranjo, was formerly a spectacularly beautiful waterfall all year round. Now, water which once would have poured over the tremendous cliff is diverted at a point some distance upriver from the cliff to flow through hydroelectric turbines off to the side. During times of heavy rainfall there is enough water for both the turbines and the natural waterfall. During the dry season there is usually some seepage from the cliff, providing a slow flow through the terraced pools at its base. The diverted water is put back into the river only 200-300 meters downstream from the falls, therefore the habitat is little changed below that point. If you explore the tall cypresses along the river bank, and the several small patches of remnant evergreen forest nearby, you should find many of the following species:

Olivaceous Cormorant	Black Vulture
Turkey Vulture	Common Black Hawk

Gray Hawk
Bat Falcon
Spotted Sandpiper (w)
Common Ground-Dove
Elegant Trogon
Green Kingfisher
Golden-fronted Woodpecker
Black Phoebe
Sulphur-bellied Flycatcher (s)
Boat-billed Flycatcher
Social Flycatcher
Great Kiskadee
Olivaceous Flycatcher
Empidonax sp. (w)
Mexican Crow
Brown Jay
Spotted-breasted Wren
Northern House-Wren (w)
Gray Catbird (w)

Clay-colored Robin
Blue-gray Gnatcatcher (w)
Solitary Vireo (w)
Red-eyed Vireo (s)
Black-and-white Warbler (w)
Orange-crowned Warbler (w)
Northern Parula (w)
Louisiana Waterthrush
Wilson's Warbler (w)
Singing Blackbird
Red-eyed Cowbird
Alta Mira Oriole
Yellow-throated Euphonia
Yellow-winged Tanager
Summer Tanager (w)
Jungle Tanager
Black-headed Saltator
Yellow-faced Grassquit
Collared Seedeater

Returning to Highway 80, turning right, and continuing a kilometer or two, you reach the center of the town of El Naranjo. Just before you reach the bridge, a branch road (paved) leads to the left (south) from Highway 80 to the settlement of El Estribo. Over the first several miles of this road you pass through vast fields of sugar cane, the region's chief crop, but if you continue you eventually come to some scattered brush-patches and wooded hillsides. You should find many of the species previously listed in this account (for El Salto and the state border area). You may find several roadside ponds (some seasonal), and if so you may lure a **Meadow Warbler** or **Altamira Yellowthroat** into view, by "pishing" or "squeaking". Raptors such as the **Laughing Falcon** often perch on snags along this road, and there is a slight chance that you might see an Aplomado Falcon along here (or on the branch road from Highway 80 to El Salto, mentioned earlier).

If you can follow one of the dirt roads which branch to the right, to the banks of the Río Naranjo, about a kilometer or less from the paved road, you should see one or two of the four kingfishers - Ringed, Belted, **Amazon,** or Green - and possibly a **Tiger Heron.** Some of these roads are impassable by vehicle, however, especially after a rain.

If you return to Highway 80 and turn left you will be proceeding westward, and will cross the Río Naranjo almost immediately. Leaving the town of El Naranjo behind, the road leads through palm forest and semi-arid brushland. At a point about two miles from the Río Naranjo, as you approach the village of El Sabinito, you come to an abrupt transition between the palm forest and the tropical evergreen forest. The luxuriant foliage of the large trees forms a partial canopy over the highway in places as you drive between a steep forest-covered hillside on the right and a roadside stream on the left. You will find adequate parking places on your left (be very careful turning across traffic), but unless you can leave several feet between your car and the edge of the road it would be preferable for you to continue to the village of El Sabinito to park. For a distance of several hundred yards in this vicinity in the woodland and woodland borders you may see many of the following birds:

Rufescent Tinamou	Brown Jay
Gray Hawk	**Spotted-breasted Wren**
White-crowned Parrot	**Blue Mockingbird**
Singing Quail	Long-billed Thrasher
Wood Owl	**White-throated Robin**
Elegant Trogon	Clay-colored Robin
Mexican Trogon	Swainson's Thrush (w)
Violaceous Trogon	**Brown-backed Solitaire**
Green Kingfisher	Tropical Parula
Vaux's Swift	Louisiana Waterthrush (w)
Wedge-tailed Saberwing	Wilson's Warbler (w)
Blue-crowned Motmot	**Fan-tailed Warbler**
Golden-fronted Woodpecker	**Red-legged Honeycreeper**
Laughing Creeper	**Scrub Euphonia**
Rose-throated Becard	**Yellow-throated Euphonia**
Masked Tityra	**Jungle Tanager**
Eastern Phoebe (w)	**Black-headed Saltator**
Boat-billed Flycatcher	**Crimson-collared Grosbeak**
Sulphur-bellied Flycatcher (s)	Olive Sparrow
Olivaceous Flycatcher	Lincoln's Sparrow (w)
Rough-winged Swallow	

If you continue westward from El Sabinito you will climb into and through an extensive area of broad-leafed tropical-oak-forest, which appears successively more luxuriant at higher elevations. Many trees are covered with bromeliads and orchids, and flocks of foraging birds are frequently encountered. The road is steep in places and has narrow shoulders, therefore parking places are at a premium. Be even *more* careful in observing all of the precautions listed for the area near El Sabinito, because traffic is heavy, and moves rapidly, and trucks and cars are often forced to run along partly *on the shoulder*. Once safely parked, however, you should be able to find many of the following, and many on the El Sabinito list:

Rufescent Tinamou	**Bronzed Woodpecker**
Collared Micrastur	**Brown Woodpecker**
White-fronted Dove	**Flint-billed Woodpecker**
Red-lored Parrot	**Laughing Creeper**
Azure-crowned Hummingbird	Spotted-crowned Creeper
Wedge-tailed Saberwing	**Barred Antshrike**
White-eared Hummingbird	Olivaceous Flycatcher
Mexican Trogon	Green Jay
Elegant Trogon	Black-crested Titmouse

Rufous-browed Peppershrike	**Fan-tailed Warbler**
Solitary Vireo	**Golden-crowned Warbler**
Black-and-white Warbler (w)	**Rufous-capped Warbler**
Yellow-rumped Warbler (w)	Audubon's Oriole
Townsend's Warbler (w)	**Blue-hooded Euphonia**
Black-throated Green Warbler (w)	**Blue Bunting**

Continuing westward you will come to a high point on the road where there is a straight stretch of highway about 1 to 1½ km. in length, with relatively open areas (usually cornfields) on both sides of the road. A small cemetery on the right "marks" the location. You should be able to park safely along here, pulling well away from the pavement and observing the precautions noted in the previous paragraph. Birding along woodland borders in this vicinity you should be able to find many of the species on the previous list.

From this point westward the forest is successively drier, and the foraging flocks of birds include many highland species. In such dry woodlands you may find many of the following:

Collared Micrastur	Hutton's Vireo
Military Macaw	Warbling Vireo
Singing Quail	**Spot-breasted Warbler**
Vaux's Swift (w)	Yellow-rumped Warbler (w)
Broad-billed Hummingbird	Townsend's Warbler (w)
White-eared Hummingbird	Black-throated Gray Warbler (w)
Azure-crowned Hummingbird	Hermit Warbler (w)
Acorn Woodpecker	Painted Redstart
Olivaceous Creeper	Hepatic Tanager
Greater Pewee	**Striped Tanager**
Common Raven	Black-headed Grosbeak
Mexican Jay	**Blue Bunting**
Bridled Titmouse	Varied Bunting
Spotted Wren	**Rufous-capped Finch**
Black-headed Thrush	**Rusty Sparrow**
Gray Silky-Flycatcher	

Eventually the road leads out of the forest and into arid grassland and dry oak-savanna at the tiny settlement of Agua Zarca. If you turn left (south) behind the village's only store you can proceed on a crushed-rock-surfaced road which is passable at all seasons. You should be able to find pull-offs along this road from which to observe some of the interesting array of birds which inhabit the adjacent arid grassland and acacia scrub. Here you may find:

White-tailed Hawk	Cassin's Kingbird
Crested Caracara	Ash-throated Flycatcher
Common Bobwhite	Gray Flycatcher (w)
Greater Roadrunner	Common Bushtit
Broad-billed Hummingbird	Curve-billed Thrasher
Say's Phoebe	Eastern Bluebird
Vermilion Flycatcher	Brown-headed Cowbird

Eastern Meadowlark	Savannah Sparrow (w)
Pyrrhuloxia	Grasshopper Sparrow
Blue Grosbeak	Lark Sparrow (w)
Brown Towhee	Chipping Sparrow

At a point 7 miles down this road is a shallow lake, Laguna Larga, which you can see off to the right as you approach. You may have difficulty finding a track or road to gain access to the lake - there is a wooden gate about 100 yards before you reach a concrete culvert and stream going under the road at about the 7-mile point - but remember to respect private property (and cattle). You should see some Bald Cypress trees in this vicinity, and there is a chance that you might find the **Military Macaw** in these trees in winter. Ducks and other aquatic species are often numerous on the lake or along its shores, and raptors may be seen in the vicinity. You should be able to find most of the following at the appropriate season:

Least Grebe	Ruddy Duck (w)
Pied-billed Grebe	Common Black Hawk
Great Egret	Virginia Rail (w)
American Bittern (w)	Sora (w)
Pintail (w)	American Coot
Mallard	Common Gallinule
Green-winged Teal (w)	Common Snipe (w)
Blue-winged Teal (w)	Spotted Sandpiper (w)
Cinnamon Teal (w)	Vermilion Flycatcher
Shoveler (w)	Common Yellowthroat (w)
Ring-necked Duck (w)	

(Ed. note: See also Christmas Count reports in *American Birds,* July, 1980 through 1984, and earlier.)

EL PALMITO - See La Capilla del Taxte.

EL SALTO - Several localities in Mexico bear this name, usually because of the presence of a waterfall in the vicinity. One of these is a large waterfall in the state of San Luis Potosí - for a discussion of that locality see El Naranjo. Another is a small town in the state of Durango, about 100 km. west of the city of Durango on Highway 40. I have not seen the Durango locality since 1950 - for species to be expected there (*if* there are still some reasonably large areas of pine or pine-oak woodlands) see Durango (FBM, 1968, pp.85-86) and the lists of frequently observed birds of the Northern Highlands sub-region (FBM, 1968, pp. 19-20).

Ensenada, Baja California Norte - 1976 up-date, based on library studies. See also FBM, 1968, p. 87.

It is about 110 km. south of Tijuana, Baja California, on Highways 1D and 1. The population is reported to be about 78,000.

Felipe Carrillo Puerto, Quintana Roo - 1976 account, based on field studies in January, 1976.

Felipe Carrillo Puerto is in the southeastern portion of the Yucatan Region, at an elevation of about 50 to 100 feet above sea level. It is about 300 km. southeast of Mérida by highway, at the junction of highways 184, 295, and 307. Its population is estimated at about 20,000 to 30,000. The climate is similar to that in Valladolid with average temperatures probably about the same and annual rainfall probably somewhat greater.

This is an important agricultural and forest products center for Quintana Roo, and is at the point where three main highways from the north and west merge into one (307) which extends southward toward Chetumal. It is a rather open town, with only moderate congestion in the business section. Residential sections merge into areas of scattered houses and small farms, which give way fairly close to town to very sparsely settled countryside. Toward the northeast and south the woodlands along the highway have remained relatively undisturbed thus far, while on the road to Valladolid there is a patchwork of cornfields, overgrown fields, patches of woodland, and areas being cleared and burned. Along highway 307, particularly south of town, there is still much woodland of rather tall trees which hold their leaves through the winter in the rather humid environment. This woodland may be cleared away rather rapidly, but patches of trees favorable for bird watching may remain.

To find many of the birds on the lists for scrubby deciduous woodland and for the more humid woodland in the Yucatan Region, drive southward along highway 307 only a few kilometers from town and find a place to pull off the road and walk into the woodlands on either side of the road. We were able to find extensive woodlands all along the highway, and small quarries within a few kilometers of town provided good pull-off places and places to park, while several dirt tracks or roads led into the forest from the highway. Working at one of these wide places, well back from the road, the visitor could observe birds moving about and flying into and out of nearby woodland edge, and could then walk along a dirt track into the forest to see the distinctively woodland species. Birds you can expect to find in such places, 3 to 5 kilometers south of Felipe Carrillo Puerto include:

Plain Chachalaca	**Citreoline Trogon**
Red-billed Pigeon	**Golden-olive Woodpecker**
Scaled Pigeon	Golden-fronted Woodpecker
Common Ground-Dove	Ladder-backed Woodpecker
White-fronted Dove	**Flint-billed Woodpecker**
Aztec Parakeet	**Barred Antshrike**
Yucatan Parrot	**Olivaceous Creeper**
Ferruginous Pygmy-Owl	*Empidonax* sp. (w.)
White-bellied Emerald	**Yellow-bellied Elaenia**

Brown Jay
Green Jay
Spotted-breasted Wren
Gray Catbird (w.)
Blue-gray Gnatcatcher
Peppershrike
White-eyed Vireo (w.)
Magnolia Warbler (w.)
Northern Parula (w.)
Black-throated Green Warbler (w.)
Common Yellow throat (w.)

Hooded Warbler (w.)
American Redstart (w.)
Singing Blackbird
Scrub Euphonia
Summer Tanager (w.)
Black-headed Saltator
Blue Bunting
Indigo Bunting (w.)
Yellow-faced Grassquit
Green-backed Sparrow

Fortín de las Flores, Veracruz - 1976 up-date, based on library studies and reports of contributors. See also FBM, 1968, p.89.

(See also Córdoba.)

Fortín de las Flores is about 280 km. from Mexico City, where Highway 125 joins highway 150D. The population is reported to be about 6300.

Directions for reaching the Cañon de Metlac are still applicable, although the turn-off may be slightly less than 2 miles from Fortín de las Flores. Add the **Spotted-breasted Wren, Orange-billed Thrush,** and **Fan-tailed Warbler** to the list of birds in the Cañon de Metlac.

Fresnillo, Zacatecas - 1976 up-date, based on library studies. See also FBM, 1968, p. 91.

It is now about 665 km. from Mexico City by road, and about 65 km. northwest of Zacatecas, on a highway numbered 45 and 49. Its population is reported to be about 45,000.

Gómez Farías, Tamaulipas - 1976 account, with the help of Fred S. Webster, Jr., based on field studies by EPE in June, 1975 and several prior years, and by FSW, Jr., in 1976 and many prior years.

See also Christmas Count reports in *American Birds,* July, 1982, and some prior years.

Gómez Farías is in the southwestern portion of the Northern Atlantic Lowlands sub-region, at an elevation of approximately 1100 feet above sea level. It is approximately 620 km. north of Mexico City by paved road, approximately 430 km. south-southwest of Brownsville, Texas, and about 45 km. north of Mante. Its population is estimated as several hundred. Weather data are not available for Gómez Farías, and conditions vary greatly within a few miles in any direction, but at the village itself one should expect very hot spring weather, hot summer and autumn weather, and generally warm winters, with annual rainfall probably around 75-80 inches. Higher in the mountains nearby it is much cooler, and in spots much rainier.

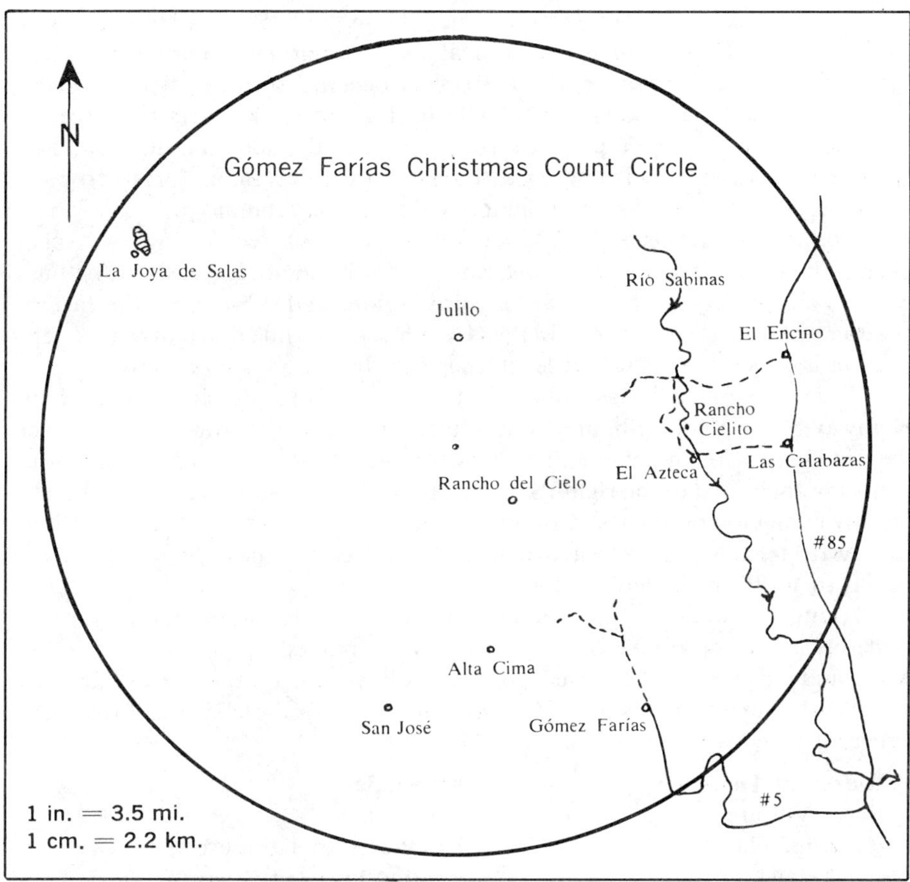

Gómez Farías is a small village situated on a long, narrow ridge of lava soil. There is but one street, running south to north for several miles, as an extension of the paved road from Highway 85. It is paved as far north as the town plaza, beyond which the dirt and gravel surface deteriorates before the road comes to a dead end a few kilometers ahead. Most of the small commercial buildings are clustered about the plaza, although a few merchants have stands along the thoroughfare. Most of the houses, thatch-roofed and set apart by stone fences, are scattered along the "main street" with intervening orchards and gardens, where hibiscus and bougainvillea, banana and papaya trees and mango trees thrive. Downslope, on each side of the main street are patches of moderately luxuriant woodlands, cultivated fields, and old clearings overgrown with brush. Beyond a deep valley to the west rises the steep, serrated front ridge of the Sierra de Guatemala, its solid green slopes of tropical evergreen forest at once tantalizing and challenging, or even forbidding.

The Gómez Farías area has been studied intensively by ornithologists and other field naturalists for at least 35 years, most of the effort having been concentrated along a few miles of the Río Sabinas and in the cloud forest around the Rancho del Cielo.

Five of Mexico's 12 vegetation zones (Leopold, 1959) can be found near Gómez Farías. Three of these are tropical plant formations not known north of the Gómez Farías region, namely, tropical deciduous forest, tropical semi-evergreen forest, and cloud forest. The bird count circle skirts the edges of extensive thorn forest, typical of the gulf coastal plain, on the east, and progresses westward and upward through tropical deciduous forest, tropical semi-evergreen forest, oak-sweet gum cloud forest, and humid pine-oak forest. The mountains reach as high as 2200 meters (about 7300 feet) above sea level in places, then slope away to the west, covered with pine-oak forest on the high western slopes. In terms of Edwards' bird regions and sub-regions the eastern portion of the circle lies mostly in the NA sub-region while much of the western portion is above the 5000-foot level, therefore in the NH sub-region.

To reach Gómez Farías from Victoria go a total of about 100 km. south on Highway 85, to a point about 40 km. south of the long Highway 85 bridge over the Río Guayalejo, and about a half-mile south of the Río Sabinas bridge. From there a branch road to the right (State Highway 5) leads about 12-14 km. west to the town of Gómez Farías. Coming from the south one goes about 33 km. northward from Mante, past a turn-off to Xicotencatl on the right, to the Gómez Farías turn-off on the left.

Along this branch road, after passing extensive fields of sugar cane, you will find dirt roads or tracks leading into low woodland. You can walk along woodland edge near the paved road or follow one of the tracks into the woodland, which extends almost uninterrupted to Gómez Farías. Birds to be expected here are:

Rufescent Tinamou	**Brown Jay**
Black Vulture	Green Jay
Roadside Hawk	Black-crested Titmouse
Gray Hawk	**Spotted-breasted Wren**
American Kestrel (w.)	Northern House-Wren (w.)
Plain Chachalaca	**White-bellied Wren**
Common Bobwhite	Northern Mockingbird
Red-billed Pigeon	Blue-gray Gnatcatcher (w.)
White-winged Dove (s.)	White-eyed Vireo
Common Ground-Dove	Orange-crowned Warbler (w.)
Groove-billed Ani	Nashville Warbler (w.)
Elegant Trogon	Yellow-rumped Warbler (w.)
Blue-crowned Motmot	Red-eyed Cowbird
Golden-fronted Woodpecker	Great-tailed Grackle
Ladder-backed Woodpecker	Altamira Oriole
Rose-throated Becard	**Crimson-collared Grosbeak**
Boat-billed Flycatcher	Rose-breasted Grosbeak (w.)
Social Flycatcher	Olive Sparrow
Great Kiskadee	Lincoln's Sparrow (w.)

At Gómez Farías you can park the car at the plaza or some other suitable place and continue a short distance on foot along the rough dirt and rock extension of the main street of the town. About two kilometers from the plaza the road curves slightly to the right, and ascends. Just before this curve a road branches to the left and descends precipitously to the floor of a deep valley. The (main) road continues a short distance beyond this fork and ends abruptly at a large clearing. Both of these roads are little more than dirt and rock tracks, impassable except for lumber trucks or the equivalent.

Among the scattered houses, gardens, orchards, brushy fields, forest and forest edge along the main dirt and rock road before it comes to a dead end, you should find many interesting tropical birds. At a propitious time, working slowly and carefully along this road, you should be able to see or hear most of the following:

Rufescent Tinamou	**Brown Jay**
Turkey Vulture	Green Jay
Black Vulture	**Spotted-breasted Wren**
Plain Chachalaca	**Blue Mockingbird**
Red-billed Pigeon	**Clay-colored Robin**
Inca Dove	Ruby-crowned Kinglet (w.)
White-fronted Dove	Cedar Waxwing (w.)
Green Parakeet	**Peppershrike**
White-crowned Parrot	White-eyed Vireo
Red-crowned Parrot	Red-eyed Vireo (s.)
Groove-billed Ani	Tropical Parula
Ferruginous Pygmy-Owl	Wilson's Warbler (w.)
Vaux's Swift	**Golden-crowned Warbler**
Wedge-tailed Sabrewing	Red-eyed Cowbird
Blue-crowned Motmot	**Singing Blackbird**
Green Woodpecker	Black-headed Oriole
Laughing Creeper	Altamira Oriole
Barred Antshrike	Hooded Oriole
Rose-throated Becard	**Scrub Euphonia**
Masked Tityra	**Yellow-throated Euphonia**
Tropical Kingbird	**Yellow-winged Tanager**
Boat-billed Flycatcher	**Black-headed Saltator**
Social Flycatcher	**Blue Bunting**
Olivaceous Flycatcher	Olive Sparrow

You should not attempt to go far, not more than about 3 km. (about 1½ mi.) beyond Gómez Farías, even if you are in excellent physical condition and have plenty of time. You would be getting farther and farther from possible medical attention, water, food, and overnight accommodations, farther from persons who speak English, and into dangerously steep and rough, rocky mountain slopes, almost impenetrable undergrowth, sink-holes, and numerous other hazardous or dangerous situations.

In case you have heard rumors of a tropical biological station in verdant mountain cloud forest in this vicinity, there is one, at Rancho del Cielo, in an isolated part of the mountains. Visitors cannot be accomodated there, however.

For much of the year only a caretaker, who does not speak English, occupies the premises. The grounds and premises are closed to everyone at such times. From time to time when work parties from the Biology Department at Texas Southmost College open the station it serves as a headquarters for especially pre-arranged study groups for a pre-determined period. Then it is closed again. One such group does the highland portion of the Gómez Farías Christmas Count. Group members are taken to Rancho del Cielo in rugged, powerful trucks, which also transport them to several surrounding mountain localities, over incredibly rough mountain "roads" or tracks.

Should you be a part of such a study group, and work in the cloud forest and nearby mountain pine-oak forest several days, you should see or hear most of the following species (in winter you could find most of the species on the NA sub-regional winter visitant list also):

Rufescent Tinamou	Olivaceous Flycatcher
Crested Guan	Coues' Flycatcher
Singing Quail	**Tufted Flycatcher**
Red-billed Pigeon	Green Jay
White-fronted Dove	**Spotted-breasted Wren**
White-crowned Parrot	Canyon Wren
Squirrel Cuckoo	Long-billed Thrasher
Least Pygmy-Owl	**Blue Mockingbird**
Wood Owl (n.)	**White-throated Robin**
Vaux's Swift	**Clay-colored Robin**
Wedge-tailed Sabrewing	**Brown-backed Solitaire**
Azure-crowned Hummingbird	**Black-headed Thrush**
Cazique Hummingbird	**Peppershrike**
Bumblebee Hummingbird	Warbling Vireo
Mexican Trogon	**Spot-breasted Warbler**
Blue-crowned Motmot	Tropical Parula
Green Woodpecker	**Golden-crowned Warbler**
Acorn Woodpecker	**Bell's Warbler**
Brown Woodpecker	Black-headed Oriole
Flint-billed Woodpecker	**Striped Tanager**
Olivaceous Creeper	**Hooded Grosbeak**
Laughing Creeper	**Black-headed Siskin**
Spotted-crowned Creeper	**Rufous-capped Finch**
Mexican Cotinga	

For bird study in the lowland areas near Gómez Farías at about 900-1000 feet elevation several places are rewarding and reasonably easy to reach. The area about half way along the branch road from Highway 85 to Gómez Farías has already been mentioned. The birds listed for that place may be found also along the Río Sabinas west of El Encino and Las Calabazas, both of which are on highway 85.

El Encino is a small village, along the highway, about 29-31 km. south of the long bridge over the Río Guayalejo. There are several houses and small stores, with a dirt road leading to your right, at right angles to the highway. Usually a highway sign indicates the name of the village. The dirt road is likely to be impassable most of the time, but you might be able to drive a few hundred feet off the highway to the far edge of the village, park there, and walk toward the Río Sabinas. Beyond the village you will pass fields of sugar cane, pastures, hedgerows, overgrown fields, scattered trees and even occasional small patches of low, scrubby woodland. Birds to be expected here are those on the NA sub-regional list for "Partially open country...outskirts of villages...". At a point about 2.7 miles from the highway the dirt road reaches the banks of the Río Sabinas. The banks are lined with big Montezuma cypress and with a band of river-edge woodland which is narrow in places and wide in others. Along the Río Sabinas you can see or hear most of the birds of the NA sub-regional list for "River-edge woodland...". Beyond the river a dirt and rock road leads generally westward through relatively level country for a short distance and then narrows into little more than a track in places, occasionally used by lumber trucks. In the plain of the Río Sabinas the birds should be somewhat similar to those seen between El Encino and the river, with a considerable number of species from the NA sub-regional lists for "Dense woodland of medium-sized trees..." and "River-edge woodland...". Once the road reaches the edge of the valley, beyond the river, it begins to climb through tropical semi-evergreen forest and tropical evergreen forest. The forest is relatively undisturbed along the side of the road, and there you can see many species of birds of the forest and forest-edge. The few clearings in the forest tend to increase the variety of birds without eliminating any forest species. Birds to be expected during a walk of a kilometer or two from the edge of the river valley are most of those listed at the end of the next paragraph, and a few other forest species.

On Highway 85, at a point about 1.8 miles south of El Encino, another dirt road goes off to the right (as you go south) to a village called El Azteca on the west bank of the Río Sabinas. At the turn-off on the highway there are two or three houses or small stores called Las Calabazas. The dirt road (impassable in wet weather) is more likely to be passable at times in dry weather than the one from El Encino to the river, but you should not try it before inquiring. (I have had a four-wheel drive Jeep stuck so tightly there that a tractor could not budge it. Finally a team of oxen pulled us out.) This road leads about two miles to the river, through pastures, cultivated fields, and a few hedgerows and scattered trees. There is a settlement on the west side of the river here, but still some river-edge woodland can be found, and one can turn right (north) after crossing the river, and walk upstream along the Río Sabinas. There is a dirt track or road between a band of riverside trees and farmlands (sugar-cane fields, cornfields, pasture) and hedgerows, and a few patches of woodland or overgrown fields. Where you can find openings in the river-edge vegetation and a gentle gravel and sand slope leading down to the water, you may see kingfishers, cormorants, and herons. Perhaps you will even see a **Tiger Bittern** or **Muscovy Duck**. About two miles upstream from El Azteca this road or track comes to the river crossing of the road from El Encino described earlier. Birds to expect along the road from El Azteca northward along the west bank of the river, and also to some extent along the road from Las Calabazas to El Azteca, include the following (see also the winter visitants list for the NA sub-region):

Rufescent Tinamou	**Blue-crowned Motmot**
Black Vulture	Golden-fronted Woodpecker
Roadside Hawk	**Laughing Creeper**
Crested Caracara	Rose-throated Becard
Plain Chachalaca	**Masked Tityra**
Common Bobwhite	**Boat-billed Flycatcher**
Red-billed Pigeon	**Social Flycatcher**
Inca Dove	Great Kiskadee
White-fronted Dove	**Brown Jay**
Green Parakeet	Green Jay
Red-crowned Parrot	**Spotted-breasted Wren**
Red-lored Parrot	**Clay-colored Robin**
Groove-billed Ani	Red-eyed Cowbird
Ferruginous Pygmy-Owl	Great-tailed Grackle
Vaux's Swift	**Singing Blackbird**
Buff-bellied Hummingbird	Altamira Oriole
Elegant Trogon	**Black-headed Saltator**
Ringed Kingfisher	**Crimson-collared Grosbeak**
Amazon Kingfisher	Collared Seedeater
Green Kingfisher	**Blue-black Grassquit**

Guadalajara, Jalisco - 1976 up-date, based on library studies and reports from contributors. See also FBM, 1968, p. 93.

It is now about 570 km. from Mexico City. In addition to highways 15 and 80, several other major highways serve the city. The population is reported to be about 1,200,000.

Expect some wintering warblers in parks and gardens, and in fields and hedgerows along the highway.

The following lists apply to the shores of Lake Chapala, especially in and around Ajijic, Chapala, and Jocótepec. They replace the Pátzcuaro lists to which we referred on page 95 (1968).

Birds on the water, in marshy areas, or along the shore are:

Eared Grebe (w.)	Louisiana Heron
Western Grebe	American Bittern (w.)
Pied-billed Grebe	White-faced Ibis
Great Blue Heron	American Coot
Little Blue Heron	Jacana
Great Egret	

Several kinds of wintering ducks frequent Lake Chapala in considerable numbers, often far from shore or on secluded portions of the lake.

Common birds of the open country, gardens, hedgerows, small patches of scattered trees, pastures, and marsh edge are:

Cattle Egret
Turkey Vulture
Black Vulture
Marsh Hawk (w.)
American Kestrel (w.)
Rock Dove
Inca Dove
Common Ground-Dove
Groove-billed Ani
Broad-billed Hummingbird
Golden-fronted Woodpecker
Vermilion Flycatcher
Cassin's Kingbird
Great Kiskadee
Empidonax sp. (w.)
Rough-winged Swallow
Barn Swallow
Tree Swallow (w.)
Bewick's Wren
Curve-billed Thrasher
Blue Mockingbird

Blue-gray Gnatcatcher (w.)
Loggerhead Shrike
Orange-crowned Warbler (w.)
Yellow-rumped Warbler (w.)
Common Yellowthroat
Wilson's Warbler (w.)
House Sparrow
Red-eyed Cowbird
Brown-headed Cowbird
Great-tailed Grackle
Red-winged Blackbird
Yellow-headed Blackbird (w.)
Streaked-backed Oriole
Blue Grosbeak
House Finch
Lesser Goldfinch
Brown Towhee
Lark Sparrow (w.)
Chipping Sparrow
Clay-colored Sparrow (w.)

Guanajuato, Guanajuato - 1976 up-date, based on library studies. See also 1968, p. 95.

The population is reported to be about 37,000.

Highway 110 to Dolores Hidalgo is now paved. Specific areas between Guanajuato and Dolores Hidalgo may have been altered.

Guaymas, Sonora - 1976 up-date, based on library studies and reports from contributors. See also FBM, 1968, p. 96.

The population is reported to be about 57,000.

There are now more tourist facilities, particularly in the vicinity of Bocochibampo Bay and farther northwest at Bahía de San Carlos. If the turn-off to Bocochibampo Bay is not well-marked, signs for Playa Miramar should lead you to the Bay.

Numerous species found in the tranquil bays and lagoons and on the associated beaches and mudflats should be added to the list (1968,p.98), including:

Yellow-crowned Night-Heron
Shoveler (w)
Osprey
American Coot
Common Oystercatcher

Black-bellied Plover (w)
Marbled Godwit (w)
Bonaparte's Gull (w)
Forster's Tern (w)
Belted Kingfisher (w)

One may walk northward across a bridge over the inlet connecting bay and lagoon (at Bocochibampo), and find roads or tracks or trails leading generally westward toward coastal headlands and then northward through scrubby, brushy vegetation. Expect dry-country birds (1968,p.97) to be numerous here, along with many transients and winter visitants in season. The following can be added to that list:

American Kestrel (w)	Lark Sparrow (w)
Inca Dove	Black-throated Sparrow
Ash-throated Flycatcher	White-crowned Sparrow (w)

Highway 40 - See La Capilla del Taxte.

Jalapa, Veracruz - 1976 up-date, based on library studies. See also 1968, p.99.
The population is reported to be about 122,000.

A by-pass around the east side of town has altered the situation. Gaining access to the coffee plantations southeast of town may be more difficult.

KABAH, Yucatán - 1984 up-date, based on field studies in June, 1978, and March 1979. See also 1976 Suppl. to FBM, p. S76 (or 1976 up-date below).
(See also Sayil and Uxmal.)

There is still no real village at the archaeological site, but there are a few buildings, such as a refreshment stand, a pavilion, overseer's house and office, or the like. Because it is only about 20-30 km. south of Uxmal, and about 10-20 km. north or northwest of Sayil, and because both Uxmal and Sayil seem very rewarding for birding, we have not studied Kabah intensively. Almost all tours proceeding from Uxmal to Sayil and Labná stop at Kabah, however, and you have an opportunity to see numerous birds as you walk from one old Maya building to another. In addition to the birds on the 1976 list you might find ground-doves, Groove-billed Ani, orioles, wintering buntings and grosbeaks, and resident grassquits. There is a chance that you might hear the **Pheasant Cuckoo** here as well, in spring or early summer, calling from the nearby scrubby woodland.

Kabah, Yucatán - New account, 1976, based mostly on reports of contributors.

Kabah is in the west-central portion of the Yucatan Region, at an elevation of about 50 to 100 feet above sea level. It is about 100-110 km. by road south of Mérida, on highway number 261. There is no well-defined town at Kabah. The climate is much like that of Mérida although annual rainfall may be slightly less and average temperatures slightly higher.

This is an archaeological site set in low, thorny, deciduous woodland, interspersed with some cultivated fields. The site is close beside the highway. It is possible to see a representative sample of the birds listed for the archaeological sites and scrubby woodland of the Yucatan Region by walking into cleared areas and around the edges of the clearing. A list of birds to be expected in the area would include the following:

Turkey Vulture	**Yucatan Jay**
Lesser Roadrunner	**Tropical Mockingbird**
Pauraque (n.)	**Peppershrike**
Fork-tailed Emerald	Black-throated Green Warbler (w.)
Turquoise-browed Motmot	**Singing Blackbird**
Golden-fronted Woodpecker	Altamira Oriole
Yucatan Woodpecker	**Scrub Euphonia**
Couch's Kingbird	Rose-breasted Grosbeak (w.)
Rough-winged Swallow	**Black-headed Saltator**
Green Jay	

LA CAPILLA DEL TAXTE, Sinaloa - New account, 1984, by Jerry and Nancy Strickling, based on field studies in November, 1982.

(See also Mazatlán.)

*Please do not fail to read the footnote below!

La Capilla del Taxte is near the upper boundary of the Northern Pacific Lowlands sub-region, at an elevation of approximately 4500 feet. It is about 1250 km. northwest of Mexico City, about 235 km. southwest of the city of Durango, and about 90 km. east of Mazatlán, on National Highway 40. Its population is only a few hundred. We have no data on rainfall or monthly mean temperatures, but the rainfall figures would probably be somewhat similar to those for Tepic (1968,p.187), while temperatures would probably be somewhat like those of Guadalajara (1968, p. 93).

This small village has served some travelers as a base point for observations of birds along a portion of Highway 40 (in the mountains of Sinaloa) which many observers consider one of the most interesting birding areas in western Mexico.

Usually birders approach the area by driving southeast from Mazatlán on Highway 15, approximately 25 km. to Villa Unión, then about one kilometer beyond, to a junction where Highway 40 leads off to the left and extends

---

***Danger:** In the April, 1984, issue of *Birding* magazine, a man from Alaska wrote that he and a companion were robbed at gunpoint by five bandits at "Rancho Libre" on the highway between Mazatlán and Durango. Presumably this is the locality treated here as Rancho Liebre Barranca (Locality 5). The writer speculated that the men may now know that this area is frequented by birders with much valuable equipment, and thus the men might do the same sort of thing in the future. There is no way you can avoid all risk of such dangerous and traumatic events (or of lesser dangers or serious inconveniences), but please see the Introduction to the 1984 Supplement for things you could do which might decrease the risk.

(generally northeastward) approximately 290 km. to the city of Durango, and eventually on to Torreón, Monterrey, and Reynosa. La Capilla del Taxte is about 65-70 km. from (northeast of) the road junction at Villa Unión.

The most favored birding localities on the Villa Unión-to-Durango section of Highway 40 are concentrated within the state of Sinaloa between a point about 50 km. from (east of) Villa Unión and a point about 100 km. from (east of) Villa Unión, at El Palmito, close to the border of the state of Durango. The highway climbs from about 50 feet elevation at Villa Unión to about 4500 feet at La Capilla del Taxte to about 6000 feet at El Palmito and the Sinaloa-Durango border. The Villa Unión-to-Durango portion of the highway is known for its spectacular scenery as well as its birds. Particularly some portions of Highway 40 between El Palmito and Durango have been acclaimed as marvels of engineering, and some are notorious for hairpin turns, narrow roadbed, narrow or non-existent shoulders and tremendous dropoffs. Rockslides, washouts, fog, even snow and ice on the road, may be encountered. (See notes in the Introduction, about mountain driving.)

We have used the location of the Hotel Villa Blanca (near marker K-234, in La Capilla del Taxte) as a bench mark from which to indicate distances to the birding locations described here. To facilitate bird-finding in this vicinity we have numbered each of the five principal locations and have numbered the maps (on the next three pages) correspondingly.

(1) To reach the first of these drive back (toward Mazatlán) a distance of about 16 km. (9.5 mi.) to a point near K-249, where you should see a road to your right (north) marked by a sign pointing to Pánuco. If you turn right, toward Pánuco, you should find a suitable place to park just after you turn. There you should be able to find various species of hummingbirds (see next list) and possibly the **Rusty-crowned Sparrow** and **Fan-tailed Warbler,** among the flowering shrubs in or near the gulley to your right as you turn off the highway.

The pavement ends only about a half-mile down this road, but the road continues as a dirt or gravel road, between a barranca on your left and a hillside rising steeply on your right. There are pull-outs, suitable for parking, however, at points about ½, ¾, and 1 mile from the main highway, and you can walk the road (with caution) as you search for birds. The pull-outs are said to have been constructed for the use of ore wagons from the formerly active mines in the vicinity of the village of Pánuco, which the road eventually reaches, about 6-7 miles from the highway. Along the first mile of this road, nearest the highway, you may find some of the following special birds, as well as many of the common birds of the Northern Pacific Lowlands sub-region (1968, pp. 7-9):

Wagler's Chachalaca	**Plain-capped Starthroat**
Military Macaw	**Dupont's Hummingbird**
Lesser Ground-Cuckoo	Lucifer Hummingbird
Fork-tailed Emerald	Broad-tailed Hummingbird

The other favorable areas for birding to be described here, locations 2-5 in southwest-northeast sequence, are *toward Durango* from (generally northeast of) La Capilla del Taxte, beginning with one about 6 miles from the Hotel Villa

Blanca (in La Capilla del Taxte) and ending with one about 20 miles from that hotel.

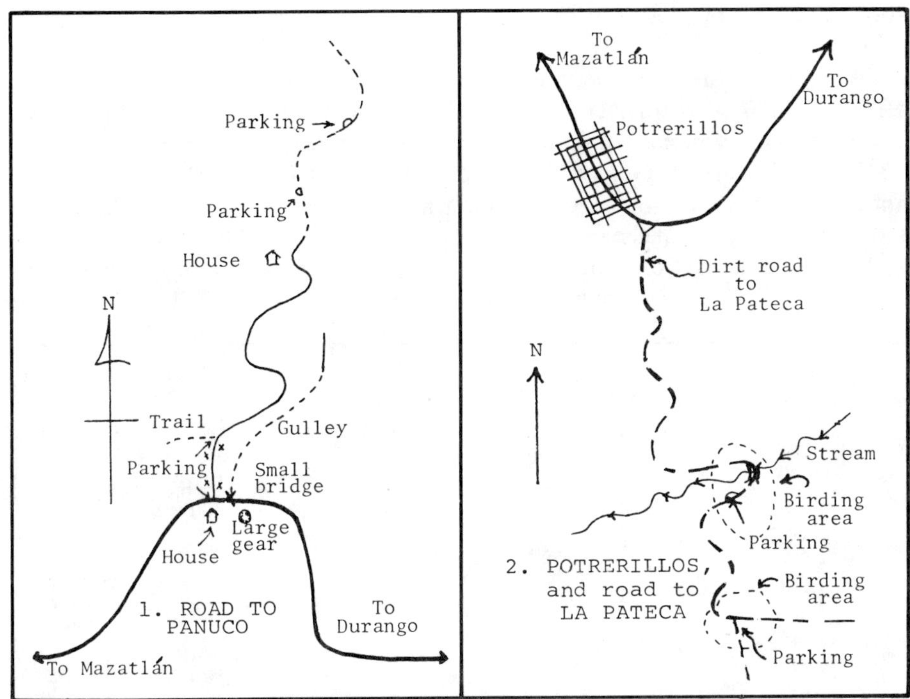

(2) To reach the first of these, an unpaved side road leading to La Pateca, drive about six miles toward Durango from the Hotel Villa Blanca, to about K-221. There, at the village of Potrerillos there is a road to your right (south) to La Pateca. At a point about a mile from the highway this side-road crosses a low-water bridge over a small stream that emerges from a broad, flat-bottomed, brushy canyon on your left, and drops into a deep ravine on your right. To find a parking space proceed about 100 yards past the bridge to a place where you can pull off to the right. Here you have a good chance of seeing several kinds of hummingbirds in addition to some of the other common birds of the Northern Highlands sub-region (1968, pp. 18-20), and possibly a few typical of the Northern Pacific Lowlands sub-region (1968, pp. 8-9).

Farther along the La Pateca road, at about 1.8 miles from Highway 40 you will come to a fork in the road where there is a cleared area suitable for parking. Species to be expected here would be much the same as those of the area just mentioned at the stream crossing, and might include some rare hummingbirds as well as the more common species. Hummingbirds which have been reported at one of these two places include:

White-eared Hummingbird	**Dupont's Hummingbird**
Berylline Hummingbird	Lucifer Hummingbird
Rivoli's Hummingbird	**Bumblebee Hummingbird**

(3) To reach the next favorable birding area in this series return to Highway 40, turn right, and drive (toward Durango) to a point about 2 miles past the village of Potrerillos, and about 8 miles from the Hotel Villa Blanca. There you should see on your left a large sign marking the Tropic of Cancer. (From this point you may possibly be able to see the Pacific Ocean, a distance of about 50 miles by road.) For the actual birding location in this vicinity proceed on Highway 40 about a quarter-mile past the Tropic of Cancer sign, to an area on your left where you may pull off and park. (Be very cautious, you'll be crossing traffic on a reverse curve, with very poor visibility.) You may be able to drive about 150 yards off the highway along a dirt track, along a "saddle" of the mountain, and park at the head of a trail which leads into the relatively dry pine and oak woodland. You should be able to find many of the species listed for the Northern Highlands sub-region (1968, p. 20).

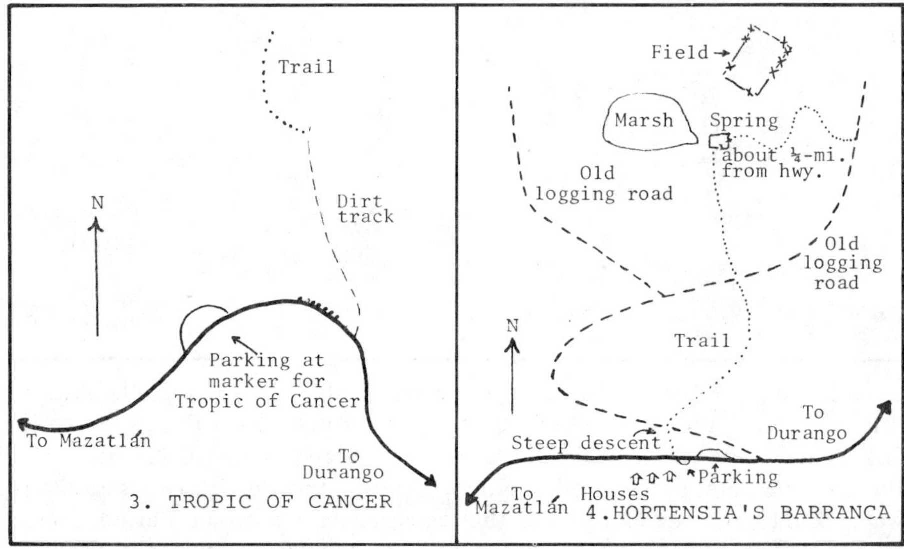

(4) Proceeding farther toward Durango you will come to a point about 3½ miles from the Tropic of Cancer, and about 13 miles from the Hotel Villa Blanca, where you can park the car and walk down an old logging road into a nearby barranca. As you approach this point on the highway you will pass a microwave (*microondas*) tower on your left and then pass marker K-212. Watch for three houses close together on your right before you reach K-213. A short distance ahead is a pull-out on your left where you can park clear of the highway. On some occasions birders have obtained permission to park in the yard of the center house of the three houses, and have informally named the barranca Hortensia's Barranca, to honor the gracious lady who lived in the house and permitted the birders to park there. Across the road from these houses you should be able to find a steep trail leading down into a wide ravine, crossing an abandoned logging road twice on the way down. You could descend on this trail *or* on the old logging road which intersects the highway a short distance beyond

the pull-out mentioned above. The trail leads to a spring, which is the water source for the local residents, and to several small cultivated fields in what is otherwise forest. In this area you should be able to find many of the common birds of the Northern Highlands sub-region (1968,p. 20). Specifically, most of the following species are to be expected here at Hortensia's Barranca, and at the Rancho Liebre Barranca (discussed next):

Turkey Vulture	**Brown-backed Solitaire**
Band-tailed Pigeon	Hermit Thrush (w)
Rivoli's Hummingbird	Ruby-crowned Kinglet (w)
White-eared Hummingbird	**Gray Silky-Flycatcher**
Eared Trogon	Hutton's Vireo
Mexican Trogon	Solitary Vireo
Common Flicker	Yellow-rumped Warbler
Gray-crowned Woodpecker	Townsend's Warbler (w)
Acorn Woodpecker	Hermit Warbler (w)
White-striped Creeper	Wilson's Warbler (w)
Olivaceous Flycatcher	**Slate-throated Redstart**
Violet-green Swallow	**Red Warbler**
Common Raven	**Bell's Warbler**
Tufted Jay	**Rufous-capped Warbler**
Steller's Jay	Hepatic Tanager
Bridled Titmouse	**Red-headed Tanager**
Bushtit	**Hooded Grosbeak**
Brown Creeper	**Rufous-capped Finch**
Northern House-Wren	Rufous-sided Towhee
Blue Mockingbird	Yellow-eyed Junco
American Robin	Chipping Sparrow

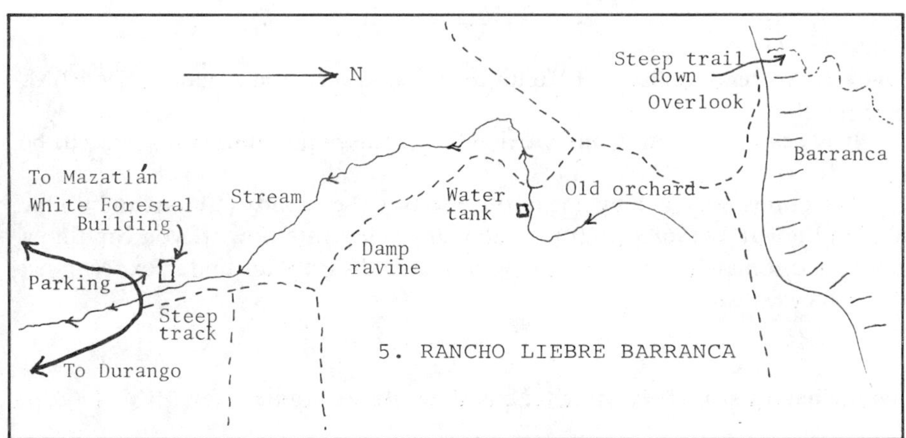

(5) (See footnote on first page of La Capilla del Taxte.) The most eastward location to be described here is probably the best known to birders - the Rancho Liebre Barranca. To reach this location continue to drive toward Durango to a

point about 20 miles from (northeast of) the Hotel Villa Blanca. On your left, at K-201, just before you reach the village of El Palmito, is an unoccupied Forestal ("Forestry Department") building, where there is ample space for parking. You should see several concrete picnic tables here. Just beyond (east of) the building there is a road, impassable to vehicles, leading (north) up the hillside. If you walk up this old road about a quarter-mile you will come to a fork. (Some trails may not be shown on Map 5, and some which *are* shown may not be obvious in the field. Check landmarks, directions and distances carefully, don't get off on side trails, and don't try to take a circle route.) The left side of the fork leads toward the Rancho Liebre Barranca, while the right side of the fork leads through oak and pine woodland toward the crest of the ridge (reaching about 7500 feet elevation).

If you proceed toward the barranca the trail leads alongside a ravine, past a water seep and storage tank which is the water supply for the village of El Palmito. From there it crosses the ravine then leads past an abandoned orchard to an overlook into the Rancho Liebre Barranca. (See note about overlooks, in Introduction.) From this point a steep trail leads down into the barranca (watch for loose gravel or stones).

All along the trail from the highway you should be able to find many of the common birds of the Northern Highlands sub-region (1968, p. 20). See discussion of Hortensia's Barranca (sub-locality No. 4) for a list of birds to be expected both at *that* barranca (which is easier to reach and possibly safer) and at the Rancho Liebre Barranca.

LAGOS DE MONTEBELLO, or **LAGUNAS DE MONTEBELLO —** see Comitán.

Lagos de Moreno, Jalisco - 1976 up-date, based on library studies. See FBM, 1968, p. 101.

It is about 430 km. from Mexico City. The population is reported to be about 34,000.

Directions for reaching one of the ponds in the vicinity ("the second visible lake on the left") (1968,p.102) probably are inaccurate now. If you can find a small pond somewhere in the area, with trees and shrubs around it, expect most of the species listed.

León, Guanajuato - 1976 up-date, based on library studies. See FBM, 1968, p. 103.

León is about 390 km. from Mexico City.

The area five miles southeast of León (1968, p. 104) may have been greatly altered.

LA PAZ, Baja California Sur - New account, 1984, based on field studies in May, 1983.

La Paz is near the southern end of the BC Region, on the coast of the Gulf of California (Sea of Cortez), approximately at sea level. It is about 1300 km. straight-line distance northwest of Mexico City and about 1480 km. by highway south-southeast of Tijuana, BCN (which is at the U.S. border). Its population is reported to be about 75,000. Average annual rainfall is about 7 inches, almost all of it March through June. Monthly mean temperatures are probably somewhat similar to those at Mazatlán, which vary from about 67 degrees F. (January-March) to about 82 degrees F. (July-September).

La Paz is a modern resort and port city , presumably with a rather crowded business section where the city borders the south side of the bay. There are many broad boulevards and avenues, however, and rather open residential areas in the southern portion of the city, where it gradually gives way to the desert, along Highway 1 south toward Rancho Buena Vista, San José del Cabo, and Cabo San Lucas. Some of the principal resort sections are north of the city, on the east side of the bay, along the road to Pichilingue where the ferry terminal is situated.

Almost anywhere along Highway 1 to the south you should be able to find a representative assortment of land birds just by walking along between the highway and the fence. Parking clear of the road is likely to be difficult because of rather narrow, sandy, sloping road shoulders, but once you find a suitable place to park you should have plenty of space to walk because the fence is generally set well back from the road. We stopped at a point about 15 km. south of the city, and found the following species in about an hour (late afternoon list by Charles R. Smith):

Turkey Vulture	Scrub Jay
Crested Caracara	Verdin
White-winged Dove	Blue-gray Gnatcatcher
Common Ground-Dove	House Sparrow
Gila Woodpecker	House Finch
Common Raven	

(Smith also saw the unique tracks of a Sidewinder Rattlesnake. No doubt other rattlesnakes are present in the area as well, so you should be cautious, especially at night and very early morning.)

Within a few minutes as we drove farther south we saw a Greater Roadrunner and an American Kestrel, as well as additional individuals of some of the above-mentioned species.

Linares, Nuevo León - 1976 up-date, based on library studies and reports from contributors. See FBM, 1968, p.105.

Linares is in the Northern Atlantic Lowlands sub-region at an elevation of about 1250 feet above sea level. It is about 860 km. north of Mexico City, and about 250 km. southwest of Reynosa, Tamaulipas (which is near McAllen, Texas) on national highway number 85 and Nuevo León state highway number

60. Its population is reported to be about 25,000. The average annual rainfall is 31 inches; 24 inches from May through October, and 7 inches from November through April. Monthly mean temperatures vary from a low of 57 degrees F. in December to a high of 81 degrees F. in August.

Birds considered specialities when occurring in south Texas are common in the vicinity of Linares, as well as a few distinctively tropical lowland birds. They are to be found along the rivers or wooded banks of irrigation ditches which cut through the scrubby woodland or semi-desert vegetation of the rolling plains and hills. The town itself is a typical small Mexican town with a rather crowded business section of low buildings close to the street, with houses and their patios situated beside small commercial establishments. Away from the center of town the houses are considerably more scattered, among numerous gardens, vacant lots, small cultivated fields and orchards, with dirt streets leading out to the edge of town. Farther afield there are widely scattered houses, larger orchards, cultivated fields, and great expanses of arid countryside, with dense growth of small, thorny trees and large shrubs. There is a large river valley beside the town, with some tributary streams leading into it, and even though there is often very little water in these streams there may be luxuriant vegetation, including large trees, along the banks.

To find the common birds of the hedgerows, orchards, gardens and cultivated fields you can drive a short distance out highway number 85 toward the north, or along state highway number 60 toward Galeana, pulling off the road and parking when you come to the edge of town. Along narrow dirt roads or trails you can expect:

Black Vulture	Black-crested Titmouse
Red-billed Pigeon	Carolina Wren
Inca Dove	Northern House-Wren (w.)
Common Ground-Dove	Northern Mockingbird
Groove-billed Ani	**Clay-colored Robin**
Golden-fronted Woodpecker	Red-eyed Vireo (s.)
Rose-throated Becard	Orange-crowned Warbler (w.)
Eastern Phoebe (w.)	Tropical Parula
Couch's Kingbird	Yellow-rumped Warbler (w.)
Sulphur-bellied Flycatcher (s.)	Great-tailed Grackle
Great Kiskadee	Brewer's Blackbird
Empidonax sp. (w.)	Hooded Oriole
Gray-breasted Martin (s.)	Collared Seedeater
Brown Jay	Olive Sparrow

Farther out on state highway 60 you can see numerous dirt roads leading off into the scrubby, thorny vegetation of the semi-desert. Pull off to the right and park along one of these roads and then walk generally north or northwest several hundred meters, to see birds along the banks of the Río Camacho. A band of larger trees shows where the river is. On favorable nights this can be a rewarding place for night birds. With a flashlight you can see the eye-shine of the Pauraques in the dirt roads or tracks. You might be able to approach one closely while others call a buzzy *per-weer* in the distance. At the same time a rapidly repeated *chip-willo* indicates the presence of the **Chip-willow.** The unobtrusive, slow thumping call of a **Wood Owl** is most likely to be heard in dense growth of rather large trees along the river, or in partly wooded areas in the outskirts of town late at night. In this area you can expect most of the species on the preceding list and the following:

Plain Chachalaca	Green Kingfisher
White-winged Dove	Wied's Flycatcher (s.)
Wood Owl (n.)	Blue-gray Gnatcatcher
Pauraque (n.)	**Rufus-capped Warbler**
Chip-willow (n.)	Indigo Bunting (w.)
Elegant Trogon	Varied Bunting

To observe a variety of birds in river-edge woodland, open fields, brushy open country, hedgerows and overgrown fields you can visit the *Ojo de Agua Vista Hermosa* several miles west of Linares on the Río Pablillos. By inquiring about a *Parque Natural* just off state highway 60 from the center of Linares a paved branch road goes left (as you go toward Galeana) from state highway number 60. About 2-3 km. along the branch road there is a left turn which leads about a half-kilometer into the recreation area. You may see signs marking the turns.

Working along trails, tracks and roads in this vicinity you should find most of the following:

Olivaceous Cormorant	Rose-throated Becard
Green Heron	Couch's Kingbird
Turkey Vulture	Great Kiskadee
Plain Chachalaca	Rough-winged Swallow
Common Bobwhite	**Brown Jay**
Killdeer (w.)	Green Jay
Spotted Sandpiper (w.)	Common Raven
Red-billed Pigeon	Black-crested Titmouse
White-winged Dove	Carolina Wren
Mourning Dove	**Clay-colored Robin**
Common Ground-Dove	Common Yellowthroat (w.)
White-fronted Dove	**Rufous-capped Warbler**
Groove-billed Ani	Red-eyed Cowbird
Ferruginous Pygmy-Owl	Great-tailed Grackle
Lesser Nighthawk	Altamira Oriole
Ringed Kingfisher	Black-headed Oriole
Green Kingfisher	Red-winged Blackbird
Golden-fronted Woodpecker	Blue Grosbeak
Ladder-backed Woodpecker	Olive Sparrow

LOS MOCHIS, Sinaloa - New account, 1984, based on field studies in May, 1983.

Los Mochis is in the Northern Pacific Lowlands sub-region at about 30 to 50 feet above sea level, only a few miles from the nearest salt-water bay. It is about 1530 km. northwest of Mexico City by road, and about 780 km. southeast of Nogales, Sonora (which is at the U.S. border) by road, on National Highway 15 and Highway 32. Its population is reported to be about 130,000. The average annual rainfall is about the same as at Topolobampo, where it is 14 inches; 13 inches from July through December and 1 inch from January through June. Temperatures are probably about the same as at Topolobampo, where they vary from a monthly mean of about 65 degrees F. (January) to a monthly mean of nearly 86 (July-September). Daylight birding hours in May: from about 5:30 or 6:00 a.m. to about 7:00 or 7:15 p.m., local time.

The city has an extensive but still crowded commercial center dealing mainly with agribusiness. Large residential subdivisions spread out particularly to the north, west and south. Still farther out, particularly to the north and east are many square miles of irrigated croplands, planted in sugar cane, tomatoes, cotton, rice, wheat, and other valuable crops. Los Mochis is an important center for trans-shipment of agricultural products, and is the westmost passenger terminal of the Chihuahua-Pacific Railroad (see Cerocahui and Chihuahua for more information about this railroad).

To find a representative sample of the typical birds of the semi-desert vegetation which undoubtedly covered much of this area before it was irrigated, you could work the area around the Motel Las Colinas, formerly the Holiday Inn. The motel is situated on the lower of twin low hills which appear almost man-made as they rise about 150 to 200 feet above the flatlands around them, on Highway 15 at its junction with Boulevard Macario Gaxiola, northeast of the city center.

You could start out in front of the Holiday Inn (which faces away from the highway) and walk up a partly overgrown road to the higher hilltop, or you could find ample parking space in what seems to be an informal dump near the highway below the hotel, and walk along a dirt road along the southwestern base of the hills.

We saw an unusually large number of Lesser Nighthawks, as we flushed 15-20 within a couple of hours. Perhaps a night-migrating flock was resting here for the day. They would fly around a while, after being flushed, and then go back to the ground or perch on a twig in full view. There were also many cottontail-type rabbits. A Burrowing Owl had its burrow near the bottom of the lower hill beside the paved road leading up to the motel.

At times walking easily along the dirt roads, and at other times working with great difficulty through the low, thorny vegetation, we found the following species:

Mourning Dove	Curve-billed Thrasher
Common Ground-Dove	Northern Mockingbird
Burrowing Owl	House Sparrow
Lesser Nighthawk	Great-tailed Grackle
Ladder-backed Woodpecker	Cardinal
Cactus Wren	House Finch

Highway 32, more or less a southward extension of Boulevard Macario Gaxiola, leads to Topolobampo, a distance of about 25 km. from Los Mochis. Several kilometers out of town, probably about halfway to Topolobampo, a side road leads to the right (as you go south) to the new airport. Beyond this turn-off, both on the side road to the airport and on the main road to Topolobampo there were vast flats, a very few of which still held a little water, which probably attract large numbers of shore birds, waders, and possibly waterfowl, in winter. Parking clear of the highway may be difficult, traffic is heavy at times, and most areas are fenced. It would not be advisable to walk out in the flats anyhow, but if you can find a safe place to park you could look out over the flats with binoculars or telescope.

In late May, in the area of dried-up flats, we saw only White-faced Ibis, Great Egret, Cattle Egret, and numerous swallows, either Violet-green or **Mangrove,** or both.

Mante, Tamaulipas - 1976 up-date, based on library studies. See FBM, 1968, p. 107.

Mante is in the southern portion of the Northern Atlantic Lowlands sub-region, at an elevation of about 280 feet above sea level. It is approximately 540 km. north of Mexico City, and about 450 km. south-southwest of Brownsville, on Highway 85 at its junction with Highway 80. Its population is reported to be about 51,000. Climate is probably somewhat like that of Tampico where annual rainfall is about 50 inches, mostly June-October, and where monthly mean temperatures drop to about 66 degrees F. in winter and rise to about 83 degrees F. in summer.

A considerable variety of tropical lowland birds may be seen in the vicinity of Mante, even though most of the original natural vegetation for miles around has been removed. Mante is strategically situated, also, to give access to the El Naranjo and Gómez Farías Christmas Count Circles, which are about 35-60 kilometers southwest and north-northwest respectively.

This is a fairly typical Mexican town, with a very busy and crowded commercial section on a very long main street. The stores and other commercial buildings are low and close to the street, and some private homes are intermingled. There are some small plazas within the business district. The main residential areas, farther out, consist of scattered houses and a very few small stores, many of the homes having large patios or gardens or overgrown fields adjacent to them. Many of the roads and streets in the outskirts of town are dirt, and lead out to widely scattered houses and vacant lots and finally to small cultivated fields, hedgerows, and overgrown fields. Outside of town there are vast fields of sugar cane and, in some years, vegetable crops such as tomatoes.

In the plazas and other small open spaces near the center of town are the following birds:

Inca Dove	Red-eyed Cowbird
Common Ground-Dove	Great-tailed Grackle

It is difficult to find a place along the edge of town to park and walk away from much human activity, but the grounds of one of the suburban motels might be suitable. The **Prevost's Mango** and **Fuertes's Oriole** have been reported in summer at a motel in southwest Mante (motel may be marked "Los Arcos"). (Ed. 1984 note: Some recent travel books do not list **any** suburban motels in Mante.) Along paths among suburban gardens, hedgerows, and overgrown fields you could find most of the following:

Black Vulture	**Mexican Crow**
Crested Caracara	Northern House-Wren (w.)
Common Bobwhite	Northern Mockingbird
White-winged Dove (s.)	**Clay-colored Robin**
Groove-billed Ani	Orange-crowned Warbler (w.)
Golden-fronted Woodpecker	Altamira Oriole
Tropical Kingbird	Collared Seedeater
Great Kiskadee	Olive Sparrow
Beardless Flycatcher	

The best way to see water birds close to Mante is to be a passenger, not the driver, and ride along some side roads north of Mante where ditches and canals parallel the road, seeing birds from the moving (at a safe speed) car. The main highway and most of the side roads are narrow with very narrow shoulders; therefore parking is not safe. Some side roads may be impassable in wet weather. Water birds are widely scattered and not numerous, but if conditions are favorable, you should be able to find:

Least Grebe	Snowy Egret
Pied-billed Grebe	American Coot
Great Blue Heron	Belted Kingfisher (w.)
Green Heron	Green Kingfisher
Little Blue Heron	Rough-winged Swallow
Great Egret	

Several distinctively tropical birds are found in the Cañon del Abra. Driving southward from the center of Mante you will see where a road branches east toward Tampico (highway number 80), at the south side of Mante. Using this junction as a zero point you would not turn, but continue southward on highway number 85 (toward Valles) about 20 kilometers until the road climbs up through a canyon. In this canyon there are two places to park, the first a large quarry on the right, and the second a grassy open area on the left at the top of the canyon. The latter spot is about 22 km. (14 mi.) from the junction in the edge of town. From either of these places you could avoid the steeper slopes while walking into the woodland or along the woodland edge. Birds to be expected in the Cañon del Abra are:

Gray Hawk	**Green Parakeet**
Bat Falcon	Buff-bellied Hummingbird
Plain Chachalaca	**Blue-crowned Motmot**
Red-billed Pigeon	Golden-fronted Woodpecker
White-fronted Dove	Eastern Phoebe

Social Flycatcher
Great Kiskadee
Brown Jay
Spotted-breasted Wren
Clay-colored Robin
Blue-gray Gnatcatcher (w.)
Ruby-crowned Kinglet (w.)
Solitary Vireo (w.)

Red-eyed Vireo (s.)
Orange-crowned Warbler (w.)
Yellow-rumped Warbler (w.)
Black-headed Oriole
Altamira Oriole
Black-headed Saltator
Olive Sparrow

If you continue southward from the canyon on highway number 85 you will soon come to Antiguo Morelos, where highway number 80 branches west and leads toward El Salto and El Naranjo. (If you go *north* from Mante on highway number 85 you would come to the Gómez Farías branch-road after about 20 miles.)

If in the south edge of Mante, you turn east on highway number 80 toward Tampico you will go through some narrow avenues of trees and then through rather barren cultivated fields to a big, steel-frame bridge over a river about 28 km. (about 17 mi.) from the road junction. The bridge is high above the river. Two gravel roads, one on each side of the river, drop steeply down to open grassy areas near river level. The gravel road on your side of the highway is *beyond* the bridge as you approach, however, and when you reach the gravel road you must turn back sharply to the right to get on it. An alternative would be to angle left across traffic on the near side of the bridge to get on that gravel road at an easy turn-angle (but still a steep descent). In any event caution, slow speed, and a sharp lookout for traffic are necessary. An option would be to pull off the highway and park a kilometer or two before you reach the bridge. Then you could walk along the woodland edge or along dirt roads or trails leading through woodland down to the river, detouring around the high, steep and crumbly banks. This Puente Magascatzín area is not as promising as some of the broader bands of river-edge woodland along the Río Sabinas, but you should find most of the birds on the preceding list, as well as numerous birds of "Partially open country...", and some parrots and other birds of "River-edge woodland..." in the NA sub-regional lists. **Mexican Crows** have nested at this bridge.

Manzanillo, Colima - 1976 up-date, based on library studies. See FBM, 1968, p. 110. For note about additional reference material about birding in the state of Colima, see Colima in this 1984 Supplement.

The population is reported to be about 21,000.

Development, and more through traffic on Highway 200, may have resulted in much alteration of specific areas mentioned in 1968. Similar habitat might be found nearby.

Remember the words of caution about swimming (FBM, 1968, pp. 110-112, and Introduction, 1976 Suppl. to FBM)

Matehuala, San Luis Potosí - 1976 up-date, based on library studies.

The population is reported to be about 29,000.

Matehuala seems to be continuing to grow in importance as a tourist stop-over on Highway 57 between the U.S. border and Mexico City. A paved highway east to Doctor Arroyo and beyond provides additional access to the dry countryside.

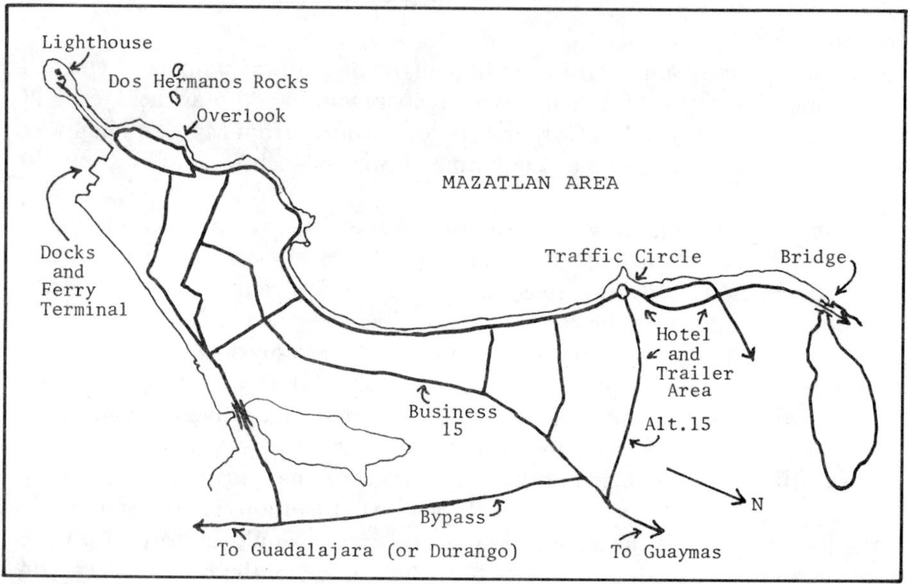

MAZATLAN, Sinaloa - New account, 1984, by Jerry and Nancy Strickling, based on field studies in November, 1982. This account replaces those of the 1976 Suppl. to FBM, (not reprinted here) p. 104, and FBM, 1968, p. 113.

(See also La Capilla del Taxte for birding localities about 100 km. east of Mazatlán along Highway 40.)

Mazatlán is situated on the sea-coast in the Northern Pacific Lowlands sub-region. It is about 1200 km. northwest of Mexico City, and about 1250 km. southeast of Nogales, Sonora (which is on the U.S. border), on National Highway 15. Its population is reported to be about 260,000. Average annual rainfall is 34 inches: 27 inches from July through September, and 7 inches from October through June. Temperatures range from a monthly mean of 67 degrees F. (January-March) to a monthly mean of 82 degrees F. (July-September).

The overall aspect of Mazatlán is that of a large resort city, with an older, crowded, commercial center in the southern portion of the metropolitan area, and numerous relatively recently constructed resort hotels and motels and trailer parks farther to the north, particularly along a curving shore drive and near more distant beaches.

Highway 15 bypasses most of the city, being situated mostly north and northeast of the business district, and mostly east of the recently developed shore areas. Therefore, the through traveler avoids most of the sections where the docks and warehouses and other commercial facilities are located.

Alternate 15, on the other hand, goes right into some of the dock areas, while circling through the southern portion, and around the western and northern portions, of the commercial district, continuing northward along the shore as the Avenida del Mar.

There are numerous ponds, inlets, and lagoons, some freshwater and some brackish, particularly toward the north, where interested observers can find many species of water birds, by following directions given below. In such places you should be able to find many of the following species, in proper season:

Eared Grebe (w)	Shoveler (w)
Least Grebe	American Wigeon (w)
Pied-billed Grebe	Lesser Scaup (w)
White Pelican (w)	Ruddy Duck (w)
Double-crested Cormorant	American Coot
Olivaceous Cormorant	Jacana
Great Blue Heron	Semipalmated Plover (w)
Green Heron	**Collared Plover**
Little Blue Heron	Wilson's Plover (w)
Cattle Egret	Killdeer
Reddish Egret	Black-bellied Plover (w)
Great Egret	Whimbrel (w)
Snowy Egret	Willet (w)
Tricolored Heron	Ruddy Turnstone (w)
Black-crowned Night-Heron	Sanderling (w)
White-faced Ibis (w)	Western Sandpiper (w)
White Ibis	Least Sandpiper (w)
Pintail	American Avocet (w)
Green-winged Teal (w)	Black-necked Stilt
Blue-winged Teal (w)	Belted Kingfisher (w)
Cinnamon Teal (w)	

In the vicinity of some of these lagoons, and particularly along beaches and in dock areas you could expect to add Heermann's Gull and Herring Gull (w).

Over inshore marine waters you can expect to see the Blue-footed Booby and the Brown Booby.

Joining these typical water birds on many occasions are the Black Vulture, Turkey Vulture, and Great-tailed Grackle, which are also very common in suburban areas and among the scattered farmlands and orchards outside of town.

Land birds are numerous among the gardens, orchards, and woodland edges in the resort areas and in open residential areas. Bird feeders in the trailer parks especially attract hummingbirds and orioles, while the gardens and hedgerows and coconut trees provide suitable habitat for many resident birds and winter visitants. Species to be expected in such areas are:

Turkey Vulture	Inca Dove
Black Vulture	Common Ground-Dove

Groove-billed Ani	Black-capped Gnatcatcher
Broad-billed Hummingbird	Loggerhead Shrike
Cinnamon Hummingbird	Bell's Vireo
Golden-cheeked Woodpecker	Yellow-rumped Warbler (w)
Tropical Kingbird	**Wagler's Oriole**
Vermilion Flycatcher	**Streaked-backed Oriole**
Great Kiskadee	Red-eyed Cowbird
Sinaloa Crow	Great-tailed Grackle
Happy Wren	Pyrrhuloxia
Curve-billed Thrasher	House Finch
Northern Mockingbird	Lesser Goldfinch
Blue-gray Gnatcatcher	

Much of the flat land along the coast away from town and the resort areas is covered by a sparse growth of **cactus** and thorny small trees and shrubs with sparse grass beneath. There are thickets of somewhat larger trees covering considerable areas in some places. Dense deciduous forest is found on a few hillsides but even there the trees are relatively small. The aspect of the countryside, except during the rainy season, is extremely arid, and most of the trees have no leaves for much of the year.

Favorable areas for bird observation are north and northeast of the city, along Highway 15, where travelers may find branch roads, most of them being dirt roads which lead off toward the west, back toward the coast. Whether on a small side road leading to a few farms or orchards or one leading to a beach, observers should be able to park and walk along the road or walk into the woods along a trail, and see most of the land birds mentioned above, as well as many of the following species:

Elegant Quail	**(Collie's) Magpie Jay**
Orange-fronted Parakeet	**Beechey's Jay**
White-fronted Parrot	**Sinaloa Wren**
Pacific Parrot	Tropical Parula
Citreoline Trogon	**Mexican Cacique**
Common (Gilded) Flicker	**Rosy Thrush-Tanager**
Ladder-backed Woodpecker	Varied Bunting
Sulphur-bellied Flycatcher (s)	Collared Seedeater

The following directions to favorable bird-finding areas are based on placing the zero-point at the large traffic circle on Avenida del Mar at Playa Las Gaviotas, because many motels and hotels and trailer parks (and favorable birding areas) are north of this point, and some are south of it, and some are east of it. This circle is about 5 to 6 miles from (north of) the heart of the old business district, and is where Alternate 15 leaves the Avenida del Mar and swings generally eastward to rejoin Highway 15 North about two or three miles inland.

Among the favorable birding areas north of this circle are some trailer parks and an inlet and lagoon. If you proceed generally northwest from the circle along the shore drive (should be marked Avenida del Mar or perhaps Sabalo Beach Road) you will come to a major fork in the road, not far from the circle. If you take the right-hand fork (actually straight ahead) you will come to several trailer parks on your right and then continue northwestward toward the above-mentioned inlet. (The left fork which may be called Av. Gaviotas, swings closer to the beach and close to hotels and restaurants and passes by the thatched-roofed building which houses the Mazatlan Arts and Crafts Center, then swings right, *crosses* the beach drive, and heads inland. Be sure to turn left at this crossing if you're on Av. Gaviotas and want to get back on the main beach drive.)

If you continue past the trailer parks and along the beach-front boulevard to a distance of about 2.5 miles northwest of the traffic circle zero-point, you will arrive at a large bridge over the inlet to a lagoon. It is possible to park safely at either end of the bridge, and walk out on the bridge (be very careful of traffic) or down a trail to your right which leads along the southeast side of the lagoon. Here you should be able to find many long-legged waders, and shore birds and ducks in season. In the nearby vegetation are some of the common land-birds. (See the first and second bird lists for Mazatlán.)

Some other favorable areas are generally *northeast* of the traffic circle zero-point. If you follow Alternate 15 inland toward its junction with regular Highway 15 North, you should see some trailer parks on your right within a few hundred meters. Continuing to a point about one mile from the traffic circle you should find some lagoons, providing much the same assemblage of birds as listed above, particularly the waders and shorebirds.

Finally, if you proceed *southward* along the beach boulevard from the traffic circle zero-point, heading back toward downtown Mazatlán, you will see lagoons and marshy areas on your left (inland). If you can find a place to park clear of the traffic you should be able to find many of the water birds listed. Just beyond the first lagoon (which is about one km. from the traffic circle) as you head toward downtown, you should see a road leading left (inland) toward the airport. You should be able to find many common land birds along this road. While here look overhead occasionally, because the **White-naped Swift** has been seen frequently in the vicinity of the airport. (This is the old airport.)

Now, you could return to the beach-front boulevard, the Avenida del Mar at this point, turn left and continue on this boulevard as it leads southeast and eventually circles around the seaward side of the downtown business section and arrives in the vicinity of the docks. There you can board the ferry to La Paz, Baja California or engage rental boats for fishing or sightseeing (this would be about 6 miles from the traffic circle zero-point). But shortly before you reach the docks you should see the Department of Tourism, and just beyond it on your right (toward the ocean) you will find a parking area and scenic overlook. (See note about overlooks, in the Introduction.) From this point you should have an unobstructed view of the *Dos Hermanos* rocks (also called Booby Rocks) about 1000 yards offshore. You can expect to see thousands of boobies - the Blue-footed and the Brown - along with Brown Pelicans and hundreds of Magnificent Frigatebirds soaring overhead. A telescope would be especially useful here. For a close look you can charter a boat which would go out and circle around the rocky island, but not make a landing there. (See note about boat trips in the Introduction.) Some regularly-scheduled sightseeing boats may pass the rocks, but you would want to ascertain in advance whether any particular boat does this or not, and whether it spends any appreciable amount of time close to the rocks. The Red-billed Tropicbird has been seen around the Dos Hermanos rocks, but you would normally have a better chance of seeing tropicbirds around Elephant Rock (see **San Blas**).

In winter, as noted in some of the foregoing lists, great numbers (and a considerable variety) of migrating water birds and shore birds appear on the lagoons, ponds, inlets, beaches, and to some extent the near-shore marine waters. Likewise, many small land birds move into the area to spend the winter or are to be seen passing through on migration, in the scrubby woodlands and other inland habitats, and even in hedgerows and thickets close to the beaches or around the ponds and inlets. Several of the most common of these are:

Warbling Vireo	Blue Grosbeak
Orange-crowned Warbler	Savannah Sparrow
Yellow Warbler	Grasshopper Sparrow
MacGillivray's Warbler	Lark Sparrow

One of the principal night birds in the vicinity of Mazatlán is the Lesser Nighthawk, which was heard calling persistently in mid-May in low, open, thorny growth near some dirt roads northwest of town. One call was a very low-pitched, soft, fluttering series of notes, uttered from the ground, and at least one individual made a strumming sound (with its wings apparently), at times, in flight.

MERIDA, Yucatán - 1984 up-date, based on brief visits in June, 1978, March, 1979, and April, 1981. See 1976 Suppl. to FBM, p. S77 (or 1976 up-date below), and FBM, 1968, p. 116.

There is now a complete, circular by-pass around the city.

The population is now reported to be about 250,000, and doubtless the city is still growing rapidly. The traveler would have to go much farther from the center of town to find relatively open areas where the birds of mixed vacant lots, yards, and weedy fields and brushland could be seen, particularly in the south toward the airport and Uxmal. A considerable amount of light and medium industry seems to be developing in that direction.

Mérida, Yucatán - 1976 up-date, based on library studies, two very brief visits in January, 1976, and reports of contributors.

Mérida is in the northwestern part of the Yucatan Region, at an elevation of about 70 feet above sea level. It is situated on highways 180 and 261, at a distance of about 1500 km. by road east of Mexico City. Its population is reported to be about 215,000. The average annual rainfall is 36 inches; 30 inches from May through October, and 6 inches from November through April. Monthly mean temperatures vary from 73 degrees F. (January) to 82 degrees F. (May-June).

In the vicinity of Mérida one may conveniently observe the characteristic birds of the more arid portions of the Yucatan Region. The aspect of Mérida is that of a very large city, spreading widely, with a crowded commercial section with many new buildings, some of them very large, but with some older homes and hidden patios interspersed among the business establishments. Many of the buildings are painted white, and there are hundreds of imported windmills throughout the city, for pumping water from underground natural reservoirs. There are some plazas and parks within the business section, and these are even more numerous and larger farther from the center of town. Farther out also there are larger patios, with numerous shrubs and trees as well as large gardens and yards visible from the streets, particularly in the areas of more expensive homes. In some other suburban areas the homes are smaller and more crowded, but even in most of those areas there are some vacant lots and small gardens and some trees. Beyond the widely scattered homes, vacant lots and weedy fields at the very edges of town, the typical vegetation is a very scrubby, thorny, dense woodland which appears rather dry for much of the year. Much of this has been cut away and replaced by vast fields of henequen, but there are still some rather extensive patches of woodland, and many hedgerows and overgrown fields.

A number of interesting birds may be seen within the city, particularly in the open residential areas in the northern section, and particularly if one can find some overgrown vacant lots near the large gardens and yards of the private homes. The traditional early morning or late afternoon would be much the best time for this - in the hot part of the day we have seen only two or three species. Under good conditions the observer can expect to see most of the following:

Black Vulture	**Tropical Mockingbird**
Rock Dove	**Clay-colored Robin**
Common Ground-Dove	Northern Parula (w.)
Ruddy Ground-Dove	Yellow-rumped Warbler (w.)
Groove-billed Ani	Great-tailed Grackle
Vaux's Swift	**Singing Blackbird**
Empidonax sp. (w.)	Hooded Oriole
Cave Swallow (s.)	**Gray Saltator**
Tropical House-Wren	

There are many dirt roads leading through the countryside where one may park the car and walk through the low woodland and beside hedgerows and some overgrown fields and cultivated fields. From the main highways leading to Campeche, to Progreso, or to Chichén Itzá, or from the "belt" highway which leads around the south, east and north sides of Mérida, a number of small roads may be found and explored. With the continuing expansion of the city, however, some of the roads which we noted earlier (Edwards, 1968,p.117) have undoubtedly been overtaken by industrial, commercial or residential development. Therefore it seems even more logical than ever for the visitor to devote most effort to the partially cleared and partially restored archaeological sites, because these have not been, and are less likely to be in the future, drastically altered by development for housing, industry or agriculture.

The well-known site most readily accessible from Mérida is still Dzibilchaltún, which can now be reached by paved road (see also Chichén Itzá, Kabah, and Uxmal, all much farther from Mérida.) There is not now so much woodland surrounding Dzibilchaltún as formerly, but bird watching within the site is still quite rewarding. Most of the characteristic birds of the rather dry country are to be found there, around the partly restored buildings, along the edges of the clearings, on tracks which go through woodland to buildings partly hidden, and around the cenote and on paths leading beyond it. The most direct way to reach Dzibilchaltún from Mérida at this time is to go north on highway number 261 toward Progreso, then turn right on a paved road at a point about 15-18 km. (about 10 mi.) from the center of Mérida, then right again after about 4 kilometers. The first turn, from highway number 261 should be just beyond a big ceiba tree and a sign to the Ceiba Golf Club. The second turn, into the site itself, should be just after a cluster of small houses. The turns may not be marked very conspicuously however, and the landmarks could be altered, so it would be worthwhile to obtain precise directions in Mérida. Dzibilchaltún can also be approached from Motul by way of Conkal, where one would take the road which leads *northwest* (*not* north to Chicxulub), and then turn left at the entrance to the site, about 10 kilometers northwest of Conkal. If you go by way of Conkal it would be well to inquire in the plaza if no signs are apparent.

In and around the abandoned old Maya city of Dzibilchaltún (or on trails elsewhere past woodlands, hedgerows, and cultivated or overgrown fields) the visitor should be able to find virtually all of the birds listed for archaeological sites and scrubby, deciduous woodland in the Yucatan region. Birds which we have learned to expect at Dzibilchaltún include:

Turkey Vulture	*Myiarchus* sp.
Black Vulture	*Empidonax* sp. (w.)
Marsh Hawk (w.)	Cave Swallow (s.)
Common Ground-Dove	Green Jay
Ruddy Ground-Dove	**White-bellied Wren**
Groove-billed Ani	**Tropical Mockingbird**
Vaux's Swift	Blue-gray Gnatcatcher
Turquoise-browed Motmot	White-eyed Vireo (w.)
Golden-fronted Woodpecker	Northern Parula (w.)
Couch's Kingbird	Great-tailed Grackle
Social Flycatcher	Altamira Oriole
Great Kiskadee	Rose-breasted Grosbeak (w.)

MEXICO CITY, Distrito Federal - 1984 up-date, based on library studies and a brief visit in January, 1976, and March, 1981. See 1968, p. 119.

The population of the metropolitan area is now reported to be about 14,000,000, including some of the suburban political entities which are immediately adjacent to, and merge into, the actual city of México. Some of the metropolitan area and contiguous towns and cities extend with little noticeable differentiation out of the Distrito Federal into the state of México. The population continues to grow rapidly, many parts of the metropolitan area are extremely congested, and the air in the Valley of Mexico is often badly polluted.

Certain residential areas still harbor a few of the common species, but the gardens in such areas are likely to be relatively inaccessible. One can expect to find relatively fewer and more crowded parks than before, and fewer opportunities for seeing any appreciable variety of birds in the parks which remain.

Visiting these parks is undoubtedly more risky than before, also, especially if you try to go into areas which are quieter and where you might see more birds. Even the parks outside of the city, such as Desierto de los Leones, are more heavily used than previously, and one should be cautious in visiting them. Note also that the alternate return route mentioned from the Desierto de los Leones to Mexico City may be closed off at night.

Numerous expressways, limited access highways, toll roads, and by-passes have been constructed within, and leading out of, Mexico City, mostly within the last 10 to 20 years, so it's essential that you have an up-to-date city map to help you find your way around. You will undoubtedly have to modify the instructions for reaching some of the birding areas mentioned in 1968 outside of the city, because of new road construction and changes. Once you reach the areas, however, you should be able to find many of the species listed, even though there will be more people around.

Minatitlán, Veracruz - 1976 up-date, based on library studies. See 1968, p. 128.
The population is reported to be about 68,000.

The locations of shallow ponds and mud flats in marshy areas may vary from year to year, and development may be encroaching on the marshes. Highway traffic has undoubtedly increased. Remember the words of caution about marshes.

MONTEBELLO — See Comitán.

Monterrey, Nuevo León - 1976 up-date, based on field studies in January, 1976. See 1968, p. 130.

(Ed. 1984 note: It is highly probable that dramatic changes have taken place in the vicinity of Monterrey since 1976, particularly in regard to reaching, and then birding in, the areas of Escobedo and Zacatecas, described in this account.)

Monterrey is in the northwestern portion of the Northern Atlantic Lowlands sub-region, close to the zone of overlap with the Northern Highlands Sub-region, at an elevation of 1760 feet. It is about 950 km. north of Mexico City, and about 230 km. south-southwest of Laredo, Texas, on Highways 85, 54, and 40. The population is reported to be about 860,000 with an additional 320,000 or so in suburbs which merge with Monterrey or with each other. The average annual rainfall is 28 inches; 21 inches from June through October, and 7 inches from November through May. Mean temperatures are probably slightly lower than those at Linares (57 degrees F. in December to 81 degrees F. in August).

There are a few tropical species of birds here which do not occur in the United States, as well as many which are common in extreme northeastern Mexico and southern Texas. In addition, numerous highland species occur on the middle and upper slopes of the nearby Sierra Madre Oriental.

Monterrey is an important industrial city, with light and heavy industry in the northern and western sections, and light industry in the eastern suburbs. There is a very congested downtown business section, with many large buildings, but some expressways and bypasses enable much through traffic to avoid the downtown streets. There are many broad boulevards, especially away from the main business section, and some rather open residential areas with large gardens, parks, and some vacant lots. Farther out, the homes (and factories) and small business establishments are somewhat scattered among vacant lots, cultivated fields, and scrubby semi-desert. A broad river valley and canal extends along (just inside of) the southern edge of the city (but does not seem promising for birds). Expansion of the city is rapid in every direction except south, where the mountain slopes are an obstacle. In south-central (downtown) Monterrey, you can find the following in Zaragoza Plaza near the Palacio Municipal and the Cathedral, mostly in summer:

Gray-breasted Martin (s)	Cave Swallow (s)
Cliff Swallow (s)	Barn Swallow (s)

Farther out, but still in crowded suburbs, especially in the north side of the metropolitan area you can see large winter flocks of White-necked Ravens, and flocks of blackbirds (Brewer's) and cowbirds (Red-eyed and Brown-headed) flying over to or from their roosts.

Birds are often numerous in small parks around the city, or in gardens and yards of open residential areas. Some motels have spacious grounds, also, and their lawns, gardens, shrubs and trees attract several species. In such places you can expect:

Inca Dove	Orange-crowned Warbler (w.)
Golden-fronted Woodpecker	Yellow-rumped Warbler (w.)
Great Kiskadee	House Sparrow
Gray-breasted Martin (s.)	Red-eyed Cowbird (w.)
Cave Swallow (s.)	Brown-headed Cowbird (w.)
Barn Swallow (s.)	Brewer's Blackbird (w.)
White-necked Raven (w.)	Hooded Oriole (s.)
Northern House-Wren (w.)	Lincoln's Sparrow (w.)

Because Monterrey is spread over a large area, most of the favorable areas for birds are several miles or more from the center of the city. Also, because of the dry climate and the intensive use of much of the land, many areas do not seem promising, superficially. But, with some effort, you can find many interesting birds in this vicinity.

If you stay overnight in the northern or northwestern part of the city, or if you bypass Monterrey en route from Laredo to Saltillo, the semi-desert is readily accessible. There are large tracts of very low, thorny, dense vegetation, or more open brushland where you can find a considerable variety of birds.

Persons coming from the north and swinging westward to by-pass Monterrey on the way to Saltillo would come in through Cienaga de Flores, and at a point about ten miles (or less) south of that town (well before reaching Monterrey) would turn right at a major intersection. This might be marked "Saltillo" or "40" or "Bypass 40" (in Spanish). Within a few kilometers along the bypass you would see many dirt roads leading off at right angles into the low scrubby woodland, and also pull-offs into "frontage" type dirt roads which go along beside the highway. (The highway is elevated and there is a rather steep descent onto the dirt roads or pull-offs.) A very large solitary mountain on the left as we drove southwestward on the by-pass toward Saltillo served as our landmark to remember the location of some of the most favorable-looking tracks and side roads. Parking beside one of these side roads you can walk along the dirt road or another track or trail through thorny, scrubby woodland or brushy semi-desert, and expect to see most of the species on the NA sub-regional list for "Partially open country...". More specifically you should expect most of the birds listed for Escobedo (next list).

(Note: In the area of the bypass, and near Escobedo, and elsewhere, there were some high-voltage power lines. The ones near Escobedo, at least, produced a *very* loud metallic humming or hissing sound.)

Farther along, as the road climbed up the mountain slopes there were pull-offs from which you could walk out into the open brushland. Convenient places near unfenced land were near kilometer marks 68 to 66. (Kilometer marks may be changed.) Birds should be much the same as those on the nearby flatlands.

The scrubby dry vegetation near the by-pass can also be approached from the south, near Escobedo, where you can find birds of a river valley near those of the semi-desert. (The area appears dry and dusty much of the time and you're never far from people or livestock, but there is a good variety of birds.) To reach Escobedo you would drive north from downtown Monterrey, or close-in suburbs, out Avenida Universidad, on Highway 85. A few miles from downtown Monterrey you would go over an overpass (highway over railroad) and then angle left onto a major street (should be marked as leading to Colombia). About three km. along the road to Colombia a road goes left, at a major intersection, to Escobedo. This road leads to the town square where you would turn right, then left, to go past the square, still heading generally northwest, on the paved road. About 2 km. from the square the pavement ends, and a short distance beyond that you go across a bumpy railroad crossing, from which point a railroad bridge over a river can be seen off to your right. At a point about 1.1 km. from the railroad crossing you can pull off the right side of the road and park near a concrete utility pole and a jog in the barbed-wire fence. Birds are usually fairly conspicuous and numerous in the river valley to your right and in the semi-desert flatland nearby. Barbed-wire fences, a deep irrigation ditch, the river itself, and the steep, crumbly banks, are obstacles or hazards, but with care you should be able to work conveniently and safely along tracks and paths, and see many of the following species:

Green Heron
Turkey Vulture
Black Vulture
Marsh Hawk (w.)
American Kestrel
Spotted Sandpiper (w.)
White-winged Dove (s.)
Common Ground-Dove
Inca Dove
Groove-billed Ani
White-throated Swift (w.)
Belted Kingfisher
Green Kingfisher
Golden-fronted Woodpecker
Ladder-backed Woodpecker
Black Phoebe
Couch's Kingbird
Great Kiskadee
Wied's Flycatcher (s.)
Empidonax sp. (w.)
Beardless Flycatcher
Cave Swallow (s.)
Barn Swallow (s.)
Rough-winged Swallow (s.)
White-necked Raven
Green Jay
Black-crested Titmouse

Verdin
Northern House-Wren (w.)
Bewick's Wren
Long-billed Thrasher
Curve-billed Thrasher
Northern Mockingbird
Blue-gray Gnatcatcher (w.)
Ruby-crowned Kinglet (w.)
White-eyed Vireo (s.)
Black-and-white Warbler (w.)
Orange-crowned Warbler (w.)
Yellow-rumped Warbler (w.)
House Sparrow
Brewer's Blackbird (w.)
Great-tailed Grackle
Pyrrhuloxia
Blue Grosbeak (s.)
Painted Bunting (w.)
Varied Bunting
Olive Sparrow
Lark Sparrow (w.)
Cassin's Sparrow (w.)
Black-throated Sparrow
Chipping Sparrow (w.)
White-crowned Sparrow (w.)
Lincoln's Sparrow (w.)

Another rewarding (and perhaps more inviting to the average visitor) area is a river valley, used as a public picnic area, within a couple hundred meters of the little town of Zacatecas. This river valley site is about 3 to 5 kilometers west or northwest of the new Monterrey airport, which is several miles northeast of downtown Monterrey, off Highway 54. To reach this place get on Highway 54, which leads to the new international airport. From *downtown* Monterrey you must go generally northeast past Apodaca, *not* east on 40 or north on 85. From the *northern suburbs* of Monterrey you *can* circle outside of the city, going north on the Laredo Highway 85, turning east toward Santa Rosa, and swinging right just before reaching Santa Rosa, to reach Apodaca; at the far edge of Apodaca when you reach Highway 54 you turn left onto it. Prior inquiry will probably be necessary. Heading northeast beyond Apodaca you come to a big Union Carbide plant on the right, later a silo-like tower of the Instituto Tecnológico (Campo Experimental) on the left, then a Pemex plant and then a paved road going off the highway at a 90 degree angle to the left (may be marked "Agua Fría" or "Zacatecas"; does not *cross* the highway). This turn-off appears to be the last paved road to the left before a big power line and the airport-road overpass which are visible farther out Highway 54. The turn-off leads about two kilometers to the small town of Agua Fría where you swing to the right down a long main street. About 1.5 or 2 km beyond Agua Fría you dip down into a river valley where you can pull off to the left or right onto grassy, sandy plots on the near side of the small river. (The paved road continues over a low concrete bridge without railings and up into the small town of Zacatecas.) From the informal picnic-parking areas it was most convenient to walk upstream on the near side of the river, or downstream on the far side, where the valley was rather flat and wide. Sandy tracks and trails lead among scattered shrubs and clumps of trees upstream, and through a more dense growth of small mesquite or mesquite-like trees downstream. A short distance upstream on the near side of the river a path leads up rather steep, sandy banks and out of the valley to a dirt road beside an irrigation ditch. You can walk along this road between an avenue of trees with cultivated fields and hedgerows nearby. Species to be expected in the vicinity of the river and the irrigation ditch include:

Turkey Vulture	White-necked Raven
Red-tailed Hawk	Black-crested Titmouse
American Kestrel (w.)	Northern House-Wren (w.)
Killdeer (w.)	Northern Mockingbird
Mourning Dove	Blue-gray Gnatcatcher (w.)
Inca Dove	Orange-crowned Warbler (w.)
Belted Kingfisher (w.)	Yellow-rumped Warbler (w.)
Green Kingfisher	House Sparrow
Golden-fronted Woodpecker	Great-tailed Grackle
Ladder-backed Woodpecker	Lesser Goldfinch
Eastern Phoebe (w.)	Lark Sparrow (w.)
Great Kiskadee	Lincoln's Sparrow (w.)
Beardless Flycatcher	

On the way back toward Highway 54 you will see a cemetery on your left as you come up a hill after passing through Agua Fría. For a look at birds of the very open scrubby desert or semi-desert you can easily pull off to the right and walk along the hilltop. The birds of this area or of the brushland (much of which is fenced) farther along toward the highway would be those of the NA sub-regional list for "Partially open country..." In 15 minutes near the cemetery we saw:

Marsh Hawk (w.)	Great-tailed Grackle
Common Raven	Vesper Sparrow (w.)
Loggerhead Shrike	Lark Sparrow (w.)
Orange-crowned Warbler (w.)	White-crowned Sparrow (w.)

The Mesa de Chipinque, which is a small relatively flat area high up on the mountain slopes more or less southwest of Monterrey has a different kind of habitat. The vegetation here is principally pine and oak and many of the birds are on the Northern Highlands sub-regional lists for "Relatively humid woodland..." and "Open pine woodland". The road to the Mesa de Chipinque is a southward extension of Avenida (or Calzada) J. Eleuterio Gonzalez, which is the major north-south avenue running along the west side of the Monterrey business section. You can reach J. Eleuterio Gonzalez by going west on Avenida (or Calzada) Adolfo Ruiz Cortines or Calzada Madero. Formerly you could reach Gonzalez by going west on Avenida Hidalgo but you might not now be able to turn left from Hidalgo onto Gonzalez. Because of the continuing construction of expressways, clover-leafs, by-passes, overpasses, and new patterns of circles and one-way streets you should inquire in detail before starting out.

You might encounter a toll gate a few kilometers out toward the Mesa, controlling access, and possibly closing off the road at night. Although a new road has presumably been built in the last few years it is probably still twisting and steep enough to be hazardous, especially at night. The Mesa de Chipinque is about 10-15 miles from the bridge over the Río Santa Catarina at the edge of the city.

You can find paths through the open areas and along woodland edge and probably into open woodland, and find most of the following species:

Turkey Vulture	Canyon Wren
Elegant Trogon	**Brown-backed Solitaire**
Common Flicker	**Spot-breasted Warbler**
Green Woodpecker	Painted Redstart (s.)
Acorn Woodpecker	**Rufous-capped Warbler**
Common Raven	Red-eyed Cowbird
Mexican Jay	Hepatic Tanager
Bridled Titmouse	**Rufous-capped Finch**
Carolina Wren	Rufous-sided Towhee
Northern House-Wren	Rufous-crowned Sparrow

Be especially careful when you might be near the tremendous drop-off at the edge of the Mesa, (preferably work on the part of the Mesa away from this edge) and review the words of caution (1968,p.132; 1976, Introduction).

The construction of a large dam, the Presa Rodrigo Gómez, about 20-25 miles south of Monterrey is a relatively new development. Roads which have been constructed to the lake and dam provide access to an interesting valley below the dam. To reach this area drive southeastward on Highway 85 toward Montemorelos and Linares and Victoria, checking mileage when you pass a group of University buildings on the left, and signs reading "Tecnológico". From this University continue 26 km. on Highway 85, and then turn left onto a paved road, where a large sign reads "Presa Rodrigo Gómez". This leads approximately 6 kilometers along the shore of the lake to the dam, below which is the Cañon de la Boca. Look for areas where you can pull off and look for birds either along the lake or in the canyon. You can see many of the birds on the NA sub-regional list for "Partially open country...". You might also find some species which are not generally common at low elevations around Monterrey, such as:

Ferruginous Pygmy-Owl	Tropical Parula
Carolina Wren	**Rufous-capped Warbler**
Red-eyed Vireo (s.)	**Crimson-collared Grosbeak**

Morelia, Michoacán - 1976 up-date, based on library studies. See FBM, 1968, p. 132.

Morelia is on Highways 15 and 43. The population is reported to be about 161,000.

Add wintering warblers and sparrows to the bird lists for suburban gardens and parks, and nearby countryside. The roads in the mountains are narrow and winding, and safe parking is difficult. The areas mentioned as national parks are poorly defined, and no tourist facilities can be expected in the parks.

OAXACA, Oaxaca - 1984 up-date by Jerry and Nancy Strickling, based on field studies in December, 1981. See 1976 Suppl. to FBM,p.S106 (or 1976 up-date below), and FBM, 1968, p. 135.

The population of Oaxaca is now reported to be about 130,000.

The Pan-American Highway, Highway 190, loops north of the main business section of the city, but no longer by-passes *all* of the congested areas. For most of its length through the northern suburbs of Oaxaca this highway is a boulevard named Niños Heroés de Chapultepec. Where this boulevard intersects Avenida Juárez there is a large motel, the *Misión de los Angeles,* on the northeast corner of the intersection. We have used this motel as a benchmark in indicating distances to some birding areas in the vicinity. The Misión de los Angeles, which opens on Avenida Juárez, is also a birding location in its own right, as is the portion of Avenida Juárez north of the motel, as it leads through residential areas, past a forestry nursery and eventually into open countryside. (1968, pp. 135-top of 136).

The Monte Albán area (1968, p. 136) is now heavily overgrazed, and denuded of most vegetation. Although it is still extremely interesting from an archaeological standpoint, you may not find many interesting birds at the site, or anywhere along the 6-mile drive up the narrow, winding road. Most of the birds listed for that area can more easily be found now at locations east of the city.

To reach the first of these, drive about 3 miles east of the Misión de los Angeles, on Highway 190, to a large monument of Benito Juárez, where Highway 175 branches off to your left and leads north to Guelatao and eventually to the Gulf of Mexico. Turn left here and follow Highway 175 about 3 miles (north) to an old bridge, near which you can park clear of the highway. In addition to many of the birds listed (1968, pp. 135-136) there is a chance you might be able to find the rare and "elusive" **Slaty Vireo.** Both this species and the somewhat more common, but even more localized, **Oaxaca Sparrow** will often respond to "pishing" or "squeaking", if nearby, but usually only momentarily, and then disappear "forever" into the brush.

If you continue northward on Highway 175 to a point about 16 miles from the junction at the Benito Juárez Monument on Highway 190, you reach La Cumbre (1968,pp.137-138). The gravel road to your left (west) at La Cumbre has been much improved since 1968, and although there has been additional logging and clearing of wooded areas, most of the birds listed for the area are still to be expected in the remaining suitable habitat.

Two specific areas are likely to be rewarding. About 1½ to 2 km. down this road from La Cumbre there is a reverse "S" curve to your right, and the road ascends sharply. Just as you enter the first part of the curve there is a relatively flat area to your left where you may safely pull off the road to park and bird (be careful turning across traffic). The Collared Towhee has been found here in the shrubs and brush adjacent to the road.

Continuing down this road you will come to a rather large sawmill on your right, situated in a rather broad high valley at about 9500 feet evevation, about 13 km. from the main Highway 175. You can safely pull off the road and park there and bird in the vicinity. (Ed. note: Although some of the sawmill employees apparently commute from Oaxaca along this road, it would still be advisable to heed the words of caution about the La Cumbre area in FBM, 1968, p. 137.) The following species seem to be common enough in suitable habitat along or near this road to be *added* to the 1968 list:

Giant Creeper	**Slate-throated Redstart**
White-striped Creeper	**Red Warbler**
Spotted-crowned Creeper	**Black-headed Siskin**
Pine Flycatcher	**Collared Towhee**

Highway 175 continues beyond La Cumbre as a paved road all the way to the Gulf of Mexico (near Alvarado) on the north, and also is paved from La Cumbre south through Oaxaca to the Pacific Ocean (at Puerto Angel) on the south. Even so, both of the long and arduous trips described in 1968, pp. 138-140, are still very long, difficult, and very time-consuming. The roads are steep and winding and narrow, and one can safely average only about 20 miles per hour of actual driving. It is hardly any more practical now to attempt such a round-trip in one day than it was in 1968.

Highway 131 to Puerto Escondido (1968, pp. 139-140) which branches off Highway 175 about 10 miles south of Oaxaca, is apparently paved as far as Sola de Vega now, and possibly farther. (Inquire in Oaxaca if interested.) Most of the birds listed for the area about 110 miles south of Oaxaca (1968, p. 140) (south of Juchatengo on Highway 131) may possibly be found along Highway 175 between Miahuatlán and Puerto Angel. We have no information as to whether they still occur along Highway 131.

Returning to a discussion of shorter trips - the area for the **Bridled Sparrow** described as about 30 miles southeast of Oaxaca (1968, p. 137) is still a relatively good birding location, but should be more accurately described as 28 miles (about 47 km.) from the Misión de los Angeles motel. You may notice that you pass through the village of Matalán not long before you reach this area, and once you arrive at the crest you should still find an area suitable for parking on your left. The signs for Nueve Puntas and Paso de Primo Fitz are probably no longer there. The "other *Aimophila* sparrows" mentioned as possibly occurring here are the **Oaxaca Sparrow** and **Rusty Sparrow,** and you may also find the **Slaty Vireo.**

If you continue about 7 km. past this area, still on Highway 190, to a point about 53 km. from the motel zero-point, you should see a microwave (*microondas*) tower on your right, and a dirt road on your left (north) where you can park clear of the road. The list of birds to be expected along the dirt road and in the nearby brushy ravines would be much the same as that for the immediately preceding area.

If you care to continue on Highway 190 an additional 28 km. past the microwave tower (a total of about 82 km. from the Misión de los Angeles motel) you would come to another favorable birding location. Nearing this point, as you descend into a rather broad, dry valley you will see several abandoned and crumbling adobe buildings on your right, beside a sandy, shallow ravine where you should be able to park. On the opposite side of the highway (your left as you approach the area from Oaxaca) there is a flat, brushy field that narrows (about ¼-mile back from the highway) into a ravine "carved" out of a hillside.

In addition to most of the birds expected in the immediately preceding two areas (including the **Oaxaca Sparrow** and **Slaty Vireo**) the **Dusky Hummingbird** and **Blue-hooded Euphonia** have been seen here.

Oaxaca, Oaxaca - 1976 up-date, from library studies.

Highway 175 (as well as 190) now goes through Oaxaca. The population is reported to be about 100,000.

Add the Tucuchillo as a night bird (Monte Albán).

Highway 175 north is paved to Valle Nacional.

Remember the words of caution in FBM, 1968.

PALENQUE, Chiapas - 1984 up-date, based on field studies in June, 1978, and April, 1981. See 1976 Suppl. to FBM, p. S106 (or 1976 up-date below), and FBM, 1968, p. 141.

The population is still reported to be about 23,000, although undoubtedly the town has grown considerably since 1976.

The bird lists of 1968 and 1976 are still very much applicable, and we have information on additional species to be expected, information on new areas, and more information on areas already mentioned.

If you walk back toward town from the parking lot at the archaeological site, as recommended in 1976, you go downhill and around a sharp curve to the right, then more or less straight ahead and down to a long, level stretch. Within a kilometer or two (of the ruins) you should come to a dirt road going left and a stream coming down the hill through the forest on your right. About 100-200 meters beyond the dirt road is the Hotel de las Ruinas on your left. Birding even a part of this area will usually be very rewarding, especially in the early morning. A round trip between the parking lot at the ruins and a point a short distance down the dirt road, should be even better. The road is very narrow and the shoulders are narrow, so be careful of traffic as you walk, and don't try to park along the road. You should be able to find most of the following species if you cover most of this area fairly carefully:

Cattle Egret	Common Black-Hawk
Turkey Vulture	Common Bobwhite
Black Vulture	White-fronted Dove

Ruddy Ground-Dove
Aztec Parakeet
White-crowned Parrot
Groove-billed Ani
White-collared Swift
Rufous-tailed Hummingbird
Blue-crowned Motmot
Collared Trogon
Violaceous Trogon
Collared Toucan
Keel-billed Toucan
Golden-fronted Woodpecker
Black-cheeked Woodpecker
Laughing Creeper
Souleyet's Creeper
Barred Antshrike
Masked Tityra
Black-crowned Tityra
Vermilion Flycatcher
Fork-tailed Flycatcher
Tropical Kingbird
Piratic Flycatcher
Sulphur-bellied Flycatcher
Boat-billed Flycatcher
Social Flycatcher
Great Kiskadee
Yellow-bellied Elaenia

Brown Jay
Spotted-breasted Wren
Lowland Wood-Wren
Gray Catbird (w)
Clay-colored Robin
Red-eyed Vireo
Grey-headed Vireo
Red-legged Honeycreeper
Wilson's Warbler (w)
Magnolia Warbler (w)
American Redstart (w)
Orchard Oriole (w)
Northern Oriole (w)
Scrub Euphonia
Yellow-throated Euphonia
Masked Tanager
Yellow-winged Tanager
Song Tanager
Crimson-collared Tanager
Summer Tanager (w)
Black-headed Saltator
Buff-throated Saltator
Gray Saltator
Rose-breasted Grosbeak (w)
Collared Seedeater
Variable Seedeater
Blue-black Grassquit

Another area where many of the above-mentioned birds may be found is the vicinity of the tourist facility known as Chan Kah (probably marked Chan Kah Cabañas, or Chan Kah Hotel), on your left about 4 km. from the town of Palenque as you go toward the archaeological site. There we heard the loud, slow whistle of the **Striped Cuckoo** from across the fields during the day, and the call of the Pauraque at night and first faint light of dawn. In January we saw wintering warblers among the ornamental plantings, along with many of the common permanent resident species. The following list of birds which we found as we birded an hour or two around the grounds of the hotel and 100 to 200 meters down the road toward the old Mayan city, one morning in June, is typical of what you can expect there:

Black Vulture
Plumbeous Kite
Gray Hawk
Red Rail
Common Ground-Dove
White-fronted Dove
Keel-billed Toucan

Masked Tityra
Great Kiskadee
Yellow-bellied Elaenia
Brown Jay
Spotted-breasted Wren
Clay-colored Robin
Montezuma Oropendola

Singing Blackbird   **Blue-black Grassquit**
Red-legged Honeycreeper   Collared Seedeater
Masked Tanager   **Variable Seedeater**
Gray Saltator

The road to Ocosingo, mentioned as a gravel road in 1976, has been paved, but in some places the pavement is breaking up and pot-holes are developing. Some areas along this road are still rewarding for birding; particularly if you know the bird voices. You will have a problem with parking, however, because the road now has raised concrete curbing which extends many miles.

One of the favorable areas is on the first mountain-side after you leave Palenque. To reach the area, either drive from the *town* of Palenque *toward* the ruins and then swing left on the road to Ocosingo, about a mile out of town, or drive *from* the ruins and swing to your right toward Ocosingo before you reach Palenque. You will go through some low hills and flatland and across a large bridge and then begin climbing up over a mountain. Once you get into the forest watch for a place where the curb is interrupted (in the vicinity of K. 6, if possible) and where you can park clear of the highway, preferably on your right. (Watch for heavy and fast-moving truck and automobile traffic on this winding road.) At this point you should be able to see other wooded hillsides and valleys off to your left. Most of the birds on the last 1976 list should be there as well as some from the third 1976 list, and there is a chance you may hear a **Boucard's Tinamou** calling.

If you continue over the top of the mountain and down the other side and a few kilometers farther you should come to a paved (perhaps broken) road leading to the right a kilometer or two to the Cascada Mizola, a large waterfall in a patch of humid woodland. This is the area mentioned in 1976 as being about 11.5 miles from the Ocosingo road junction near Palenque. There are now some concession stands and other signs of much heavier use than before, and you will have to pay admission, but in 1981 it was still possible to see some of the birds on the lists for the Chan Kah motel and the Palenque ruins.

The vast marshes of the Río Usumacinta near Palenque are a major attraction for birders in this area, and the marshy areas mentioned in 1976 presumably are still favorable for seeing most of the species on the fifth and sixth 1976 Palenque lists. However, parking is difficult and one must be very careful because of relatively narrow shoulders, narrow road surface, and heavy, fast-moving traffic of large trucks and buses. An alternate area, off the main highway and closer to Palenque, and offering much the same assortment of species as the above-mentioned area, is near La Libertad. To reach this marsh drive from Palenque or the ruins toward the railroad tracks and the Palenque railroad station, which is on the way generally northward toward Highway 186. About one km. after you cross the railroad tracks turn right toward La Libertad, more or less paralleling the railroad tracks at first. You should pass a plywood factory on your right shortly after you turn. Drive about 40 km. from the turn, to the village of La Libertad. A short distance beyond the village you should find some marshy and swampy areas on both sides of the road, and should be able to find places where you can park clear of the road and look for birds of the marshes, ponds, and low-lying fields and pastures. You should inquire locally about the condition of the branch road from near Palenque station to La Libertad, because if it is not paved it could be very muddy and perhaps impassable to ordinary automobiles in the rainy season. An alternate approach to this area, from farther northeast on Highway 186, is to turn south off Highway 186 at a large Pemex gasoline station toward Tenosique. After you go through and beyond the small town of Emiliano Zapata watch for a fork in the road, and take the right-hand fork toward La Libertad (*not* the left fork toward Tenosique). Then watch for the small ponds and marshy areas shortly before you reach La Libertad. In this area you should be able to find many of the birds on the fifth and sixth 1976 lists, and perhaps have a chance of seeing a **Sungrebe, Tiger Heron** or **Chestnut Hawk** as well.

Palenque, Chiapas - 1976 up-date, based on field studies in January, 1976, and reports from contributors.

Its population is reported to be about 23,000.

The area for birds along the roadside about four miles from the town of Palenque (1968,p.142) is still satisfactory. One can reach this same type of habitat by walking along the road a distance of a kilometer or two *back toward* the town of Palenque *from* the archaeological site. Many birds which are on the list for the ruins and forest edge (1968,p.143) should be seen here. Several other species should be added to the "roadside" list, including:

Cattle Egret	*Empidonax* sp. (w.)
Common Black Hawk	**Brown Jay**
Gray Hawk	**Montezuma Oropendola**
Aztec Parakeet	Orchard Oriole (w.)
Squirrel Cuckoo	Painted Bunting (w.)
White-collared Swift	

There is also the possibility of seeing some of the rarer falcons, kites, hawks, hawk-eagles and vultures in this area as they begin soaring in late morning on a hot day.

In the small town of Palenque one should see the **Gray-breasted Martin** and the Great-tailed Grackle. Some birds in or near the upland fields between the town of Palenque and highway number 186 are:

Turkey Vulture	**Fork-tailed Flycatcher**
Roadside Hawk	Tropical Kingbird
American Kestrel (w.)	Meadow Warbler
Ruddy Ground-Dove	Eastern Meadowlark
Pit-Sweet (n.)	Botteri's Sparrow
Acorn Woodpecker	

In January, 1976, the gates to the archaeological site opened at 7 a.m. Opening time may change again.

For the parking lot, the partly cleared area of the archaeological site, and the edges of the dense woodland, add the following to the first list (1968,p.143):

White Hawk	**Swallow-tailed Swift**
Bat Falcon	**Long-tailed Hermit**

Little Hermit
Chestnut Woodpecker
Black-cheeked Woodpecker
Cinnamon Cotinga
Olivaceous Flycatcher
Slate-headed Tody-Flycatcher
Green Honeycreeper
Black-and-white Warbler (w.)
Yellow Warbler (w.)
Black-throated Green Warbler (w.)

Magnolia Warbler (w.)
Louisiana Waterthrush (w.)
Wilson's Warbler (w.)
American Redstart (w.)
Masked Tanager
Summer Tanager (w.)
Gray Saltator
Black-faced Grosbeak
Variable Seedeater

You might find the hanging, tube-shaped nest of the **Swallow-tailed Swift** on ceilings or inner walls of the ruins.

Remember that some birds including some listed (1968,p.143) will be heard but seldom seen. Expect this to be true of:

Little Tinamou
Spotted Wood-Quail
Short-billed Pigeon
Ruddy Quail-Dove
Massena Trogon

Tody Motmot
Black-faced Antthrush
Lowland Wood-Wren
Nightingale Wren

Most have distinctive calls or songs which are described in Edwards (1972).

Birds of the marsh can be seen in many places between Villahermosa (1968,p.216; 1976,p.S119), and Palenque. There are also some extensive marshes and, at times, flooded fields and shallow ponds along the highway between Palenque and Escarcega to the northeast. Some portions of the countryside along this same stretch of highway are a little higher or drier, and consist of grassland dotted with scattered trees. The wet areas and dry areas may be intermingled so that birds of the two habitats may be seen from one vantage point. Some favorable places for this are on highway number 186 about 15 miles east of its junction with the Palenque branch road. Scan the marshes and grassland with binoculars and telescope. Birds of the wet portions of the countryside include:

Olivaceous Cormorant
Great Egret
Little Blue Heron
Snowy Egret
Cattle Egret
Louisiana Heron
Black-bellied Tree-Duck
Turkey Vulture

Yellow-headed Vulture
Common Black Hawk
Chestnut Hawk
Limpkin
Jacana
Black-necked Stilt
Ringed Kingfisher
Belted Kingfisher (w.)

Birds to be expected in the drier places are:

Black Vulture
White-tailed Kite
Roadside Hawk
Gray Hawk
Bat Falcon

Aplomado Falcon
American Kestrel (w.)
Groove-billed Ani
Vermilion Flycatcher
Fork-tailed Flycatcher

Tropical Kingbird	Eastern Meadowlark
Red-eyed Cowbird	**Yellow Grass-Finch**
Great-tailed Grackle	Botteri's Sparrow

Along the road which goes from Palenque toward Ocosingo one can find many of the birds which occur at Palenque. A short initial section of the road (about 3-5 miles) is paved, but beyond that it may be dirt or crushed rock, one-lane in places because of erosion or slides, and dusty or muddy. Parking is a problem. Information about road conditions should be obtained in advance. About one mile after you leave the outskirts of the town of Palenque, going toward the ruins, the road toward Ocosingo branches to the left. From there it leads through mostly open country, about three miles, and then goes into low hills with many wooded areas. At a point about 11.5 miles from where you left the road to the ruins, a side road to the right leads about a half-mile to a waterfall. If you can find safe parking somewhere within the first few miles from Palenque and walk along a trail or track into the forest or along woodland edge and nearby hedgerows you may see or hear many of the following:

Little Tinamou	**Keel-billed Toucan**
Collared Micrastur	**Blue-crowned Motmot**
Short-billed Pigeon	**Laughing Creeper**
Blue Ground-Dove	**Masked Tityra**
Aztec Parakeet	**Streaked Attila**
Squirrel Cuckoo	**Long-billed Gnatwren**
Violaceous Trogon	**Green Shrike-Vireo**
Collared Toucan	

PATZCUARO, Michoacán - 1984 up-date by Jerry and Nancy Strickling, based on field studies in November, 1982. See 1976 Suppl. to FBM, p. S109 (or 1976 up-date below), and FBM, 1968, p. 144.

(Review the words of caution in regard to marshes, boat trips, exertion at high elevations, etc.)

The population is reported to be about 70,000.

As you enter Pátzcuaro from the north, whether originally on the road from Quiroga or from Morelia, the highway leads to a Y-fork, with a Pemex gasoline station in the angle of the Y. The right fork becomes the highway to Uruapan, while the left fork leads to the center of Pátzcuaro and to a bypass which swings around west of the center of Pátzcuaro. (The residential-resort-business area on the flatland around the Y-fork and the railroad station is sometimes known as El Lago, as distinct from Pátzcuaro proper which is mostly on the hillsides overlooking the lake. For birds of the El Lago and other residential areas see FBM, 1968, p. 145.)

To proceed to open fields, pastures, and marshes near Lake Pátzcuaro, or to go to the docks at the south end of the lake, you should angle right at the Y-fork as if heading for Uruapan, then turn right again at a point only about 300 feet from the Y-fork, just before you reach the railroad station. After crossing the railroad tracks here (watch for trains) and proceeding about a half-mile you

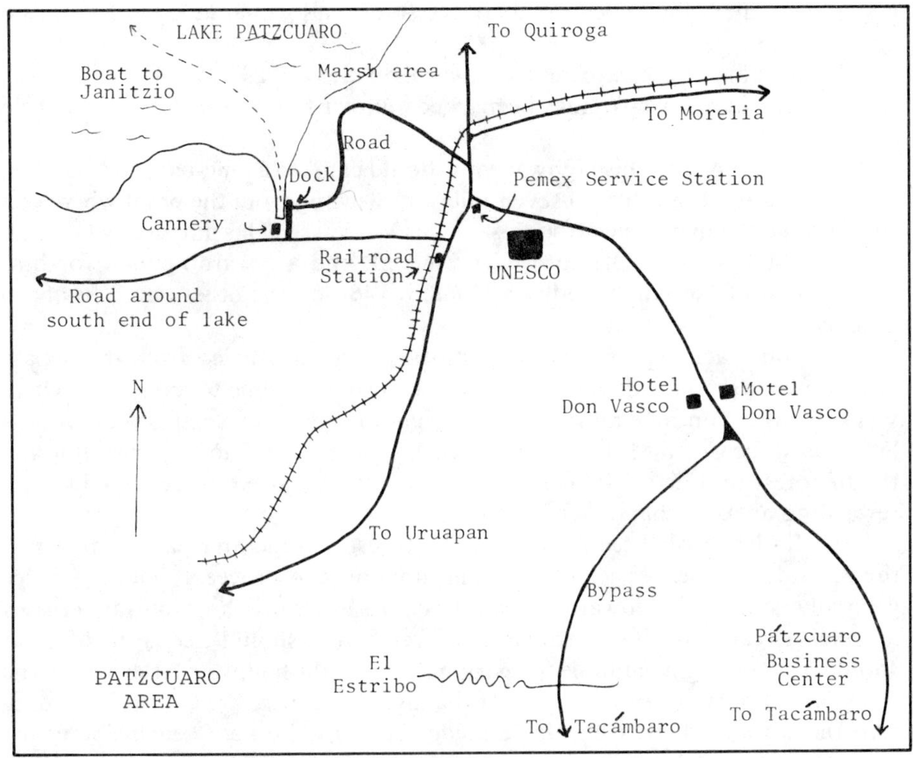

will come to another road leading to your right. If you continue straight ahead at this point you will skirt the south side of the lake and go on to relatively open fields and pasture lands where you should be able to find the common birds of the open country (1968, p.147). If you turn right instead you will arrive at the boat docks where you may charter a boat to explore the lake (1968, p.168), or take one of the regular passenger launches to the island of Janitzio. Or you can swing right again at the docks and proceed to drive through marshy areas generally south and southeast of the lake (1968, p.147) and after a long "circle" eventually rejoin the main highway from Quiroga and Morelia, and reach the original Y-fork at the north end of town. These marshes past the boat docks may provide opportunities for seeing the **Black-polled Yellowthroat,** Sedge Wren, Meadow Warbler, Savannah Sparrow, and other birds of marshes, marshy shores, and moist grasslands. Another special feature of this area is the distinctively dark-colored Song Sparrow, more of a marsh bird here than in many other parts of its wide range.

To proceed to the center of Pátzcuaro, or to El Estribo or to birding areas in the mountains south of town on the road to Tacambaro, swing left at the Y-fork. This road climbs past the UNESCO center on your right, then past the Best Western - Posada de Don Vasco. About a quarter-mile past the Posada de Don Vasco a new bypass highway leads to your right, circling around the west side of Pátzcuaro. About 1½ miles past the junction, and on the bypass, you should see a sign on your right indicating a cobblestone road which leads to El Estribo (1968, p.145).

Continuing southward and eastward on the bypass you will eventually rejoin the main highway (it may be marked number 120) to Tacámbaro and Ario de Rosales.

Driving south on this highway you should come to a pine-oak woodland on your right after about five to seven miles, measuring from the point where you first entered the bypass near the Posada de Don Vasco. This pine-oak woodland (1968, p.146) is still relatively well preserved, and a rewarding area for bird study. Most of the pine woodland (1968, p.146), on the other hand, has been destroyed.

As you reach a point about 12 miles south (measuring from the bypass junction near the Posada de Don Vasco) you should come to a junction where you can either continue more or less straight ahead to Ario de Rosales, or turn left toward the Cerro Moluca area (1968, p. 146-147) and Tacámbaro. Although the fir forest on Cerro Moluca has been largely destroyed, there are still some rewarding areas in that general vicinity.

To find one of these areas, a moist forest of pine and oak, turn left at the Ario de Rosales - Tacámbaro road junction and proceed about 1½ miles generally southward toward Tacámbaro. Just before the highway crosses a small stream flowing through a culvert, you should see a wide road shoulder on the right, suitable for parking clear of the highway. At this point the pine-oak woodland lies to the left of the highway. There are two trails leading into the woodland, both on the left side of the road, one on each side of the stream. You should find most of the species listed for pine-oak woodland (1968, p.146). If you should inadvertently pass the wide road shoulder, and the stream, you may see a K-3 marker on your right.

Beyond this area the road descends toward, through, and beyond the town of Tacámbaro, and into the Central Pacific Lowlands sub-region, through mostly cleared and cultivated countryside.

Pátzcuaro, Michoacán - 1976 up-date, based on library studies and reports from contributors.

The population is reported to be about 38,000.

The mixed pine and oak woodland indicated (1968,pp.145-146) as being about five miles south of Pátzcuaro, to your right as you go south toward Tacámbaro, is still relatively well preserved, and a rewarding bird study area. The pine woodland supposed to be just across the road may have been cleared away. There is an area of scattered pines and shrubby growth about two miles *back* toward Patzcuaro, that is, about *three* miles south of the plaza in Patzcuaro. Some of the species on the list for mixed pine and oak woodland (1968,p.146) can be expected in pine woodland and brushy woodland edge as well. Species to be added to this category are the Yellow-bellied Sapsucker (w.), Bushtit, and Painted Redstart.

Apparently the water level in Lake Pátzcuaro is now lower, and marshes are farther from the road, but year-to-year fluctuation is to be expected (1968,p.147).

Progreso, Yucatán - 1976 up-date, based on library studies and reports from contributors. See FBM, 1968, p. 149.

Progreso is in the northwestern portion of the Yucatan Region, approximately at sea level. It is about 35 km. (22 mi.) north of Mérida on highway 261. Its population is reported to be about 18,000. Average annual rainfall is reported to be only 19 inches, with most of the rain falling in summer and early autumn. Monthly mean temperatures vary from a low of 73 degrees F. (January) to a high of 80 degrees F. (June-September).

This is a convenient place to see some of the water birds of coastal Yucatán. It is a small resort town, with a central business section of moderately small buildings and a large central plaza. The main plaza is a short distance from the shore, and in the intervening area one finds mostly business establishments. Except in the few blocks of the central area there are large gardens, vacant lots, and small orchards scattered among the houses and small stores throughout the town. At the waterfront there are some port facilities including a long jetty projecting at right angles to the shoreline. Much of the resort section of town stretches along a shore drive which extends eastward from near the port area and jetty. Farther from the shore a road extends much farther eastward through residential areas. Small dirt roads, many of them private, lead to the beach from this inland road. Outside of town the soil is sandy and the orchards, gardens, and overgrown fields of the residential and resort areas give way to some areas of natural vegetation of low, rather thorny trees or large shrubs in a rather dense growth, along with more and more henequen fields or coconut plantations.

A short distance south of Progreso, and usually noticeable on both sides of the highway, there is a shallow mangrove lagoon more or less parallel to the coastline. Some water birds are here, but it is difficult to find sufficiently wide places to pull off and park safely and watch birds from well off the road. Many of the birds on the list for lagoons in the Yucatan Region should be here, and the following should be most in evidence along with numerous other water birds and shore birds in winter:

Little Blue Heron	Spotted Sandpiper (w.)
Great Egret	Belted Kingfisher (w.)
Reddish Egret	Tree Swallow (w.)
Black Vulture	**Mangrove Warbler**
Lesser Yellowlegs (w.)	Yellow-rumped Warbler (w.)
Greater Yellowlegs (w.)	Great-tailed Grackle

At the main plaza the **Gray-breasted Martin** and Cave Swallow might be in evidence around the large buildings to the left as you come in from Mérida, except in winter. From the main plaza one can proceed northward a short distance to the shore and then drive eastward along the shore drive, or swing directly eastward from the plaza and later work back north to the beaches east of town. Birds are usually visible out over the water or along the beaches, and it should be convenient to park along the broad shore drive and observe birds out near the jetty, with binoculars and light telescope. Among species to be expected are:

Brown Pelican	Western Sandpiper (w.)
Magnificent Frigatebird	Herring Gull
Black Vulture	Laughing Gull
Black-bellied Plover (w.)	Black Tern (t.)
Killdeer (w.)	Royal Tern
Spotted Sandpiper (w.)	Sandwich Tern (w.)
Willet (w.)	Least Tern (s.)
Sanderling (w.)	Great-tailed Grackle

Among the scattered gardens, orchards, coconut plantations, and vacant lots east of town the visitor should be able to find a firm place to pull off of the road and park. In such a place the following birds are to be expected:

Common Ground-Dove	*Empidonax* sp. (w.)
Ruddy Ground-Dove	**Yucatan Wren**
Groove-billed Ani	**Tropical Mockingbird**
Lesser Nighthawk	**White-lored Gnatcatcher**
Pauraque (n.)	Magnolia Warbler (w.)
Vaux's Swift	Yellow-rumped Warbler (w.)
Cinnamon Hummingbird	Red-eyed Cowbird
Golden-fronted Woodpecker	Great-tailed Grackle
Vermilion Flycatcher	**Singing Blackbird**
Tropical Kingbird	Hooded Oriole

The road from Progreso eastward to the village of Chicxulub Puerto is now paved, and the continuation of that road as a one-lane sand road or track now extends eastward to Telchac Puerto and San Crisanto and beyond (1976,p.S84,S85). An experienced driver with proper vehicle for soft sand, and perhaps deep mud in the rainy season, might be able to go for miles along this road, preferably after checking locally about condition of the road, and other traffic. The narrow road goes past lagoons, and near the seashore on one side, and low woodlands, brushy fields, coconut plantations, and cultivated fields on the other side. There one should see many of the birds on all of the lists for the Yucatan Region except the humid forest. Some special birds which you might find east of Chicxulub Puerto are:

Zenaida Dove	**Mangrove Vireo**
Cinnamon Hummingbird	**Mangrove Warbler**
Mexican Sheartail	Meadow Warbler
Mangrove Swallow	Cardinal
Yucatan Wren	**Yellow-faced Grassquit**
White-lored Gnatcatcher	Olive Sparrow

———————————

Puebla, Puebla - 1976 up-date, based on library studies. See FBM, 1968, p. 152.

This city is situated on Highways 119, 150, 150D, 190, and 190D. The population is reported to be about 400,000.

———————————

Puerto Juárez, Quintana Roo - New account, 1976, based on field studies in January, 1976.

Puerto Juárez is in the northeastern corner of the Yucatan Region, approximately at sea level. It is about 320 km. (199 mi.) by highway east of Mérida, at the northeast end of highway 180, just east of its junction with the northern end of highway 307. Its population is estimated as a few thousand. Figures for temperature and rainfall are not at hand, but weather conditions are probably much like those on Cozumel Island (1976,p.S73).

The sandy shores of the Caribbean Sea are accessible, with some difficulty, in the vicinity of Puerto Juarez, and the medium-height woodlands characteristic of the eastern portion of the Yucatan Region, considerably more humid than those around Chichén Itzá, for example, are accessible along the highways about 20 to 30 kilometers and beyond toward the southwest and south.

The town seems to consist partly of many scattered houses over a distance of several kilometers along highway number 180 and extending to the outskirts of Cancún which is situated on highway number 307. The commercial center of Puerto Juárez is a concentration of restaurants and other small businesses and some dwellings where the road ends at the small dock along the shore. A passenger launch or passenger-only ferry makes trips from this dock to nearby Isla Mujeres. Up and down the coast from this terminal point in Puerto Juárez are narrow beaches, backed by overgrown fields and some small coconut groves. This does not appear to be a good place to observe many birds of the seashore.

To see land birds in the rather humid woodlands in this vicinity the visitor can drive to the places mentioned under Cancún, or drive back toward Valladolid on highway number 180 (or stop enroute from Valladolid to Puerto Juárez). Much land has been cleared between Valladolid and Puerto Juárez, and along the eastern half of this stretch of highway the cleared land is used largely for cattle ranching. There are still large areas of woodland, however, of a moderate height, rather humid, and largely evergreen. There are numerous small palm trees amid dense undergrowth, along with many trees which have been tapped for chicle. One favorable place in this kind of habitat was about 34 km. (21 mi.) by road southwest of the main dock at Puerto Juárez. There was a very large quarry (on the right as you drive from Puerto Juárez toward Valladolid) with ample space to park. From here one could find dirt roads or tracks leading into the woodland, where most of the birds on the list for humid woodland in the Yucatan Region should be found. If this area has been cut over or trails blocked off, there should be other patches of woodland and other tracks or trails in the vicinity. Birds observed on our only visit to this area (mid-day, late January, 1976) included:

Wedge-tailed Sabrewing	**Gray-headed Vireo**
White-bellied Emerald	Magnolia Warbler (w.)
Flint-billed Woodpecker	**Rose-throated Tanager**
Brown Jay	**Jungle Tanager**
White-eyed Vireo (w.)	

PUERTO VALLARTA, Jalisco - New account, 1984 on the basis of field studies in May, 1983.

Puerto Vallarta is situated on the shores of the Pacific Ocean, at the southern end of the Northern Pacific Lowlands sub-region. It is about 970 km. by shortest road-distance west of Mexico City, and about 460 km. by road south of Mazatlán, on National Highway 200. Its population is reported to be about 80,000 and appears to be increasing rapidly. The average annual rainfall is probably about the same as that of Manzanillo, where it is about 41 inches, 37 inches from June through October, and 4 inches from November through May. Temperatures are probably slightly lower than at Manzanillo, varying probably from a monthly mean in the low 70s (degrees F.) (January-March) to a monthly mean of about 83 degrees F. (July-August). Daylight birding hours in late May: from about 6:00 a.m. to about 7:00 p.m., local time.

This is a large resort town or small city with a rather long, narrow, and very congested commercial section, with very confusing traffic patterns. Somewhat more open residential areas extend into the low hillsides to the east (inland). Most of the large tourist hotels and condominium developments are situated on the beach northwest of the main commercial section. Although this area was no doubt rather open a few years ago, and set somewhat apart from the commercial center, it is becoming very crowded in its own right, and now merges into the old commercial portion of the city. Now there is a rather abrupt transition near the ferry dock in the north end of town, with mostly mangrove swamps and cultivated fields northward, and a long line of hotels and condominiums southward.

If you wish to see the birds of the ocean front, you could go to the beach "behind" one of the hotels north of the business district, or to the ferry dock beyond most of those hotels. You might find a public road to the beach or get permission to go through the gardens of the Holiday Inn or the Fiesta Hotel and walk north on the beach to the river mouth, or go behind the Hotel Playa de Oro or Posada Vallarta and walk south.

Looking far out over the ocean, along the beach, and in the shallow waters or muddy areas at the mouth of the river, especially at low tide and when the river is not in flood, you should see many of the following:

Brown Pelican	Laughing Gull (w)
Blue-footed Booby	Common Tern (w)
Brown Booby	Least Tern
Magnificent Frigatebird	Killdeer
Great Blue Heron	Whimbrel (w)
Green Heron	Greater Yellowlegs (w)
Little Blue Heron	Spotted Sandpiper
Snowy Egret	Willet (w)
Tricolored Heron	Sanderling (w)
Heermann's Gull	Black-necked Stilt

A favorable area for observing land birds and some water birds of the Pacific coastal plain is in and near an elaborate resort-housing development named Nuevo Vallarta. This is particularly convenient if your lodgings are north of the business section of Puerto Vallarta. To reach it drive about 7-8 km. generally north on Highway 200 from the ferry dock, past the airport on your left, to the toll bridge across the Río Ameca. This river forms the boundary between the states of Jalisco and Nayarit. Cross this bridge and continue about 2.5 to 3 km. (mostly on a raised road-bed) to a broad avenue or boulevard going left. You should see a large pull-off on the right (partly washed away when we were there, but possibly reconstructed later) and a sign pointing left to Nuevo Vallarta. From this pull-off, or from the shoulders of the boulevard going left you could see or hear some interesting birds. Preferably, however, after turning left toward Nuevo Vallarta drive about ½-km. to a dirt road on your right, before you stop and park (clear of both roads). If you walk 200 to 300 hundred meters down the dirt road and back, birding as you go, you should find most of the following species:

White-tailed Kite	**Social Flycatcher**
Elegant Quail	Great Kiskadee
Killdeer	**Sinaloa Wren**
White-winged Dove	**Happy Wren**
Ruddy Ground-Dove	Townsend's Warbler (w)
Common Ground-Dove	Great-tailed Grackle
Groove-billed Ani	**Streaked-backed Oriole**
Lesser Nighthawk	**Gray Saltator**
Golden-cheeked Woodpecker	**Blue-black Grassquit**
Tropical Kingbird	**Striped-headed Sparrow**

If you continue on the broad avenue or boulevard toward Nuevo Vallarta you should come to a large traffic circle or cloverleaf just before the road goes over a high bridge over a large canal. If you turn to the right at this point, and drive about 2 or 3 km. you should enter an elaborate, broad boulevard with tropical ornamental plantings and landscaping, and numerous short dead-end streets with small canals between them, to your left. If you turn left at such a street, particularly if there are some vacant lots and some natural woodland on the street, you should find some interesting birds. In a few minutes late one May afternoon we saw:

Black-bellied Tree-Duck	Great Kiskadee
Elegant Quail	**Mexican Cacique**
Killdeer	**Streaked-backed Oriole**
Black Tern	**Striped-headed Sparrow**

One of the side roads to the left leads across a second bridge over the above-mentioned large canal and to another boulevard closer to the beach and parallel to the first. You can turn left after crossing the main canal and drive back on this boulevard to the seaward side of the first-mentioned Nuevo Vallarta high bridge. Then, to return to Puerto Vallarta, turn left at this point, cross the high bridge back to the cloverleaf or traffic circle, drive on straight ahead out to Highway 200, turn right and go back to the toll bridge and on to Puerto Vallarta. Before returning to Puerto Vallarta, however, while you're on the seaward side of the large, main canal you could drive down one of the side roads almost to the beach. There we saw thousands of small crabs walking and scurrying on the little-used, but paved, roads. There were hundreds of Black Terns apparently "hawking" insects above the low woodland, and Brown Pelican, Magnificent Frigatebird, Black Tern, Common Tern, and Least Tern over the beach and surf.

Near the airport terminal I found several interesting birds, including several individuals of western Mexico's distinctive chestnut and black (not white and black) Collared Seedeater. To find the area on foot from the terminal building, walk straight out the front door of the terminal, across the parking area and traffic circle, across a large square of lawn bordered on all four sides by short, paved streets, and still going straight away from the terminal follow the road which leads away from the terminal from one side of the square lawn. This road goes through some trashy areas and low brushy trees and almost marshy situations (you should stay on the road). It may lead eventually back to the highway closer to town. On the lawn, in the ornamental plantings, and along a part of the small road, I found the following:

Turkey Vulture	**Happy Wren**
Ruddy Ground-Dove	House Sparrow
Tropical Kingbird	Great-tailed Grackle
Great Kiskadee	Collared Seedeater
Sinaloa Wren	**Blue-black Grassquit**

Birding beyond the other end of town, generally southward on Highway 200, is quite different. There is virtually no coastal plain, as the highway winds along the sides of hills which come right down to the ocean. Within the first few kilometers south of town we saw a few wooded ravines on the left, most of them developed with villas and condominiums, but we didn't investigate them because we had been warned about "bad" dogs, and because we found extremely interesting, and less crowded, birding areas elsewhere. We had difficulty finding our way onto the highway in the first place, from the maze of one-way streets downtown. You may find that you should drive generally southward on *Insurgentes* (if it's not *one-way north*), but it's highly advisable to get directions and a local map before you set forth - toward Mismaloya Beach and Boca de Tomatlán, and El Tuito in the mountains.

About 10 km. south of the edge of town there is a small pull-out to the right where you can park and look out at two gigantic rocks (see note about overlooks in the Introduction) where many Magnificent Frigatebirds gather.

A short distance beyond this pull-out is Mismaloya Beach where the highway dips down into a rather narrow river valley and crosses a bridge. We used this bridge (at K. 202) as a zero point for measuring distances to some rewarding birding areas in the mountainous country farther south.

Before you reach the bridge, however, as you come down to the bottom of the hill to the beach on your right, watch for a side-street going left to "Lomas de Mismaloya". This mainly cobblestone road shortly begins to wind steeply up a wooded hillside, into a(n) (abandoned?) housing development. (Parking is hazardous - besides normal precautions you should "chock" your wheels.) In a few minutes on the hillside we saw:

Citreoline Trogon	**Sinaloa Wren**
Russet-crowned Motmot	**Rufous-backed Robin**
Golden-cheeked Woodpecker	**Mexican Cacique**
San Blas Jay	

From this point the highway continues generally southwestward along the coast almost to the mouth of the Río Tomatlán, and then turns and winds up the precipitous hillsides on the Puerto Vallarta side of the river valley. (Rock slides are frequent from Puerto Vallarta to the top of this stretch of highway.) To find other favorable birding areas continue several km. past a locally well-known place called Chico's Paradise (Paraiso), to a place, with 2 or 3 small buildings, called La Puerta. This is about 14 to 17 km. from the bridge zero-point at Mismaloya. As you approach La Puerta you will swing around a wide curve to your left, see trees (we hope) on a hillside to your left, and also trees ahead bordering a small stream which goes under the highway at a small bridge, and beyond that a fairly straight, level, long stretch of road through open terrain on each side. A short distance beyond the stream you can pull completely off the road to either side at a break in the curbing (preferably go right). If you park here and work your way back to and across the small bridge and into the woods going up the hillside (watch traffic), you should find most of the following species:

Turkey Vulture	**Sinaloa Wren**
Black Vulture	**Blue Mockingbird**
Orange-fronted Parakeet	**Rufous-backed Robin**
Groove-billed Ani	**White-throated Robin**
Masked Tityra	Red-eyed Vireo
Tropical Kingbird	**Mexican Cacique**
Thick-billed Kingbird	Red-eyed Cowbird
Social Flycatcher	**Striped Tanager**
Great Kiskadee	**Black-headed Siskin**
Western Pewee	**Striped-headed Sparrow**

Farther along, at a point about 25.2 km. from the Mismaloya bridge, and before you reach Tuito, you should see a large area, and a break in the curbing where you can safely pull off the road and park on your right. This is on a rather long, straight, level stretch of road at the top of a mountain, just after you pass K. 177, after several kilometers of winding, climbing mountain road.

You can bird both sides of the road along this level stretch easily and safely. You can also work back toward Puerto Vallarta a few hundred meters, to places where you can look down on the tree-tops, so long as you are cautious about fast-moving traffic, narrow road-shoulders, and very steep slopes. There is an adequate pull-out, about 500 meters back, on your right as you go back.

Among the pines, oaks, and madrones of these mountain woodlands you should be able to see or hear most of the following:

White-fronted Dove	**Berylline Hummingbird**
Military Macaw	Elegant Trogon
Pacific Parrot	**Russet-crowned Motmot**

Gray-crowned Woodpecker	**Sinaloa Wren**
Acorn Woodpecker	**Happy Wren**
Ladder-backed Woodpecker	**White-throated Robin**
Masked Tityra	Western Bluebird
Social Flycatcher	**Golden Vireo**
Greater Pewee	Grace's Warbler
Tufted Flycatcher	Gray Saltator
Green Jay	**Black-headed Siskin**
Barred Wren	Chipping Sparrow

Querétaro, Querétaro - 1976 up-date, based on library studies. See FBM, 1968, p. 153.

It is on highways 45, 45D, and 57. The population is reported to be about 113,000.

There are some new suburban or out-of-town motels and hotels, which may provide favorable habitat for a variety of birds.

RANCHO BUENA VISTA, Baja California Sur - New account, 1984, based on field studies in May, 1983.

This small settlement and associated hotel is near the southern end of the BC Region at sea level on the Gulf of California. It is about 1250 km. straight-line distance from Mexico City, about 1590 km. by highway south-southeast of Tijuana, BCN (at the U.S. border), and about 110 km. by road south-southeast of La Paz, BCS, and is just off National Highway 1. The population probably varies from a few dozen to about 100 or 200, consisting mostly of the registered guests at, and the support personnel for, the Hotel Rancho Buena Vista on the beach. Average annual rainfall is probably about the same as that at La Paz, where about 7 inches of rain falls from July through February, and almost no measurable amount the rest of the year. Temperatures are probably somewhat similar to those of Mazatlán, where there is a variation from a monthly mean of about 67 degrees F. (January-March) to a monthly mean of about 82 degrees F. (July-September). Daylight birding hours in May: from about 5:15 a.m. to about 6:30 p.m., local time.

Rancho Buena Vista consists mostly of a set of motel-type buildings and recreational facilities among coconut palms and some lawns and gardens, with service buildings and the homes of some of the employees and other associated persons nearby. Just a few hundred feet inland from the main hotel building is the natural semi-desert of the area, flanking the dirt road which leads from the hotel to the highway.

To find Rancho Buena Vista from La Paz drive about 100 to 105 km. south on Highway 1 to a Pemex gasoline station on your right (and most of the town of Barriles on your left). About 3 km. beyond the Pemex station watch for a (perhaps obscure) sign indicating a turn to your left onto a dirt road to the Rancho Buena Vista. Follow this road about a kilometer to the hotel grounds. If you're driving from Cabo San Lucas or San José del Cabo proceed about 70 to 75 km. from San José del Cabo, then watch for the sign on the right for Rancho Buena Vista. If you go beyond it you would soon come to the Pemex gasoline station (now on your left), and could turn around there and go back about 3 km. to the branch road.

You can find a reasonable number of birds just by walking along the dirt road to the highway in early morning. More rewarding, however, would be a walk to the broad, flat (dry in May, but flash floods can happen) river valley and flood plain about 200-300 meters east and northeast of the hotel. To reach it you can walk 50-100 meters up the dirt road toward the highway and then go to your right where you can see open areas or a trail, down into the valley. Walking off-trail in the typical thorny desert scrub is extremely difficult. Alternatively you could walk out to the beach in front of the hotel, turn left and walk up the beach a couple hundred meters or so, and turn inland up the valley. Working through this river valley in early morning you should be able to find most of the following species:

Turkey Vulture	Cactus Wren
California Quail	**Gray Thrasher**
White-winged Dove	Blue-gray Gnatcatcher
Common Ground-Dove	Black-tailed Gnatcatcher
Common Poorwill (n)	Loggerhead Shrike
Xantus's Hummingbird	House Sparrow
Gila Woodpecker	Scott's Oriole
Ladder-backed Woodpecker	Hooded Oriole
Ash-throated Flycatcher	Cardinal
Scrub Jay	Pyrrhuloxia
Verdin	House Finch

On the beach near the hotel you can expect to find Brown Pelican, Magnificent Frigatebird, Laughing Gull, Least Tern, and perhaps other gulls and terns and shorebirds, especially in winter.

Other species which we did not see in the dry river valley but which are regular in the vicinity are Mourning Dove, Greater Roadrunner, Common Raven, and Brown-headed Cowbird; several species of wintering warblers, grosbeaks, and finches are to be expected in season.

(Walking or even driving very far from the highway is not advisable because of the possibility of getting stuck in deep sand, or getting lost in the confusing network of unmarked sand roads and trails.)

Among the palms and ornamental shrubs in the hotel gardens the common birds were House Sparrow, Hooded Oriole, and House Finch.

RANCHO LA ESTANCIA, Chihuahua - New account, 1984, based on field studies in May, 1983.

This working cattle ranch, hunting resort, and ranch-style motel is in the Northern Highlands sub-region, at an elevation of approximately 7300 feet above sea level. It is about 1650 km. northwest of Mexico City by road, about 140 km. by road west of Chihuahua, and about 32 km. by road north and west of the town of Cuauhtémoc. From the turn-off on Highway 23 the ranch is about 12 km. west or northwest by dirt and gravel road. There is no real town immediately adjacent to the ranch, but there are a few houses in a cluster, probably on the ranch property, about a mile from the motel, and there are some Mennonite farming communities within 10 to 20 km. The climate is probably slightly colder and slightly wetter than that at Bustillos, which is in the same general vicinity, but at a somewhat lower elevation. The average annual rainfall at Bustillos is about 15 inches, about 12 inches from July through October and about 3 inches from November through June. The temperatures at Bustillos vary from a monthly mean of about 40 degrees F. (December-January) to a monthly mean of about 67 degrees F. in June and July.

Daylight birding hours in May: from about 6:00 or 6:15 a.m. to about 7:30 to 7:45 p.m., local time.

Rancho La Estancia is situated at the base of the eastern slopes of the main Sierra Madre Occidental range, where the mountains rise from the high plains of central Chihuahua. The steep, rocky hillsides and narrow, boulder-strewn canyons in the vicinity appeared very dry in mid-May, and were covered with a rather low growth of oaks, junipers, and manzanilla, along with some large pines. Some hillsides and hilltops were mostly covered with jumbled rocks and boulders and scattered junipers. Not far east of the ranch there were level (irrigated?) croplands, where we saw Red-winged Blackbirds, Western Meadowlarks, and a Burrowing Owl. Farther east and farther south respectively are two large shallow lakes, Laguna Bustillos and Laguna (de los) Mejicanos, which are dry or nearly dry in summer, but provide a winter home for thousands of migratory waterfowl.

Birds were numerous and active around the hotel. On an early morning walk around the grounds, and a short distance up the hillside or down into the small stream valley (flash floods?) behind one row of motel rooms, you should find most of the following:

Turkey Vulture	American Robin
Gray Hawk	Common Yellowthroat
Mourning Dove	Wilson's Warbler (w)
White-winged Dove	Brown-headed Cowbird
Common Flicker	Western Tanager
Cassin's Kingbird	Black-headed Grosbeak
Western Pewee	House Finch
Violet-green Swallow	Rufous-sided Towhee
Mexican Jay	Brown Towhee
Mexican Chickadee	Chipping Sparrow
Bridled Titmouse	

In late morning, working our way up the canyon in which the motel is situated, after crossing the small stream valley behind one row of motel rooms, we found many birds were still active. The trail is rough and rocky and steep in places, a strenuous climb at this elevation, but if you walk slowly, listen, and occasionally scan the cliffs rising on your right, you should find most of the above -mentioned species, and most of the following as well:

Red-tailed Hawk	Black-eared Bushtit
Prairie Falcon	Canyon Wren
White-eared Hummingbird	Hutton's Vireo
Elegant Trogon	Warbling Vireo
Steller's Jay	Painted Redstart

A somewhat different assortment of birds may be seen in the broad flat valley which opens out a mile or two below the hotel. Working mostly near a cluster of farm buildings and small houses and a small pond and stream near one side of the valley, and in the vicinity of water leaking from the concrete and rock dam of an artificial lake on the other side of the valley, we found the following species:

Turkey Vulture	Mexican Jay
Killdeer	Rock Wren
Band-tailed Pigeon	American Robin
Mourning Dove	Western Bluebird
Common Flicker	Starling
Black Phoebe	Common Yellowthroat
Cassin's Kingbird	Brown-headed Cowbird
Barn Swallow	Brown Towhee
Common Raven	Lark Sparrow

Another area which we found to be favorable for birding was a side canyon off to the right as we went down the road to a point about 300-400 meters from the hotel grounds. Walking up a cattle trail on the more gently sloping (but still steep) right side of the side canyon, we could see birds nearby and also look across the side canyon to some steep cliffs, where Turkey Vultures were coming to roost, where White-throated Swifts flashed through the air, and where a pair of Common Ravens were putting on a courtship display. Other species in the area in late afternoon were:

Prairie Falcon	Violet-green Swallow
Common Flicker	Bridled Titmouse
Acorn Woodpecker	Canyon Wren
Cassin's Kingbird	Painted Redstart

RANCHO LIEBRE BARRANCA - See La Capilla del Taxte.

SALTILLO, Coahuila - 1984 up-date, with the help of Aldegundo Garza de León, based on continuing field studies by Sr. Garza de León who lives in Saltillo. See 1976 Suppl. to FBM, p. S110 (or 1976 up-date below), and FBM, 1968, p. 154.

The population of Saltillo was listed in 1983 as 350,000. There is some heavy industry in Saltillo, in addition to the light industry and other businesses mentioned in 1976.

The road signs and locality markers mentioned in 1976, p. S110, were still properly in place in late 1983. Be alert to the possibility that such signs may not be permanent, however.

As we have learned more about the area it has become apparent that there are more birding possibilities than indicated in 1968, p. 155. See 1976, pp. S110-S111, and also add species to the 1968 lists, as follows:

To the list of birds for the open desert or semi-desert add Red-tailed Hawk, Harris's Hawk, Scaled Quail, Cactus Wren, House Wren, Curve-billed Thrasher, and Black-tailed Gnatcatcher.

To the list of birds expected mostly, or only, in winter, add Marsh Hawk, Ruby-crowned Kinglet, and Eastern Meadowlark.

Additional owls and nightjars to be expected are Barn Owl, Burrowing Owl, and Lesser Nighthawk.

Sr. Garza de León has a private museum of mounted birds of about 600 species of Mexican birds, displayed in exhibit cases at Aldama Poniente No. 552 (roughly translated - 552 West Aldama St.). Birders who would like to see these life-like specimens (about 60% of all species of Mexican birds) might be able to visit the collection on Thursday afternoon.

Saltillo, Coahuila - 1976 up-date, based on field studies in January, 1976.

It is about 870 km. (540 mi.) north of Mexico City, on Highways 40, 54, and 57. The population is reported to be about 161,000.

As Highway 57 leads eastward out of Saltillo and later swings southward toward Matehuala and Mexico City it goes 10-15 kilometers through relatively flat, open country with very little vegetation. There are a few patches of trees, or large shrubs, and some plantings around suburban motels, and here one should find the species listed in 1968 (pp.155-156).

Beyond this relatively flat area, continuing toward Matehuala, Highway 57 begins to climb and is relatively narrow and winding. There are several bridges, and one or more signs reading *Puente Chorro,* then a small shrine on the right, and then a sign reading *Los Lirios.* Beyond the *Los Lirios* sign (any signs may be missing), and before you reach the top of the climb, is a fairly large area on your left where you can pull off and park. Among the low juniper trees, grass and thorny shrubs, and small pinyon pines of the mountainsides here expect birds from the open-country lists (1968,pp.19,155-156).

The birds of the mountain forests in the vicinity of Saltillo are more readily accessible than in past years. One way to reach some of these forests is to go out Highway 57 as described above, toward Matehuala and Mexico City, cross the flat country close to Saltillo, make the winding climb up the open mountain slopes, and then at the top of this long ascent turn left onto a branch (paved) road toward San Antonio (de las Alazanas). This high point is about 20 to 30 kilometers from the junction of by-pass and business route 57 at the edge of Saltillo. (Beyond the turn-off, which may not be marked, the *main* highway, 57, descends into a broad valley.) The branch road to the left also descends into a broad open valley, proceeding about 22 km. (14 mi.) to the town of San Antonio de las Alazanas. The road continues as a paved road several kilometers beyond San Antonio (with some rough detours around bridge construction), then becomes a gravel road which soon begins to climb through a narrow valley. The natural vegetation here is pinyon pine and yucca, some of it replaced by orchards, while farther up-slope is a forest of larger pine trees. At still higher elevations we could see a mixed forest of pine and Douglas fir, much of it recently burned. Depending on the situation one should be able to follow this gravel road up and up past a place called Siberia, past a playground-picnic area on the left, over the Puerto de las Cumbres, and down through forests of pine and Douglas fir to a broad open valley where there is a village called Mesa de las Tablas. (The road ends not more than a few kilometers beyond the village of Mesa de las Tablas, abruptly becoming a sharply descending, narrow dirt track.) It is in the general vicinity of Puerto de las Cumbres and Mesa de las Tablas that other observers and I have seen the **Maroon-fronted Parrot.** These big parrots apparently come into the area only when the pinyon nuts are ripe, however, probably mostly from late August or September to late December or early January. Even then they may be far away from the road, or flying high above the mountain slopes.

To be expected in these areas from Saltillo to Mesa de las Tablas are many of the birds in the Northern Highlands Sub-region lists (1968,pp.19-20). We found the *Western* Meadowlark in grassland near San Antonio de las Alazanas.

See also Christmas Counts from Mesa de las Tablas in the July 1981 and 1983 issues of *American Birds.*

San Andrés Tuxtla, Veracruz - 1976 up-date, based on library studies. See FBM, 1968, p. 156.

The road distance from Mexico City has been shortened somewhat by new highway construction. The population is reported to be about 24,000. Catemaco was formerly included under San Andrés Tuxtla. (Ed. 1984 note: For complete information about Catemaco see San Andrés Tuxtla (FBM, 1968, pp. 156-159) and Catemaco (1976 Supplement, p. S96; and this 1984 Supplement, in alphabetical sequence).

SAN BLAS, Nayarit - 1984 up-date, with the help of Robert A. Behrstock, based on field studies by Behrstock in December, 1982, and at least three times before that. See also 1976 Suppl. to FBM, p. S112, and FBM, 1968, p.159.

The highway from San Blas to the Highway 15 junction, called Highway 54 in 1968 and 1976, is now numbered "11" on some maps, while Highway 54 is shown extending only from Saltillo to Guadalajara, nowhere near San Blas. Be prepared to substitute 11 for 54, or to continue using 54, whichever you find appropriate. In this 1984 Supplement we will generally continue to use 54.

San Blas is situated at the western end of Highway 54 (or 11, or both).

Population figures are confusing, and almost certainly inaccurate. 1968 figures indicated a population of about 1600; 1976 figures indicated about

32,000; 1984 figures indicate 32,000. Anyhow it's a small coastal town, not nearly as large as Puerto Vallarta to the south or Mazatlán to the north.

In addition to the river or estuary trips mentioned in 1976, p. S112, and 1968, pp. 160-161, you can charter a boat for a pelagic trip if you wish (see note about boat trips). The following is based on an account of such a trip, by Robert Behrstock:

A boat trip to Piedra Elefante (Elephant Rock) for pelagic as well as near-shore species can be readily and inexpensively arranged. Elephant Rock is a small rock island 8 miles or so northwest of San Blas. You should be able to find a boatman (and boat) by inquiring at the Hotel Las Brisas or the Hotel Casa Morales. The boatman can advise you about favorable departure time, whether the ocean is too rough on any particular day, the duration of the trip, point of departure, and the cost of the trip. Ordinarily the boat goes rather slowly, and you should expect to devote most of a morning to the round trip.

Once underway you will pass some rocks just as you leave the harbor at San Blas. You should have a good chance to photograph boobies and pelicans as you go by these rocks. Once you have reached Piedra Elefante your boatman will probably circle the rock island a few times, and then return to San Blas, possibly swinging close to a shrimp trawler if any are in the area, giving you a chance to see some interesting birds attracted to the trawler.

The main attractions of the island are Brown Boobies, Blue-footed Boobies, and a few Red-billed Tropicbirds. If you don't see the tropicbirds flying near the island as you approach and circle it, study the landward face of the rock for the "tell-tale" streamer-like tail-feathers projecting from vertical cracks in the rock.

Common species to be expected are Brown Pelican, Magnificent Frigatebird, and various gulls and terns. In winter, you might find Manx (Black-vented) Shearwater, Black Petrel, Least Petrel, Parasitic Jaeger, Ruddy Turnstone, and several kinds of terns. In fall and spring watch for Black Terns and phalaropes as well. In summer you may see Sooty Terns.

There is a possibility you may see whales, porpoises and dolphins (including the Pacific Bottlenose Dolphin), Whale Shark, Manta Ray, and perhaps a sea turtle.

Back on shore, note that you can probably see Elephant Rock from the old fort on the hilltop near the estuary (Estero San Cristóbal). Also you might find Barn Owls in the church behind the fort. The natural marshy and swampy areas along the road which goes away from the highway across from the fort have been partly converted into shrimp ponds but should still be favorable for shore birds and waders particularly in fall, winter, and early spring.

The paved road leading along the shores of Matanchen Bay, beginning near the old Hotel Colón provides access to water birds such as gulls and terns and some shore birds on one side of the road, and some of the land birds mentioned in 1968, p. 160, on the other side.

For great numbers of shore birds and waders in winter you could study the mud flats at the end of Matanchen Bay closest to the main part of town. The species to be expected include:

Great Blue Heron   Little Blue Heron

Great Egret	Ruddy Turnstone
Snowy Egret	Least Sandpiper
Tricolored Heron	Western Sandpiper
Yellow-crowned Night-Heron	Long-billed Curlew
Semipalmated Plover	Long-billed Dowitcher
Snowy Plover	Black-necked Stilt
Wilson's Plover	American Avocet
Whimbrel	

The marshy, swampy areas in the flatlands along Highway 54 before you reach the Estero San Cristóbal (driving *toward* San Blas from Highway 15) have also been partly converted into ponds managed for aquaculture. As a result you might not see as many individuals or species as before, especially of the secretive birds, but many shorebirds and waders will still be in evidence in winter.

It is more difficult to find a dirt road through undeveloped countryside close to town then it was in 1968. (Some dirt roads in the vicinity of San Blas may be covered with water at high tide. Even when they appear dry you may become bogged down, walking or driving. Be careful!)

An area where you should find most of the species listed in 1968, p. 160, and the first 1976 list, and numerous others, is northwest of the village of Singayta. To reach this area drive east on Highway 54, about one kilometer from San Blas across the "river crossing" (Estero San Cristóbal) to a brick road going left into the village of Singayta. Turn left onto this road and follow it as it swings still farther left through the village; then park where the road leaves the north-western part of the village. Beyond this point the road deteriorates into a dirt road or wide trail and then into a muddy track or trail. If you follow this track northwest from the village you go through cornfields, hedgerows and woodlands, to mangrove swamps and marshes. Birds to be added to the lists mentioned above are raptors, ducks, trogons, warblers and finches, specifically some of the following:

Common Black Hawk	American Coot
Collared Micrastur	**Citreoline Trogon**
Black-bellied Tree-Duck	Orange-crowned Warbler (w)
Green-winged Teal (w)	Northern Waterthrush (w)
Gadwall (w)	MacGillivray's Warbler (w)
Pintail (w)	Wilson's Warbler (w)
Blue-winged Teal (w)	American Redstart
Shoveler (w)	

Other favorable areas farther inland are near the small town of Navarrete which is on Highway 54 between San Blas and the Highway 15 junction. If you can turn off on a side road, and then stop and study any hedgerows, overgrown fields, small ponds, or patches of woodland where you can park clear of the road, you should be able to find some resident land birds, perhaps even a **Lesser Ground-Cuckoo**, several species of wintering warblers, orioles, grosbeaks, and finches, and perhaps some shore birds and waders as well.

San Blas, Nayarit - 1976 up-date, based on library studies and reports from contributors. See 1968, p. 159.

San Blas is about 35 km. from highway 15, and about 70 km. from Tepic. The population is reported to be about 32,000.

Because this area is famous for birds, you might (by inquiry and good judgment) find a reliable guide who knows birds fairly well, and who knows where to find them at the moment. At the "river" crossing mentioned (1968,p.160) one may still obtain a boat with boatman-guide for a cruise through the mangrove swamps along this estuary, which is called the Estero San Cristóbal. There are other places where similar trips may be arranged, trips which visit different areas or approach the same area in a different way. (Safety standards and degrees of danger may vary greatly from boat to boat and trip to trip. Judge this in advance. Our mention of boat trips is not a recommendation!) Some guides know how to find the **Boat-billed Heron** and the **Common Potoo** and perhaps the **Rufous-necked Rail**, as well as other bird specialties of the San Blas area. The bird list for the swamps and estuaries (1968,p.161) should also include Snowy Egret, American Bittern (w.), Belted Kingfisher (w.), **Laughing Creeper, Mangrove Swallow, Gray-breasted Martin** (s.), Northern Waterthrush (w.).

Another convenient area to find land birds is the old fort and other ruins near the San Cristóbal estuary crossing, on the side toward town. You can park on the right as you go away from town, just before reaching the estuary, and walk up the very steep cobblestone road (or you can drive). From the top there is a view of the San Blas area. Meanwhile you have a chance to see parrotlets, hummingbirds, trogons, motmots, flycatchers, swallows and wrens. Across the highway from the fort, and still on the town side of the estuary, a road leads away from the highway and between marshy areas, where you may see waders and other marsh birds.

Another favorable area is along highway number 54 after you come down out of the hills (going toward San Blas from highway number 15) and before you reach the Estero San Cristóbal. There may be wet marshes and shallow ponds here at times, or grassy areas and mud flats at other times. One should find many of the following waterbirds, as well as numerous shorebirds, in this area and along the above-mentioned road opposite the ruined fort:

Pied-billed Grebe	White Ibis
Green Heron	Roseate Spoonbill
Little Blue Heron	Common Gallinule
Great Egret	Jacana
Snowy Egret	Black-necked Stilt
Cattle Egret	American Avocet (w.)
Louisiana Heron	Great Kiskadee
Wood Stork	Rough-winged Swallow (w.)
White-faced Ibis (w.)	**Mangrove Swallow**

Although not stressed in the 1968 book, a variety of shore birds and other water birds, such as the Brown Pelican, Blue-footed Booby, Brown Booby, **Collared Plover,** and various sandpipers, may be seen on or from the beaches, especially in winter.

Birds to be added to the list for overgrown fields, hedgerows, etc., are:

Turkey Vulture	Golden-cheeked Woodpecker
White-winged Dove	Rose-throated Becard
Mexican Parrotlet	Vermilion Flycatcher
Squirrel Cuckoo	**Rufous-backed Robin**
Broad-billed Hummingbird	Blue-gray Gnatcatcher (w.)
Cinnamon Hummingbird	Blue Grosbeak (w.)
Russet-crowned Motmot	Lesser Goldfinch

Many Christmas Bird Counts have been conducted in the San Blas area, and the most recent ones have been reported in the April issues of *American Birds* beginning with April, 1973 (July issues after 1976).

SAN CRISTOBAL DE LAS CASAS, Chiapas - 1984 up-date, based on field studies in March and April, 1981. See 1976 Suppl. to FBM, p. S113 (or 1976 up-date below), and FBM, 1968, p. 162.

(See words of caution in FBM, 1968.)

The population figure posted for San Cristóbal is 93,500. The original bypass south of the business center is gradually being absorbed into the town, and a new "periférico" or beltway has been built.

Southeast of town the point where the periférico comes back to the main Highway 190, just as that highway begins to climb into the mountains, is the point mentioned in FBM, 1968, p. 163, "2½ to 3 miles from the main plaza in town". As you approach this point, coming from town, on the old bypass you should see a small dirt road angling left, still on the floor of the valley. If you bird along this road you should see most of the species on the second 1968 list, and perhaps a few from the third list.

The area specified as three miles (from the edge of the valley) farther along into the mountains southeastward, has been opened up and altered too much to be very rewarding now. But there are numerous other areas where the birds on the third 1968 list can be found, beginning about a kilometer or two beyond the altered area. You should be able to find a place where you can pull into a small side road or onto a very broad shoulder, close to a wooded area. If there are some small cultivated patches nearby, and mixed pine and oak woods and hedgerows you should see most of the birds on the third 1968 list, and some on the fourth list. In about an hour of birding from the roadside in such a place about 10-15 km. from town (stay well off the pavement) we found:

Band-tailed Pigeon	**Rufous-collared Robin**
Common Flicker	Eastern Bluebird
Acorn Woodpecker	Hutton's Vireo
Greater Pewee	Townsend's Warbler (w)
Rough-winged Swallow	House Finch
Unicolored Jay	Rufous-sided Towhee
Steller's Jay	Yellow-eyed Junco
Bushtit	Andean Sparrow

If you continue to a point about 15-20 km. from San Cristóbal where the road begins definitely to descend toward Teopisca you should begin to see relatively intact woodland, mostly of oak and madrone. There are several places where you can pull off into the woods and park in an open space and walk along a dirt road or track. If you do this before you go very far down the slope toward Teopisca, you will have a better chance of finding some pines along with the oaks, and therefore of finding a greater variety of birds. Species to be expected are those of the above list and of the third 1968 list.

The road to Chanal, described in FBM, 1968, p. 114, is now much easier to find than in 1968. The first part of it is now a broad, paved highway, branching left (as you head southeast toward Comitán) at a conspicuous road junction about 10 to 15 km. after you leave San Cristóbal. (Signs for Ocosingo or Chanal or both should be in evidence here.) The highway follows a different route than the old road did, however, therefore you are not likely to find the particular ridge-top locality described in FBM, 1968, p. 164. The road does go over the mountain in that general vicinity, however, and we saw at least one small dirt road swinging off into woodland to the right, near the top of the ascent, perhaps 5 to 10 km. from the Highway 190 junction, going away from San Cristóbal. Birding in the mountain-top woodland along one of these small dirt roads you should find most of the birds in the third and fourth 1968 lists.

The area described in FBM, 1968, p. 165, as a wooded ravine about 5 miles west of San Cristóbal appeared (in 1981) to be still a favorable place for birding, although undoubtedly some deterioration has occurred, due to tree-cutting and increased grazing. The **Chestnut-collared Swift, Black-capped Swallow, Highland Thrush, Pink-headed Warbler,** and perhaps the **Rusty Sparrow** might be less likely to occur there now than formerly.

San Cristóbal de las Casas, Chiapas - 1976 up-date, based on library studies and reports from contributors.

The population is reported to be about 26,000.

The specific area 2½ to 3 miles southeast, the one three miles farther southeast than that, and the one about five miles west of town, may no longer be rewarding. Kilometer marks undoubtedly have been changed. The landmarks for finding the road to Chanal are no longer in evidence, and although the proper road can be found with some effort, the ridge-top area mentioned (1968,p.164) and most of the former pine forest along the road to Chanal have been altered greatly. Apparently only a few patches of woodland remain along this road, so your chance of finding characteristic forest species is much reduced. Wooded areas along the *main highway* about 15-30 kilometers southeast of San Cristóbal de las Casas are still promising, however. One can pull off the road and park and walk into mixed woodlands of pine and oak and expect to find many of the birds listed (1968,pp.164-165).

Remember the words of caution (1968,pp.162-163; also 1976 Introduction.)

SAN JOSE DEL CABO, Baja California Sur - New account, 1984, based on field studies in May, 1983.

(See also Cabo San Lucas.)

San José del Cabo is situated on the sea-coast at the southern end of the Baja California Region. It is on National Highway 1, and is about 1200 km. straight-line distance northwest of Mexico City, and about 1670 km. by highway south-southeast of Tijuana, BCN (at the U.S. border). Its population is reported to be about 10,000 but it is almost certainly more than that, and presumably growing rapidly. The average rainfall is probably about the same as that of La Paz, which is about 7 inches per year, almost all of it falling from July through February, and only about 0.05 inches from March through June. Temperatures are probably somewhat similar to those of Mazatlán (or perhaps somewhat warmer) which vary from a monthly mean of about 67 degrees F. (January - March) to about 82 degrees F. (July-September). Daylight birding hours in May: probably from about 5:30 a.m. to about 6:45 p.m., local time.

This is a rather large resort town, situated where Highway 1 reaches the coast (if you're coming from the north) and swings westward along the shores of the southern tip of Baja California. There is a large and crowded business section mostly extending north and south in a narrow belt along Highway 1 as it comes from the north. Most of the hotels and condominiums and many of the resort homes are situated between the shore and the westward extension of Highway 1. Expansion of the resort section seems to be proceeding rather rapidly westward along Highway 1 toward Cabo San Lucas, particularly between the highway and the seashore. Except in this southwestern part of the town there is a rather abrupt transition between commercial or residential areas and the low, thorny, sometimes dense, vegetation of the surrounding semi-desert. Some areas north of town seem to be irrigated, and devoted to growing crops of vegetables and fruits.

Our birding in and near San José del Cabo was restricted to the vicinity of the Hotel El Presidente (on the beach in the southwestern suburbs) and the vicinity of the Hotel Palmilla (about 9 km. west of town on a rocky headland south of Highway 1).

The Hotel El Presidente is situated beside a large, presumably freshwater, lagoon, where we were able to see a considerable variety of water birds even in May. Doubtless there would be larger numbers of wintering waterfowl there from about October through March. The lagoon is close to the east end of the hotel (left end as you go in the main front entrance), and it's possible to rent a canoe or paddle boat and go out on the lagoon. Much safer, and more satisfactory all around was to walk out on the beach "behind" the hotel and walk generally eastward along the partially open shore of the lagoon, separated at this point from the ocean by a strip of land only a couple of hundred to a few hundred feet wide. Our list of birds for this lagoon was as follows, mostly seen as we walked a few minutes along the shore after we returned from an hour or so of hard work in a canoe, in a strong wind, with a broken paddle:

Eared Grebe	Snowy Egret
Brown Pelican	Cattle Egret
Double-crested Cormorant	Ruddy Duck
Great Egret	American Coot

Bonaparte's Gull
Caspian Tern
Least Tern
Lesser Nighthawk
Gila Woodpecker

Violet-green Swallow
Belding's Yellowthroat
House Sparrow
Hooded Oriole

Where there are ornamental plantings around the hotel, and along the streets in the vicinity, you should be able to find the following species and perhaps some others typical of suburban areas and desert borders:

Common Ground-Dove
House Sparrow

Hooded Oriole
House Finch

Another area favorable for shore birds in fall, winter and early spring, also for some sea birds, and for more of the typical birds of the desert and mixed desert borders and gardens, can be reached by driving westward on Highway 1 about 8 or 9 km. from the center of San José del Cabo, going toward Cabo San Lucas. You should see the public beach "Palmillas" on your left about 6 or 7 km out of town, and then a short distance beyond that a dirt road leading through a gate on your left with a sign marking the Hotel Palmilla. This dirt road leads about 1 km. to the hotel on a bluff overlooking the ocean. You might see the hotel from the main highway, two or three kilometers before you reach the entrance road.

Looking out to sea or down toward the rocks below from the hotel terrace you should be able to see terns, gulls, pelicans, and shore birds, particularly in winter. We saw Common Tern, Least Tern, and Wandering Tattler. Around the grounds on the landward side of the hotel where there were lawns and ornamental plantings we saw Common Ground-Dove, House Sparrow, Hooded Oriole, and House Finch. To see more of the typical birds of the semi-desert you should be able to walk out along the dirt entrance road, and find such species in the low, thorny vegetation on each side. Particularly in the early morning you should be able to find many of the species listed for the Hotel Cabo San Lucas (see Cabo San Lucas).

San Luis Potosí, San Luis Potosí - 1976 up-date, based on library studies. See FBM, 1968, p. 166.

It is approximately 415 km. north of Mexico City, by new, shorter highways, and is situated on highway number 49, 57, 70, and 80. The population is reported to be about 230,000.

The habitat types indicated (1968,p.167) as being from 5 to 15 or 20 miles out, and 30 to 40 miles out, toward the northeast, should still be accessible, although possibly more acreage is being overgrazed, cleared and cultivated, replaced with cultivated varieties of grass, fenced, or otherwise altered.

San Miguel de Allende, Guanajuato - 1976 up-date, based on library studies and reports from contributors. See FBM, 1968, p. 168.

It is approximately 275 km. northwest of Mexico City, 48 km. north of Highways 45 and 45D, and 35 km. west of Highway 57. It appears to be on Highway 51, as well as Guanajuato Highway 49. The population is reported to be about 24,000.

There is a lake several kilometers south of San Miguel, where some water birds might be expected.

In an irrigated area about 20 or 30 kilometers north of town the following species have been reported:

Harris's Hawk	Common Yellowthroat
Green Kingfisher	Orchard Oriole
Common Flicker	Eastern Meadowlark
Golden-fronted Woodpecker	House Finch

There has been a local Audubon Society in San Miguel, the only one in Mexico.

SAYIL, Yucatán - New account, 1984, based on field studies in June, 1978, and March, 1979, and reports from George and Janet Cobb, who live near there. (See also Uxmal.)

Sayil is an archaeological site in the Yucatan Region, perhaps 25 to 50 feet above sea level. It is on a branch paved road a few kilometers east of Highway 261, and about 110 to 120 km. south of Mérida. Its climate is probably very much like that of Mérida, although average annual rainfall is possibly greater at Sayil.

There was no real village here in 1979, just two or three small houses on the site. This was shortly after the branch road was paved, therefore it seems likely that additional houses and small souvenir stands might be there now.

To reach the site from the north, drive south from, or past, Uxmal on your right, past Kabah on your left and right, to a conspicuous junction with a paved road going left. This junction is probably 25 to 30 km. south of Uxmal. Turn left onto the branch road and drive a few kilometers to the Sayil entrance and parking lot on your right. You should find a dirt road leading from the parking lot a couple hundred meters (in a direction away from the paved road) and then swinging left as it leads in front of the long, low Palace on your left. Once you reach the area near, or in front of , the Palace you should see one or more dirt tracks or roads leading still farther from the highway into the woodland (tracks more or less perpendicular to the long axis of the Palace). The vegetation here seems somewhat more luxuriant than that at Uxmal, and some species of birds generally associated with more humid areas seem to be more common here than they are at Uxmal. If you follow one of the tracks leading from the Palace (be careful to keep your bearings) and also work around the clearing near the Palace, and around the parking lot and entrance road you should see many of the birds listed for Kabah and Uxmal, and possibly even the **Olivaceous Creeper, Laughing Creeper, White-eyed Flycatcher,** or **Yellow-throated Euphonia.**

SUDZAL, Yucatán - Special note, 1984, based on reports from contributors.

Soon after the 1976 Supplement was published the rewarding birding area described there (that part *not* reprinted below) was almost completely converted from dense, thorny low woodland to cultivated fields of henequen or corn or both. Therefore you can no longer expect to find a great variety and concentration of birds there. If you can find patches of woodland and hedgerows near Sudzal, or any of the other small towns in that part of Yucatán, you should find some of the birds listed in the Yucatán regional write-up.

Sudzal, Yucatán - New account (part), 1976 - Based on field studies in January, 1976.

Sudzal is in the north-central portion of the Yucatan Region, probably about 50 to 100 feet above sea level. It is about 80 km. by road east of Mérida, on a paved road between Kantunil on Highway 180 about 10 kilometers to the south, and Izamal, a much larger town about 9 kilometers to the north. The population of Sudzal is estimated to number a few hundred. Climatic conditions should be much the same as those at Mérida (1976,p.S77).

Sudzal is a very small town or large village, with a large open grassy field in the center as a plaza, and houses along the streets which border the plaza, and houses and small stores extending from the center of town, particularly along the paved road which connects Kantunil with Izamal. The town is set in a mixture of henequen fields, small cornfields, and large patches of low, thorny deciduous woodland typical of this part of the Yucatan Region. Since the town is so small and the houses and commercial buildings close together, there is a rather abrupt transition to the countryside.

Tamazunchale, San Luis Potosí - 1976 up-date, based on library studies. See FBM, 1968, p. 169.

The elevation is now listed as about 400 feet above sea level. The population is reported to be about 12,000 by one source and about 63,000 by another, the former probably being much closer to the actual figure. Annual rainfall is probably somewhat higher than estimated earlier, probably reaching a total of 70 to 80 inches per year, most of the rain falling from May or June through October.

The area (1968,p.170) in the edge of town along the highway toward Mexico City may no longer be suitable for many birds. The road mentioned (1968,p.171) as turning off to the right just before you reach the river when coming from Mexico City may be the road (perhaps unpaved) which goes generally east to Huejutla which is on Highway 105 between Tampico and Pachuca. If so, expect more traffic now and fewer places to pull off and park in relatively undisturbed areas. The areas (1968,pp.171-172) along the highway toward Valles must have been altered considerably if not obliterated as bird-watching areas. The road to Xilitla is now paved Highway 120 continuing generally southwest beyond Xilita to San Juán del Río, where one may enter Highway 57D northwest of Mexico City. There are now many orange groves along this road, between Highway 85 and Xilitla.

Add Northern House-Wren and Blue-gray Gnatcatcher to the list of winter birds.

Tampico, Tamaulipas - 1976 up-date, based on field studies in January, 1976. See FBM, 1968, p. 173.

Tampico is situated on the Gulf of Mexico, approximately at sea level, in the southeastern corner of the Northern Atlantic Lowlands sub-region, where it meets the Central Atlantic Lowlands sub-region. It is about 520 km. north-northeast of Mexico City, and about 600 km. south of Brownsville, Texas. It is at the east end of Highways 80 and 70, while Highway 180 goes through the city. Its population is reported to be about 180,000. The average annual rainfall is 49 inches; 39 inches from June through October, and 10 inches from November through May. Monthly mean temperatures vary from a low of 66 degrees F. in January to a high of 83 degrees F. in August.

The vicinity of Tampico provides an opportunity to see some tropical land birds which do not reach the United States, and to see large numbers, as well as a variety of species, of widely distributed water birds. This is a modern city with a number of large buildings and narrow, congested streets in the long downtown business section. A large industrial section is concentrated in the southern part of the city, and in the southwestern and northern suburbs. There are railroad yards, refineries, oil wells, and port facilities, designed for extracting and handling petroleum and petroleum products, for which Tampico is a major center. The principal residential areas are in the western part of the city, extending along the highway which leads in from a northwesterly direction. Many small business establishments are intermingled with private homes. The city extends to the shore of the Gulf of Mexico. Some beaches are accessible, although they do not provide the major ornithological attractions of the area. Out in the countryside the gardens and parks of the open residential areas give way to some small farms, ranches, and pastures, but much of the surrounding area is marshland, or higher ground with industrial or residential development. The natural vegetation of this area would consist of thorny shrubs and small trees on high ground, larger and more luxuriant trees along some stream valleys and lower ground, and marsh and swamp plants in shallow ponds and flatlands along the Río Tamesí and Río Pánuco.

To see representative land birds of the area you can work around the grounds of one of the suburban motels or in the vacant lots, overgrown fields, hedgerows, and open residential areas nearby. You can now find patches of woodland and overgrown fields between the outskirts of town and the airport more easily than farther out on highway number 80 toward Altamira. Birds to be expected in these open suburban areas include:

Great Egret	Common Bobwhite
Turkey Vulture	White-winged Dove
Black Vulture	Common Ground-Dove
Crested Caracara	Groove-billed Ani
American Kestrel (w.)	Pauraque (n.)

Golden-fronted Woodpecker	Orange-crowned Warbler (w.)
Eastern Phoebe (w.)	Common Yellowthroat (w.)
Tropical Kingbird	Red-eyed Cowbird
Social Flycatcher	Great-tailed Grackle
Great Kiskadee	**Singing Blackbird**
Mexican Crow	Altamira Oriole
Brown Jay	Eastern Meadowlark
Black-crested Titmouse	**Gray Saltator**
Spotted-breasted Wren	Cardinal
Gray Catbird (w.)	**Yellow-faced Grassquit**
Northern Mockingbird	Collared Seedeater
Blue-gray Gnatcatcher (w.)	**Blue-black Grassquit**
White-eyed Vireo	Olive Sparrow
Red-eyed Vireo (s.)	Lincoln's Sparrow (w.)

The **Altamira Yellowthroat** and the **Fuertes's Oriole** are two of the specialties of the vicinity of Tampico, and the latter, particularly, *may* be found between the city and the airport, but the best chance of seeing these two birds is southwest of the city on the highway to Valles. The **Altamira Yellowthroat** is more likely to be found in the marshes or in weedy growth around marsh edges. The **Fuertes's Oriole** frequents shrubs or trees around marsh edges.

There are some shallow ponds and wet flats off highway number 80, north and northwest of Tampico, and you might also find marshes and ponds in the western suburbs of Tampico. The most rewarding areas for water bird observation, however, are generally west and southwest of Tampico along Highway 70 (formerly Highway 110). There you could find extensive shallow ponds, mudflats and marshy or swampy areas at intervals on both sides of the highway, out to a distance of about 20 miles, measuring from the first large bridge (toll) on Highway 70 southwest. Water levels, locations of concentrations of birds, and light conditions vary, but we have found ample water and numerous birds in good light in both winter and summer.

The highway is narrow and uneven, with narrow shoulders, and is heavily used by large trucks and buses. Consequently it is difficult to park safely or even walk safely along the road after parking elsewhere. You should not venture into the marsh, either. Frequently road construction and short detours can be a problem. Fortunately, there are some places where you can park safely, walk well away from the road, and see numerous birds in good light, including possibly the **Fuertes's Oriole** and other land birds.

One such place was about 9 km. (about 5 to 6 miles) out beyond the toll bridge. There you could find a dirt road or two leading off the highway, enabling you to park and walk near hedgerows away from the road and at the same time get a view out across the marshes. A telescope would be especially helpful here.

Other favorable places were scattered about 18 to 22 km. out the Valles highway from the toll bridge. There were some reasonably good places to park, some hedgerows for land birds, places to walk away from the road, and marsh birds in the background.

Birds to be expected in these marshes and nearby hedgerows and grassy higher ground, in summer and usually all year round are:

Pied-billed Grebe	Common Gallinule
Olivaceous Cormorant	American Coot
Anhinga	Jacana
Great Blue Heron	Black-necked Stilt
Green Heron	Laughing Gull
Little Blue Heron	Gull-billed Tern
Reddish Egret	Caspian Tern
Great Egret	Royal Tern
Snowy Egret	Black Skimmer
Cattle Egret	**Aztec Parakeet**
Louisiana Heron	Ringed Kingfisher
Yellow-crowned Night-Heron	Green Kingfisher
Wood Stork	Couch's Kingbird
White-faced Ibis	Great Kiskadee
White Ibis	**Mexican Crow**
Roseate Spoonbill	**Altamira Yellowthroat**
Black-bellied Tree-Duck	Great-tailed Grackle
Turkey Vulture	**Fuertes's Oriole**
Osprey	Red-winged Blackbird
Crested Caracara	Botteri's Sparrow
Red Rail	

With the advent of autumn the numbers and variety of water birds are greatly augumented by transients and winter visitants of species which breed farther north. Some of these arrive as early as the first week in July, and may not leave the following year until June, and a few stay all summer as non-breeding birds. Species to be expected only from fall to spring (w.), generally, are:

White Pelican	Lesser Yellowlegs
Gadwall	Least Sandpiper
Pintail	Western Sandpiper
Blue-winged Teal	Long-billed Dowitcher
American Wigeon	American Avocet
Shoveler	Herring Gull
Lesser Scaup	Ring-billed Gull
Ruddy Duck	Black Tern
Black-bellied Plover	Common Tern
Ruddy Turnstone	Forster's Tern
Long-billed Curlew	Belted Kingfisher
Marbled Godwit	Eastern Phoebe
Spotted Sandpiper	Orange-crowned Warbler
Willet	Yellow-rumped Warbler
Greater Yellowlegs	Lincoln's Sparrow

In early spring, especially April, you may see flocks of hawks migrating northward in soaring, circling flight, high overhead. These are principally

Swainson's Hawks and Broad-winged Hawks, sometimes numbering in the hundreds or thousands.

Tapachula, Chiapas - 1976 up-date, based on library studies and reports from contributors. See FBM, 1968, p. 176.

Its elevation is much less than the 500 feet indicated in 1968, probably being closer to 50 feet above sea level. It is still on Highway 200, and at the end of Highway 225. The population is reported to be about 61,000.

The road to Puerto Madero, the road to Talisman Bridge, and the road going generally north of town still provide areas of considerable interest. To avoid confusion over the new airport omit reference to the airport in the directions (1968,pp.177-178) for bird-finding on the Puerto Madero road. The idea is to follow the main highway toward Puerto Madero.

For another bird-watching area accessible by paved (but not so heavily traveled) road one could go about 15-20 kilometers northwest of Tapachula, on highway 200 toward Arriaga, and turn left on the road to Mazatán. You should then find a place to pull off and park near areas of very open woodland. Expect many of the species on the SP sub-region lists (1968,pp.12-14).

Taxco, Guerrero - 1976 up-date, based on library studies. See FBM, 1968, p. 180.

The population is reported to be about 27,000.

The areas mentioned in 1968 may have been altered, but bird lists should be applicable, once suitable habitat has been found. Many slopes around Taxco are extremely steep with loose rock, gravel, or dirt. Watch your footing when walking, and watch for rock-falls or slides when driving.

Tehuacán, Puebla - 1976 up-date, based on library studies. See FBM, 1968, p. 182.

Situated on Highway 125, Tehuacán is about two or three miles from the main part of old Highway 150 and about 20-30 miles straight-line distance from the new Highway 150D. The population is reported to be about 48,000.

The reference to "regular Highway 150 north of Tehuacán" (1968,p.183) applies to the portion between Tehuacán and Córdoba. The areas "five miles northeast" (this should read "five miles toward Córdoba from Tehuacán") and "16 to 16½ miles north" may have been altered, but if those *types* of habitat can be found nearby, the bird lists should be applicable. Kilometer mark 278 probably has been moved away from the place mentioned (1968,p.184).

Tehuantepec, Oaxaca - 1976 up-date, based on library studies and reports from contributors. See FBM, 1968, p. 184.

Highway numbers in town are 185 and 190. The population is reported to be about 13,000 by one sourcebook, and about 101,000 by another. The correct figure is probably closer to the former.

The bridge two miles west of the main Tehuantepec River crossing (1968,p.185) should be there but the open area and woodland nearby may have been altered. There should be numerous areas of scrubby woodland west of town however. Add **Lesser Roadrunner** to the list for this habitat. The rock formation at about 28 miles east of the main river crossing (1968,p.186), should be there but the marsh or swampy area nearby may have been modified. Wading birds should be numerous around seasonal ponds, flooded fields, and ditches or canals with water in them.

In mid-autumn you might find thousands of Scissor-tailed Flycatchers migrating through the area.

TELCHAC PUERTO, Yucatán - Special note, 1984.

Soon after the 1976 Supplement was published, construction of a "Puerto Abrigo" was apparently being considered, and may have been initiated, just beyond the area described as being about 2 km. west of Manolo's Corner. Such construction presumably would involve digging a channel from the ocean to the lagoon mentioned in the discussion, and then dredging and deepening a portion of the lagoon. Whether or not this has been done, you still may be able to find most of the birds listed for the area, provided you can bird along undisturbed portions of the lagoon shores and in mixed fields, woodland borders, hedgerows and coconut plantations.

Telchac Puerto, Yucatán - New account, 1976 - based on field studies in January, 1976.

Telchac Puerto is in the northern portion of the Yucatan Region, approximately at sea level. It is about 65 km. northeast of Mérida by paved road (but is not on a major numbered highway). It is about 28 km. north of the much larger town of Motul and about 14 km. (about 9 mi.) north of Telchac *Pueblo*. The population of Telchac *Puerto* numbers a few hundred, including some who live in vacation homes for only a part of the year. Average temperatures and annual rainfall are about the same as in Mérida (1976,p.S77).

This is a very small town or large village with a small grassy field-play-ground-plaza in the main part of town, with three or four sand streets paralleling the ocean front, and some cross streets. The town extends farther along the shore than it does inland, and there are larger yards and more scattering of homes as one goes beyond two or three blocks from the plaza. There are numerous vacant lots and some coconut plantations in the edge of town, giving way to henequen fields and more coconut plantations and low shore growth along the coast. These are separated from the very low, scrubby, thorny woodland and henequen fields, which are farther inland, by a long narrow mangrove swamp and series of lagoons paralleling the coast.

The main road coming into Telchac Puerto from Telchac Pueblo goes to the seashore less than a hundred meters north of the north side of the plaza. The beach is also accessible in places from the sand road nearest the beach and parallel to it. The visitor may walk from this road to the beach, particularly near the outskirts of town. There is usually some shorebird activity along the beach.

With a suitable vehicle and a driver experienced on sand (and mud, in season) the visitor may go west or east along the one-lane sand road or track which extends roughly parallel to the shore (see also Progreso, 1976, p.S79). This narrow road intersects the north-south paved road in Telchac Puerto at "Monolo's Corner", (a translation of the local name for the corner one block south of the south end of the town plaza and about 2½ blocks south of the seashore). To provide for two-way traffic on this coast road (trucks loaded with salt use it often) there are pull-outs at intervals. It might be wise to inquire locally about road conditions and traffic.

One favorable area for observing a variety of water birds and land birds is a large, rather open lagoon accessible at a point about two kilometers west of Telchac Puerto. Another is among the "salt pans" and nearby waters in the vicinity of the village of San Crisanto, about 10 kilometers east of Telchac Puerto. The San Crisanto salt pans are likely to be at their most interesting in the fall, winter and spring, while the lagoon west of Telchac Puerto can be expected to be of continuing great interest all year round.

To reach the lagoon close to Telchac Puerto turn west at Manolo's Corner (one block south of the south end of the plaza) and drive about 2 km. (about 1.2 mi.) to a place where you will see a coconut grove on the right (north side), a pull-off area on the left, a dirt road or track going off to the left, and a henequen field ahead to your left. If you walk down the dirt road to the south you will come to the edge of an extensive lagoon within 300 to 400 meters. A rough stone causeway with some large, open-water gaps in it extends out into the lagoon, but the preferred way to see birds in this area is to walk east along the shores of the lagoon. Water levels vary from season to season, so the visitor may have to walk through higher, brushy, grassy areas to avoid high water or soft wet sand or mud at times.

Birds to be expected in this mixture of habitats are:

Brown Pelican	Spotted Sandpiper (w.)
Magnificent Frigatebird	Laughing Gull
Green Heron	**Zenaida Dove**
Little Blue Heron	Common Ground-Dove
Great Egret	**Ruddy Ground-Dove**
Snowy Egret	Groove-billed Ani
Louisiana Heron	**Cinnamon Hummingbird**
Pintail (w.)	**Mexican Sheartail**
Turkey Vulture	Belted Kingfisher (w.)
American Kestrel (w.)	**Barred Antshrike**
Yucatan Bobwhite	Couch's Kingbird
Killdeer (w.)	Great Kiskadee
Greater Yellowlegs (w.)	*Empidonax* sp. (w.)

Tree Swallow (w.)	Common Yellowthroat (w.)
Mangrove Swallow	Great-tailed Grackle
Yucatan Wren	**Singing Blackbird**
Tropical House-Wren	Hooded Oriole
Tropical Mockingbird	Summer Tanager (w.)
Blue-gray Gnatcatcher	Cardinal
Mangrove Vireo	Olive Sparrow
Mangrove Warbler	Savannah Sparrow (w.)

To reach the lagoons and salt pans (and some mangrove-swamp edges) near San Crisanto, turn *east* at Manolo's Corner. Drive along the narrow sand road a distance of about 9.5 km. (about 6 mi.) to the village of San Crisanto. Turn right at the plaza and go two or three hundred meters south to a point where you can park, and walk out onto a causeway past the salt pans, the shallow ponds in which sea water is evaporated to yield the residual salt. If you go through San Crisanto toward the east instead of turning to the salt pans, you would also come to lagoon edge and flats, but we found fewer birds there than along the causeway south of the village. A list of birds to be expected in the vicinity of San Crisanto would include:

Brown Pelican	Ruddy Turnstone (w.)
Great Egret	Sanderling (w.)
Louisiana Heron	Western Sandpiper (w.)
Little Blue Heron	Black-necked Stilt
Turkey Vulture	Herring Gull (w.)
Common Gallinule	Laughing Gull
Lesser Yellowlegs (w.)	Forster's Tern (w.)
Greater Yellowlegs (w.)	Royal Tern
Spotted Sandpiper (w.)	Groove-billed Ani
Willet (w.)	

For studying the wide variety of land birds near Telchac Puerto one of the small dirt roads leading off into the dense brush and very low woodland to the south of town should be rewarding. One of the most favorable for birds leads west from the main highway, just south of the mangrove lagoon which is just south of Telchac Puerto. Coming in *from* the south one would look for the last dirt road or track on the left before the mangrove swamp-lagoon, which lies on both sides of the highway. Driving *toward* the south from Telchac Puerto one would turn off at the first dirt track on the right after passing through the mangrove area; you would see successively a double utility pole of concrete, then a black utility pole, then a single unpainted concrete utility pole, all on the right - the last one being close to the turn-off. You may see an "80 km." highway speed sign by the lane, and a small Army barracks may soon be built nearby. One may park beside the road or down the lane. From there one can walk along branching roads and trails through the cactus and other thorny shrubs and very small trees, past tiny ponds or remnants of ponds.

Along the track one can expect most of the birds on the list for scrubby, deciduous woodland in the Yucatan Region, and a few on the lagoon list.

Specifically, in this area, you can find:

Little Blue Heron	*Myiarchus* sp.
Great Egret	*Empidonax* sp. (w.)
Louisiana Heron	Green Jay
Black Vulture	**Yucatan Wren**
Roadside Hawk	**Spotted-breasted Wren**
Plain Chachalaca	**Tropical Mockingbird**
Killdeer (w.)	**White-lored Gnatcatcher**
Lesser Yellowlegs (w.)	**Peppershrike**
Greater Yellowlegs (w.)	White-eyed Vireo
White-winged Dove	**Mangrove Vireo**
Common Ground-Dove	Magnolia Warbler (w.)
Aztec Parakeet	Palm Warbler
Groove-billed Ani	Northern Waterthrush (w.)
Cinnamon Hummingbird	Great-tailed Grackle
Buff-bellied Hummingbird	**Singing Blackbird**
Mexican Sheartail	Hooded Oriole
Belted Kingfisher (w.)	Red-winged Blackbird
Golden-fronted Woodpecker	Summer Tanager (w.)
Yucatan Woodpecker	Indigo Bunting (w.)
Vermilion Flycatcher	Painted Bunting (w.)
Couch's Kingbird	Collared Seedeater
Great Kiskadee	

Tepic, Nayarit - 1976 up-date, based on library studies and reports from contributors. See FBM, 1968, p. 187.

(Ed. 1984 note: The area on the road to Jalcocotán may have been altered greatly.)

It is about 800 km. west of Mexico City on Highways 15 and 200. The population is reported to be about 88,000.

The pond and nearby wet meadows (1968, p. 188) once found between the main part of town and an overpass (highway over railroad), on the way to Guadalajara may have been modified. Likewise the quarry area about four miles from Loma Park (1968, p. 188) may have been greatly altered. As a substitute, common birds of the mountain slopes can be found in a wooded area along the branch road which goes to Jalcocotán. This road branches left off highway number 57 about one mile from Tepic as you go generally northwest from Tepic toward Mazatlán. The branch road may or may not be marked (state) highway number 66, or Jalcocotán, or otherwise. At a point about seven miles from the main-highway junction, as you wind down the road toward Jalcocotán, a dirt road branches to the left into a woodland of mixed pine and oak. You can park here and walk up the dirt road, or find a path into a moist ravine or canyon. You may see a large rock where the dirt road branches off. Birds to be expected here include:

Black Vulture	Turkey Vulture

White-fronted Dove	**Orange-billed Thrush**
Orange-fronted Parakeet	Ruby-crowned Kinglet (w.)
Berylline Hummingbird	**Golden Vireo**
Olivaceous Flycatcher	Orange-crowned Warbler (w.)
Coues' Flycatcher	Yellow-rumped Warbler (w.)
Western Flycatcher	MacGillivray's Warbler (w.)
Rough-winged Swallow	Wilson's Warbler (w.)
Sinaloa Wren	**Slate-throated Redstart**
Happy Wren	**Rufous-capped Warbler**
Blue Mockingbird	Varied Bunting (w.)
White-throated Robin	Black-headed Siskin
Brown-backed Solitaire	Lesser Goldfinch

The discussion of bird watching at about "15 to 30 miles southeast of Tepic," (1968, p. 189) toward Guadalajara, should still be generally applicable, with some clearing to be expected. The high point may be slightly less than 20 miles from Tepic. At or near this point a paved road goes left to Santa María del Oro.

TEZIUTLAN, Puebla - New account, 1984, by Robert A. Behrstock, based on field studies in January, 1984, and several times before that. Replaces the 1976 account (not reprinted here) and the 1968 account.

Teziutlán is in the Central Highlands sub-region at an elevation of about 6600 feet. It is approximately 340 km. east of Mexico City, and about 100 km. southwest of the coastal town of Nautla, on Highways 129 (shown on some maps as 125) and 131. Its population is reported to be about 53,000. The average annual rainfall is 69 inches, 52 inches from June through October, and 17 inches from November through May. Temperatures vary from a monthly mean of 53 degrees F. (December-January) to a monthly mean of 65 degrees F. (May).

It is a small, rather compact city, with a huge church on an attractive square, and a large indoor market supplemented by many large stores. Lying beyond the business district is a sprawling fringe of residential areas, small agricultural plots, and light industry. Most of the relatively level land in the area has been planted in corn, fruit trees, and other crops. Days and nights are often quite chilly, and the entire region can be buried in fog for days on end, especially when a *norte* brings cold air which enhances cloud formation.

As in many areas, timber cutting, firewood gathering, and clearing of land for farming have made inroads into some important birding areas, but an interesting variety of habitats can still be found within a short distance of Teziutlán. The areas likely to be most interesting to the birder are some moist "pockets" of cloud forest northeast of town, and the dry pine or pine-oak woodland west of town.

In the former, moisture-laden air cools as it rises up the slopes of the Sierra Madre Oriental, forming dense fog, clouds, and rain. Here, towering Sweet Gum trees and stately tree ferns rise from carpets of smaller ferns and soft green mosses, a fitting backdrop for the haunting songs of the **Brown-backed Solitaire** and the **Slaty Solitaire.** The cloud forests here are characterized by dense undergrowth, and by many epiphytes in the forest canopy. The trails which penetrate these forests are steep and usually muddy. Birds may be seen infrequently, and then only briefly. Nonetheless, if your timing is right, and you proceed with reasonable care and at a slow pace you should be able to find some interesting species. On foggy mornings, there may not be much activity until an hour or two after dawn, but on the other hand, activity may have waned considerably by late morning, especially on bright days.

To reach an interesting area of cloud forest northeast of town drive out Highway 129 toward Nautla. At a point about 5 or 5½ miles from Teziutlán on this twisting, turning descent toward the Gulf Coast, the highway crosses a bridge over the small Río Frío (there is no sign naming the river). You should continue about 100 yards beyond the bridge and pull off and park clear of the highway on a broad, nearly level space on your right. The area on both sides of the highway near the Río Frío was formerly a favorite area for finding cloud-forest species, especially the trail leading down the canyon from the main highway, and the trail leading uphill along the river. Extensive fencing has recently put these areas off-limits to birders - it's not possible now to go on either of these trails. Nevertheless, if you bird along the highway (watch for fast-moving vehicles) outside the fence you should be able to see or hear a reasonably large sample of the species in the area, many of them easier to find if you're *not* on a narrow forest trail:

Sulphur-bellied Flycatcher (s)	Black-throated Green Warbler (w)
Greater Pewee	Louisiana Waterthrush (w)
Gray-breasted Martin	Wilson's Warbler (w)
Unicolored Jay	**Bell's Warbler**
American Dipper	**Rufous-capped Warbler**
Highland Wood-Wren	**Blue-hooded Euphonia**
Brown-backed Solitaire	Hepatic Tanager
Warbling Vireo	**Common Bush-Tanager**
Spot-breasted Warbler	**Black-headed Saltator**

By carefully scanning the treetops and woodland borders, and listening, it's possible you'll find some of these more elusive species as well:

Cazique Hummingbird	**Azure-hooded Jay**
Garnet-throated Hummingbird	**Gray Silky-Flycatcher**
Olivaceous Creeper	**Highland Shrike-Vireo**
Spotted Creeper	**Striped Tanager**
Spotted-crowned Creeper	**Hooded Grosbeak**

Even if you can find the person(s) authorized to give permission to cross the fences, it's not advisable unless you are rugged and experienced on steep, muddy trails, and are fluent enough in Spanish to convince any challenger that you have proper authorization. Communal, disputed, and shifting ownerships confuse the picture.

When you leave the vicinity of this river crossing, if you continue to drive northeastward (away from Teziutlán) still on the winding, descending Highway 129, you will reach a point about 21 km. (about 13 mi.) from Teziutlán where there is a well-marked turnoff to your left toward Hueytamalco. Just after turning left (generally north) you should find several successive places where you can pull off and park clear of the highway (be especially careful if you park on the downhill side of the road). Here, and at similar pulloffs farther on, you can look, almost at eye level, into the tops of large epiphyte-festooned trees which form the forest canopy. Clumps of mistletoe are a great attraction for euphonias here. Our cumulative list for several winter visits to this area includes the following (on a single visit under favorable conditions you can expect to find many of them):

Emerald Toucanet	Audubon's Oriole
Golden-olive Woodpecker	**Blue-crowned Tanager**
Boat-billed Flycatcher	**Blue-hooded Euphonia**
Social Flycatcher	**Scrub Euphonia**
Townsend's Warbler (w)	**Yellow-throated Euphonia**
Black-throated Green Warbler (w)	**Yellow-winged Tanager**
Wilson's Warbler (w)	**White-winged Tanager**
Black-and-white Warbler (w)	**Striped Tanager**
Nashville Warbler (w)	**Black-headed Saltator**
Northern Oriole	

This area, being at a lower elevation, is often not as foggy as the vicinity of the Río Frío crossing, or as Teziutlán itself.

If you continue to drive several kilometers farther toward Hueytamalco, you will see numerous cornfields along the roadside. In winter these appear dry and barren, but seed-eating birds, both resident and wintering species, often are abundant there, and the endemic **Brush Yellowthroat** is relatively common.

The yellowthroats, along with a bewildering assortment of small brown birds, mostly of the following species, will often respond to "squeaking" or "spishing".

Rose-breasted Grosbeak (w)	**Blue-black Grassquit**
Blue Grosbeak (w)	Lesser Goldfinch
Indigo Bunting (w)	Lark Sparrow (w)
Yellow-faced Grassquit	Chipping Sparrow (w)
House Finch	Lincoln's Sparrow (w)
Collared Seedeater	

If you drive *westward* out of Teziutlán on Highway 129 toward Zaragoza you will find some attractive piney ridges separated by moist ravines. One such small piney knoll, which has been especially productive in late afternoon, is located just a few miles out of Teziutlán. There is a conspicuous tower (possibly radio or microwave) near this knoll, and a very good parking area on the left (south) side of the road. From here you can walk out into the adjacent pine woods. Numerous species, many of which we think of as typically western, have been observed in this area, generally in mixed flocks. Some of the birds to be expected are:

Greater Pewee	White-breasted Nuthatch
Buff-breasted Flycatcher	American Robin
Mexican Chickadee	Eastern Bluebird

Cedar Waxwing   Hermit Warbler (w)
Spot-breasted Warbler   **Red Warbler**
Olive Warbler   Hepatic Tanager
Yellow-rumped Warbler   Pine Siskin
Black-throated Gray Warbler (w)   **Black-headed Siskin**
Townsend's Warbler (w)

Farther along on the highway toward Zaragoza you will see other pine woodlands and moist ravines, and if you can find suitable places to pull off and park completely clear of the highway there is a chance that you could find some of the following:

Rivoli's Hummingbird   Steller's Jay
Bumblebee Hummingbird   **Black Robin**
White-throated Flycatcher (s)   **Highland Honeycreeper (s)**

Returning (generally eastward) toward Teziutlán you should see, on the left side of the highway, a row of cypress trees with white-painted trunks, as you near the outskirts of the city. The dirt road which branches off to the left (as you go toward Teziutlán) leads to cornfields, apple orchards and scrubby woodland. If you stop occasionally along this road, park clear of the road, and walk along well off the road you can expect to see a variety of small birds, some of which are on the piney-knoll list, as well as towhees which show a blend of plumage characteristics of the **Collared Towhee** and the Rufous-sided Towhee.

You can find additional orchard and woodland and associated vegetation types (though somewhat disturbed) on Highway 131, generally east of Teziutlán. To find one such area drive almost directly south out of Teziutlán on Highway 131, which soon swings generally eastward then southward again toward Perote. At a point a few kilometers from Teziutlán you should see a dirt road (may be marked "Rancho El Angel") branching off to the left. If you turn left and proceed on this side road you should see a suitable place to pull off and park to your left not far from the main highway. From this point a fairly steep trail descends into a ravine. If you follow this trail, or if you walk along (well off) this road you can expect to find an interesting mixture of highland and mid-elevation species, including some of the following:

Squirrel Cuckoo   **Slate-throated Redstart**
Greater Pewee   **Blue-hooded Euphonia**
White-throated Flycatcher   **Hooded Grosbeak**
Buff-breasted Flycatcher   Lesser Goldfinch
Bushtit   Lincoln's Sparrow
Russet Thrush   House Finch
Gray Silky-Flycatcher

Farther out Highway 131 toward Perote, in suitable habitat, you can expect to find many of the species on the "piney-knoll" list.

See also Christmas Counts in *American Birds*, July 1981-1983.

Tizimín, Yucatán - New account, 1976, based on field studies in January, 1976.

Tizimín is in the northern portion of the Yucatan Region at an elevation of about 50 to 100 feet above sea level. It is about 160-170 km. east of Mérida by paved road (but is not on a major numbered highway), and about 50 km. north of Valladolid, which is on Highway 180. Its population is reported to be about 18,300. The climate is similar to that in Valladolid (1976,p.S92); perhaps slightly cooler and slightly more humid.

Tizimín is one of the larger towns in the Yucatan Region, and is in the center of a cattle-ranching and farming area, as well as being near areas to the east where lumbering is still a major enterprise. There is a crowded business section in Tizimín, with a typical town plaza near the center. Crowded commercial buildings and homes extend particularly along the four principal roads which radiate from the plaza. Near the edge of town most of the buildings are private homes, and these become more scattered farther out, gradually giving way to small farms and then mostly to open ranch country. To the east and west of town there are only scattered remnants of the moderately tall, humid, and partly evergreen woodland which probably once covered the entire area.

A favorable place for bird watching in the vicinity of Tizimín was at the edge of a relatively small patch of woodland about 31 km. (about 19 mi.) out on the road toward Colonia Yucatán, measured from the main plaza in Tizimín. During the last few kilometers of the drive one can expect to see some old ruins (not unearthed) on the right, then a large power line crossing the highway, and then a very obvious patch of woods on the right, where dirt roads branch off to the left and right. There is space to park off the paved road without blocking the dirt roads.

If the dirt roads are not closed the visitor may expect to find, along the one to the south, most of the following:

Turkey Vulture	**Spotted-breasted Wren**
Black Vulture	**White-bellied Wren**
Red-billed Pigeon	**Tropical Mockingbird**
Aztec Parakeet	White-eyed Vireo (w.)
Vaux's Swift	Black-and-white Warbler (w.)
Turquoise-browed Motmot	Northern Parula (w.)
Golden-fronted Woodpecker	Magnolia Warbler (w.)
Ladder-backed Woodpecker	Black-throated Green Warbler (w.)
Barred Antshrike	American Redstart (w.)
Laughing Creeper	**Singing Blackbird**
Rose-throated Becard	**Black-cowled Oriole**
Couch's Kingbird	Altamira Oriole
Social Flycatcher	Hooded Oriole
Great Kiskadee	**Yellow-winged Tanager**
Empidonax sp. (w.)	Summer Tanager (w.)
White-eyed Flycatcher	**Jungle Tanager**
Rough-winged Swallow	**Black-headed Saltator**
Green Jay	Rose-breasted Grosbeak (w.)
Yucatan Jay	Collared Seedeater
White-browed Wren	

There are other patches of woodland closer to Tizimín along the road to Colonia Yucatán. At some of these places dirt roads go off into, or beside the woods. The visitor could expect to see a considerable number of the birds on the preceding list by walking along one of these roads or tracks.

West of Tizimín on the paved road which leads to Buctzotz and eventually to Motul and Mérida there is a rather large tract of woodland at a point about 25 km. (about 15 mi.) from the zoo (and large Pemex station nearby) which is on the western edge of Tizimín. Driving west from Tizimín the visitor should see a large quarry on the right at about 25 kilometers distance from the zoo. There is space to leave the car off the road at the quarry. By walking along the edge of the woodland west of the quarry, well back from the road, or perhaps finding paths or tracks into the wooded area, one should be able to find some of the birds on both woodland lists for the Yucatan Region. In a half-hour in this area on January 21, in late morning, we saw:

Turkey Vulture	**Spotted-breasted Wren**
Ruddy Ground-Dove	**Peppershrike**
Rose-throated Becard	Red-eyed Cowbird
Couch's Kingbird	**Singing Blackbird**
Social Flycatcher	**Black-cowled Oriole**
Empidonax sp. (w.)	Altamira Oriole
Green Jay	**Black-headed Saltator**

North of Tizimín you may find numerous birds in patches of low woodland along the highway. You might also be able to reach an area frequented by the American Flamingo and other water birds.

For land birds, as you drive northward toward Río Lagartos, watch for pull-offs where you can gain access to trails or dirt roads which lead through the low woodland. Expect to find most of the birds listed for "Partially cleared archaeological sites...or dense, scrubby, deciduous woodland".

At a point about a mile and a half south of the town of Río Lagartos, a shell road or sand and dirt road turns right (as you go north) and goes toward a very long, narrow, east-west lagoon, sometimes called the Río Lagartos, the same as the name of the town. This road leads across the lagoon to the village of Los Colorados, and on to other areas along the coast. According to recent reports some of the favorable areas for viewing flamingos have been closed to the public, but it seems likely that you could at least drive *toward* Los Colorados (if road conditions permit) five to ten miles to a bridge over the lagoon. There you might find the American Flamingo and other water birds flying over the bridge in the morning or late afternoon. Many flamingos have been reported in the vicinity of Los Colorados in November as well as in summer, but they may be absent in some months. Access to more secluded areas might depend on obtaining permission from the appropriate salt company's headquarters in Merida.

Before you reach the bridge you may find places to see many species of the near-coastal, scrubby woodland, including:

Yucatan Bobwhite	**Yucatan Jay**
Zenaida Dove	**Mangrove Vireo**
Yucatan Woodpecker	**Orange Oriole**

The **Mangrove Warbler** would occur in the mangrove swamps.

TOPOLOBAMPO, Sinaloa - New account, 1984, based on field studies in May, 1983. Replaces the brief statement of FBM, 1968, p. 191.

(See also Los Mochis.)

Topolobampo is situated on the shores of the Gulf of California, in the west-central portion of the Northern Pacific Lowlands sub-region. It is approximately 1550 km. northwest of Mexico City by road, and about 25 km. south-southwest of Los Mochis, at the end of what is presumably Highway 32.

Driving to Topolobampo from Los Mochis you begin to see some broad, open, flatlands beginning about 15 km. from Los Mochis (about 10 km. from Topolobampo). For further information about these flats, which might be flooded in winter, see Los Mochis.

As you drive the last kilometer or two into Topolobampo from Los Mochis the highway goes through mangrove swamps on both sides of the road. These were rather dry and stagnant in early May, and from the standpoint of birding or safe parking, other areas were more favorable (and probably would be at any season).

Continuing into town you could swing left at a busy, major junction to go to the crowded commercial section, or swing right to go on out toward a long, narrow peninsula where there are some docks, warehouses, and other port facilities on each side of the road.

If you go right you will skirt a rather narrow inlet on your right bordered by mangroves. Here we found ample parking clear of the road, and saw Heermann's Gulls in full adult plumage. In winter you might see waterfowl, waders, or shorebirds, in addition to gulls and terns.

Continuing on the right branch road, when you reach an area where you can see the bay (and out toward the Gulf of California) on your left, and a broad lagoon with mangroves far out on your right, you should find ample space to pull off the road and park and look for water birds on both sides of the road. In early afternoon in May we saw there:

Magnificent Frigatebird	Heermann's Gull
White Ibis	Laughing Gull
Osprey	**Mangrove Swallow**

On your right, especially in winter and early spring, might be a good place to see considerable numbers and variety of wintering waterfowl for which the area is well-known. Alternatively, you might have to inquire locally (Los Mochis hotels?) to learn about more secluded areas for ducks.

Torreón, Coahuila - 1976 up-date, based on library studies. See FBM, 1968, p. 191.

Torreón is on Highway 40, and close to Highways 30 and 49. The population is reported to be about 223,000.

TULUM, Quintana Roo - 1984 up-date, based on field studies in April, 1981. See 1976 Suppl. to FBM, p. S89 (or 1976 account below).

The archaeological site of Tulúm is now about 320 km. east-southeast of Mérida by way of Highway 180 and the three-year-old short-cut from that highway at Nuevo X-Cán past Cobá to Tulum.

It now appears that the road (now paved) to Cobá from near Tulum leaves Highway 307 *between* the village of Tulum and the junction for the archaeological site, *not southwest* of the village of Tulum as indicated in 1976.

To find the archaeological site of Tulum as you come from Cobá, drive south about 47 kilometers from Cobá to Highway 307. Turn left onto Highway 307, go 1.9 km., then turn right at a large road junction, and drive 0.8 km. to the big parking lot at the site. To find the Tulum site from Cancún go about 125 or 130 km. south on Highway 307, to the turn-off, turn *left* and proceed 0.8 km. to the Tulum site. As you come from Cancún you should see the Xel-Há turn-off (left) after about 110 km. - don't turn left here; instead continue about 13.5 km. straight ahead to the turn-off to the Tulum site.

The ambience of the Tulum archaeological site has changed considerably since 1976. The parking lot was crowded with buses and cars in April, 1981, and there were many small souvenir shops and some food stands on the edge of the parking lot and across the street. Hundreds of people strolled around the ruins, the shops, and the parking lot. It is not likely that a birder would now find the birds listed in 1976 around the parking lot or nearby. Although the archaeological site is sometimes crowded with tour groups as implied above, you still might see a few birds there such as the **Ruddy Ground-Dove,** Groove-billed Ani, Rough-winged Swallow, and perhaps some wintering warblers and finches, in the proper season.

We don't have any information about the road mentioned in 1976, as going south from the parking lot to the shore.

Tulum, Quintana Roo - New account, 1976, based on field studies in January, 1976.

Tulum is in the eastern portion of the Yucatan Region. (The archaeological site of Tulum extends out onto a rocky promontory which rises well above the waters at the edge of the sea, while most of the rest of the land in the area is closer to the level of the sandy beach. The village of Tulum is a few kilometers or less inland on low-lying, level terrain, close to sea level.) It is approximately 370-390 km. east of Mérida via Highways 261 and 184 (through Felipe Carrillo Puerto) and 307, and about 90 to 100 kilometers farther from Mérida via Highways 180 and 307 through Cancún. It is about 125-135 km. south of Cancún and about 90-100 km. northeast of Felipe Carrillo Puerto. (If the road from Tulum to Cobá should be extended and paved to the vicinity of X-Cán on Highway 180, it would provide a short-cut to Tulum from Mérida.) The population of the village of Tulum seems to be only a few hundred. Average annual rainfall and temperatures are probably about the same as those on Cozumel Island (1976,p.S73).

Approaching from the north along Highway 307, the visitor first arrives at a road junction where there is a restaurant and other buildings on the southeast corner, and a gasoline station a short distance beyond that. On the northwest corner, there is a large military or government building. By turning east here and proceeding a distance of two or three kilometers more or less the visitor arrives at a large parking lot next to the ancient Maya walled city of Tulum, which is partly restored.

(Ed. note, 1984: This paragraph, and some distances *not* reprinted verbatim from 1976.) If, at the original road junction, you continue straight ahead on Highway 307, rather then turning left, you would soon pass the junction with the road to Cobá, branching to your right, and still continuing straight ahead you would next come to the village of Tulum. Continuing southward beyond there would take you toward Chunyaxché and Felipe Carrillo Puerto.

The visitor will presumably wish to work mostly around the archaeological site of Tulum rather than the village. The site itself is a relatively small, grassy, walled area, with one of its principal buildings situated on a rocky promontory overlooking the Caribbean Sea. Around the site (except toward the sea), and extending up and down the coast, and inland, are rather low and humid woodlands, interrupted in places by cultivated fields and overgrown fields. One should be able to find birds within the walled area or in the nearby trees outside of the walls, or around the edges of the parking lot, or in ditches or other low wet places near the parking lot. Also a road goes south from the parking lot, more or less parallel to the shore, presumably reaching the beach eventually. There should be suitable places to pull off this road and park and look for birds.

In an extensive study of the Tulum site and its environs, you can expect to find most of the birds on the Yucatan Region lists for "Partially cleared archaeological sites..." and "Moderately tall, humid forest...". For specific names refer to our list for Cobá and the following list for wooded areas 50 to 100 kilometers north of Tulum along highway 307:

Gray Hawk	**Brown Jay**
Plain Chachalaca	Green Jay
Red-billed Pigeon	**Yucatan Jay**
Scaled Pigeon	**Spotted-breasted Wren**
Ruddy Ground-Dove	**Tropical Mockingbird**
White-fronted Dove	**Peppershrike**
Aztec Parakeet	White-eyed Vireo (w.)
White-fronted Parrot	**Mangrove Vireo**
Yucatan Parrot	Black-throated Green Warbler (w.)
Groove-billed Ani	**Singing Blackbird**
Golden-fronted Woodpecker	Alta Mira Oriole
Rose-throated Becard	Hooded Oriole
Couch's Kingbird	Cardinal
Social Flycatcher	Rose-breasted Grosbeak (w.)
Empidonax sp. (w.)	Blue Grosbeak (w.)

TUXTLA GUTIERREZ, Chiapas - 1984 up-date, based on a very brief visit in March, 1981, and reports from contributors. See 1976 Suppl. to FBM,p.S118(or 1976 up-date below), and FBM, 1968, p. 193.

The population figure posted for Tuxtla Gutiérrez is about 180,000.

The first 1968 list is probably too large for the current situation unless one goes much farther from the center of town. The gardens around the old Zoo and the suburban hotel mentioned probably yield fewer species than before because of development crowding closer to or perhaps into these once-peripheral areas.

El Suspiro is no longer a favorable area for observing unusual birds. The cloud forest which was there has been destroyed, and replaced mainly by cornfields.

El Chorreadero may still be a favorable area for observing birds of the scrubby woodland east of Tuxtla Gutiérrez. Remember if you try to go there from Tuxtla, the side road may not be marked, and you will have to turn across traffic on a winding road.

Some places in the Sumidero area are still undoubtedly favorable for finding interesting and unusual birds, although quite possibly these will not be the same ones mentioned in FBM, 1968, pp. 196-198, and some of the rarer species may no longer be real possibilities. (See note about overlooks.)

The area called El Zapotal has been altered considerably, but the alterations have probably improved the potential for birding. A new zoo has been established there on approximately 10 hectares (about 25 acres) of a 100-hectare area, the remaining 90 hectares having been dedicated as a *Reserva Natural*. The ZOOMAT (Zoológico Miguel Alvarez del Toro) is primarily for exhibition and study of animals native to the state of Chiapas, and is reputed to be the best of its kind in Mexico. The road to the zoo and nature preserve at El Zapotal presumably goes south and uphill from the Libramiento Sur (bypass south of the business section). You should inquire locally for more precise directions.

The area between Ocozocoautla and the huge lake behind the Mal Paso Dam (which is north of Ocozocoautla, which is west of Tuxtla Gutiérrez) still offers some interesting birding in places. Dr. Miguel Alvarez del Toro has informed me (September, 1983) that there are some coffee plantations along this road, and that there is a small reservation at Km. 17 (presumably 17 km. north of Ocozocoautla) "where there are many birds during the good season" (presumably spring and summer). You may have to inquire in Ocozocoautla as to how to find the road north toward Mal Paso.

Tuxtla Gutiérrez, Chiapas - 1976 up-date, based on library studies and reports from contributors.

The population is reported to be about 69,000.

Many species of birds may still be found in the vicinity of the Zoo, Museum, and botanical gardens. The Museum is considered the outstanding museum in southern Mexico.

Details about El Zapotal, El Chorreadero, El Sumidero, and El Suspiro should be checked locally.

The Zoo has not been moved to the area of El Zapotal, and the woodlands there have apparently not been greatly disturbed recently so the discussion and bird lists (1968,pp.194-195) should be generally applicable.

The discussion of the road (now paved) to the Sumidero (1968,pp.196-198) is still applicable, although there is persistent cutting of trees, charcoal burning, cultivation of plots of land, and clearing of roadside brush, resulting in alteration of some of the places mentioned. The visitor should be alert for "new" areas which may support a variety of birds, perhaps one of the relatively level and partly open spaces beside the road on the side away from the steep drop-offs. Add Tucuchillo (n.) to the list of birds to be expected.

Remember the words of caution (1968,pp.197-198; 1976, Introduction).

The construction of new roads and modifications or abandonment of previously-existing roads have made the El Suspiro discussion obsolete. You cannot expect to find the cloud forest by following the directions (1968,pp.198-200), but instead should obtain new directions (and information on road conditions) in Tuxtla Gutiérrez, if possible. You should still be able to find grassy fields with scattered trees, and hedgerows and woodland edge nearby, north or northwest of Berriozabal (and elsewhere), and the list (1968,p.199) should apply. If you are able to find humid forest the list (1968,p.200) applies.

A fifth area mentioned (1968,p.200) is still of uncertain status. This is the road from near Ocozocoautla to the shores of a huge lake backed up behind the Malpaso Dam. Most of the forest has been cut away from readily accessible places, but you might still be able to find some forest about 16 miles from Ocozocoautla on the way to the lake. Prior inquiry might be helpful.

Uruapan, Michoacán - 1976 up-date, based on library studies. See FBM, 1968, p. 201.

Its population is reported to be about 83,000.

Highway 37 south of Uruapan is paved all the way to the Pacific Coast, connecting with coastal Highway 200.

UXMAL, Yucatán - 1984 up-date, based on field studies in June, 1978, March, 1979, and April, 1981, and reports from George and Janet Cobb. See 1976 Suppl. to FBM, p. S91 (or 1976 up-date below), and FBM, 1968, p. 203.

There is still no real town or village at Uxmal, but there are probably 100 to 200 or more employees of the major hotels, and workers at the archaeological site. There have been some changes in the arrangement of roads, and in access to the archaeological site. Highway 261 now passes within 100 meters or less of the site, with just a very short branch road (to the right as you go south from Mérida) to the big parking lot and elaborate main entrance to the site.

The 1976 bird lists are still applicable. We can now be more specific about the location of good birding roads, trails, and other areas.

The large parking lot (sandy dirt with many scattered trees) at the main entrance to the archaeological site, affords an opportunity to see an interesting variety of orioles and large flycatchers (and their nests, in proper season) as well

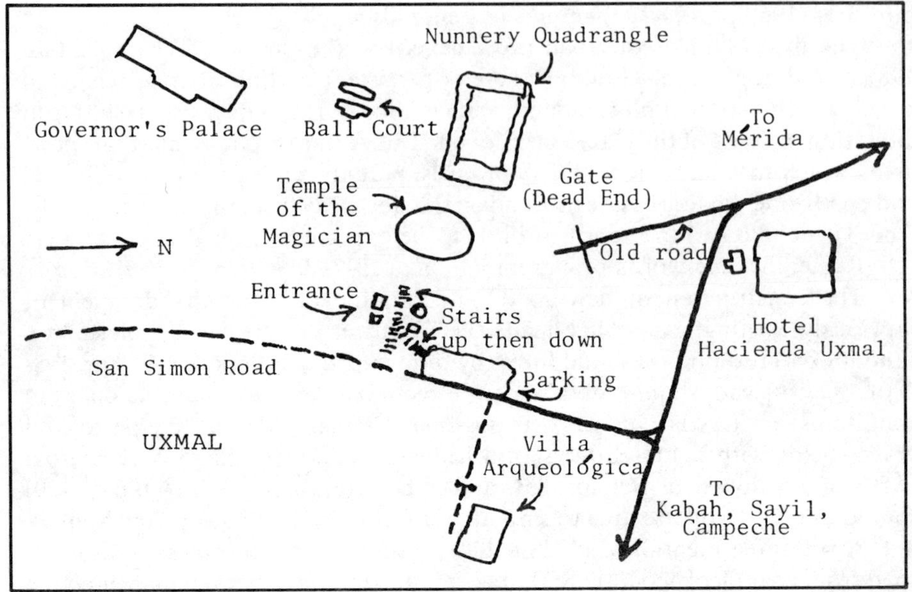

as several other species. The weedy low woodland borders (and utility wires) along the very short, branch, paved road to the parking lot from the main highway provide opportunities to observe many species at leisure, especially wintering finches. In the parking lot along the branch road you should find most of the following:

White-winged Dove	Great-tailed Grackle
Common Ground-Dove	**Orange Oriole**
Ruddy Ground-Dove	Alta Mira Oriole
Turquoise-browed Motmot	Hooded Oriole
Golden-fronted Woodpecker	**Gray Saltator**
Couch's Kingbird	Rose-breasted Grosbeak (w)
Boat-billed Flycatcher	Blue Grosbeak (w)
Social Flycatcher	Indigo Bunting (w)
Great Kiskadee	Painted Bunting (w)
Clay-colored Robin	**Blue-black Grassquit**
Blue-gray Gnatcatcher	

To reach the parking lot and nearby woodland borders from Mérida or from the Hotel Misión Uxmal or from the (Hotel) Hacienda Uxmal go generally south on Highway 261 to a branch road about 100 to 200 meters south of the Hacienda Uxmal entrance. Turn right onto this road and go 100 to 200 meters to the parking lot. To reach the area from the Villa Arqueológica just go out the Villa's entrance road and you will see the branch road and the parking lot.

To find species not so often seen in open areas, as you walk down the branch road from the highway, continue past the parking lot along a dirt road extension of the paved branch road. If you walk no more than 500 to 1000 meters along this dirt road you should find most of the birds on the second 1976 list, as well as the

Turqoise-browed Motmot, Yucatan Jay, and others from the first 1976 list.

Another area, apparently little-used by visiting birders, is outside the northern boundary of the maintained portion of the archaeological site. To reach this go about 100 to 300 meters (measuring from the Hacienda Uxmal entrance) generally north on Highway 261 to the point where an old, paved (now dead-end) road joins the highway on the left. About at this point or a short distance farther north, a dirt road or track (perhaps strewn with trash) leads left into the low woodland. Along this track you should have a good chance of seeing many of the birds in the second 1976 list and some in the first 1976 list.

See also Christmas Counts in *American Birds,* July 1981-1983.

Uxmal, Yucatán - 1976 up-date, based on library studies and reports from contributors.

Uxmal is in the northwestern portion of the Yucatan Region, at an estimated elevation of 50 to 100 feet above sea level. It is about 80 km. south of Mérida, on a short spur road just west of Highway 261 (formerly 180). Its population is estimated at several dozen to a hundred or more. The climate is much like that of Mérida (1976,p.S77).

At Uxmal most of the typical birds of the drier portions of the Yucatan Region are common, and some of the more unusual ones may be seen here as well. The overall aspect is that of a partially cleared and partially reconstructed archaeological site, with a few small contemporary buildings near the entrance, and some hotels nearby with a number of houses and other buildings clustered near these tourist facilities. The cleared portion of the archaeological zone is surrounded by a very low, scrubby, thorny woodland of shrubs and small trees, on very rocky, but rather level terrain. This type of woodland extends outside of the zone where it is interrupted in places by cultivated fields and overgrown grassy fields. Some of the old Maya buildings have been almost completely restored, some have been cleared off and restoration begun, while others are still merely piles of jumbled stones covered by the natural low woodland.

It is convenient to divide the birds of this area into two groups according to the type of habitat in which they occur most frequently, but there is much overlap. The first group includes those which are more common in cleared areas of the ruins and on the hotel grounds. The second group includes those most common in the natural vegetation and woodland edge and hedgerows.

In the first group, around the ornamental gardens of the hotels, and among the orchards and vegetable gardens and yards of the nearby houses, or in the cleared areas of the archaeological zone, the following species appeared to be most common:

Turkey Vulture	**Turquoise-browed Motmot**
Black Vulture	Couch's Kingbird
Common Ground-Dove	Great Kiskadee
Ruddy Ground-Dove	*Empidonax* sp. (w.)
Groove-billed Ani	Cave Swallow
Lesser Nighthawk	Rough-winged Swallow
Vaux's Swift	Green Jay

Yucatan Jay	Great-tailed Grackle
Gray Catbird (w.)	**Singing Blackbird**
Tropical Mockingbird	Altamira Oriole
Clay-colored Robin	Hooded Oriole
Peppershrike	**Gray Saltator**
Northern Parula (w.)	Blue Grosbeak (w.)
Hooded Warbler (w.)	Painted Bunting (w.)
American Redstart (w.)	

In the second group, to be found along dirt roads or trails through the scrubby, thorny woodland, or along the edges of overgrown fields, or in relatively undisturbed portions of the archaeological zone, most of the species in the preceding list are included, and the following in addition:

Plain Chachalaca	**Yucatan Wren**
White-fronted Dove	**White-browed Wren**
Aztec Parakeet	**Spotted-breasted Wren**
Lesser Roadrunner	**White-bellied Wren**
Ferruginous Pygmy-Owl	Blue-gray Gnatcatcher
Fork-tailed Emerald	White-eyed Vireo (w.)
Buff-bellied Hummingbird	**Mangrove Vireo**
Golden-fronted Woodpecker	Common Yellowthroat (w.)
Boat-billed Flycatcher	**Black-headed Saltator**
Social Flycatcher	Cardinal
Yucatan Flycatcher	Rose-breasted Grosbeak (w.)
Olivaceous Flycatcher	Blue Bunting
Gray-breasted Martin	Olive Sparrow

Valladolid, Yucatán - New account, 1976, based on a brief visit in January, 1976.

Valladolid is in the central portion of the Yucatan Region, at an elevation of about 70 feet above sea level. It is about 160 km. east of Mérida, on Highway 180. The population is reported to be about 15,000. The average annual rainfall is about 47 inches, 35 inches from May through October, and 12 inches from November through April. Monthly mean temperatures vary from 72 degrees F. (January) to 81 degrees F. (May).

Valladolid is spread over a wide area, with closely-packed houses and small commercial establishments centered around a large town plaza. Near the edges of town the crowded residential sections give way to more scattered houses. Farther out there is a gradual transition to scattered cornfields and other farmlands and patches of woodland, and finally to large tracts of the rather low, scrubby woodland, typical of this area. The woodland is somewhat taller and more humid and less thorny than that near Mérida, and there are fewer henequen fields and more pastures, cornfields, and cattle ranches, particularly toward the east and south of Valladolid. The paved roads going east to Puerto Juárez, and south to Felipe Carrillo Puerto lead into areas of higher rainfall, presumably more favorable for a wide variety of typically tropical species, but habitat destruction has proceeded rapidly there as elsewhere. The visitor should, however, be able to find dirt roads or tracks leading away from the highway, and past woodlands, overgrown fields, hedgerows, and croplands. A walk along such a track, particularly in the early morning, should be rewarding. The birds to be expected would be principally those on the Yucatan Region list for "partially cleared archaeological sites..." although the farther east or south you go the more species you might find from the list for "Moderately tall, humid forest...". Toward the north bird-finding opportunities along the highway seem fewer than in other directions, at least within 10 to 20 miles of Valladolid. To the west of town the locality of Chichén Itzá is about 40 km. away, and there is much low woodland with numerous side roads or tracks along the highway between Valladolid and Chichén Itzá.

Valles, San Luis Potosí - 1976 up-date, based on field studies in January, 1976. See FBM, 1968, p. 205.

Valles is in the southwestern part of the Northern Atlantic Lowlands Sub-region, where it meets the Central Atlantic Lowlands Sub-region, at an elevation of 300 feet. It is about 470 km. north of Mexico City, on Highways 85 and 70. Its population is reported to be about 24,000. Climatic data are not available, but conditions are probably much like those in Tampico, where average annual rainfall is 49 inches, most of it from June through October, and where monthly mean temperatures vary from 66 degrees F. (January) to 83 degrees F. (August).

Many of the characteristic birds of the flatlands of the Northern Atlantic Lowlands Sub-region occur in the vicinity of Valles. This town is not as important an overnight stop between southern Texas and Mexico City as it once was. It is still very important as a rail center and agricultural center, shipping considerable quantities of the agricultural commodities of the region, such as cattle and fruit. The town extends along highways number 85 and number 70 west more than in other directions, with crowded commercial and residential sections along the west side of highway number 85. Farther out houses are scattered, and intermingled with vacant lots, overgrown fields, and some gardens. There are a few motels or hotels in town, with some gardens and scattered trees. There are two large resort-type hotels a few miles from town, with very extensive grounds, including large grassy areas (formerly or presently golf courses), overgrown fields, orchards, and woodlands. The countryside around Valles shows a mixed vegetational picture, with numerous cultivated fields, but also extensive plains and hillsides covered with grass and small trees and shrubs. This shrubland or mesquite-grassland has a dense growth of trees in some areas and is quite open in others, and is often used for pasture. Farther from town there are a few fairly large tracts of deciduous woodland with medium-sized trees, and some moderately luxuriant river-edge woodland.

Around the parks and plazas, and gardens and grounds of the hotels and motels in Valles one can expect to see most of the following species:

Turkey Vulture	White-winged Dove
Black Vulture	Common Ground-Dove
Common Bobwhite	Groove-billed Ani

<table>
<tr><td>Golden-fronted Woodpecker</td><td>Red-eyed Cowbird</td></tr>
<tr><td>Tropical Kingbird</td><td>Great-tailed Grackle</td></tr>
<tr><td>Great Kiskadee</td><td>Altamira Oriole</td></tr>
<tr><td>Northern Mockingbird</td><td></td></tr>
</table>

The extensive grounds, gardens, orchards and woodlands of the two out-of-town resort-type hotels mentioned above provide opportunities for observing the common birds of the Valles area. To reach the closer of these two hotels check mileage where highway number 70 comes from Tampico and meets highway number 85, near the south end of Valles. Then go south on highway number 85 slightly less than seven miles to the second of two large ornamental gates on the right. Shortly before you reach the two gates there is a sharp curve in the highway, then a small bridge, then another sharp curve. To reach the hotel parking lot you would turn to the right, into the second gate (may be marked "Hotel Covadonga"). We found that a walk around the hotel was rewarding, through the gardens and large shade trees. Also many birds were active along a dirt road which led behind the hotel, between the golf course and an orange grove, and on to woodland growing along the river (caution at the river banks). You could expect to see most of the following by working around the hotel and along the dirt road:

<table>
<tr><td>Red-billed Pigeon</td><td>Green Jay</td></tr>
<tr><td>Inca Dove</td><td>Spotted-breasted Wren</td></tr>
<tr><td>Common Ground-Dove</td><td>Northern House-Wren (w.)</td></tr>
<tr><td>White-fronted Dove</td><td>Clay-colored Robin</td></tr>
<tr><td>Green Parakeet</td><td>Blue-gray Gnatcatcher (w.)</td></tr>
<tr><td>Red-crowned Parrot</td><td>Ruby-crowned Kinglet (w.)</td></tr>
<tr><td>Red-lored Parrot</td><td>Red-eyed Vireo (s.)</td></tr>
<tr><td>Groove-billed Ani</td><td>Black-and-white Warbler (w.)</td></tr>
<tr><td>Ringed Kingfisher</td><td>Orange-crowned Warbler (w.)</td></tr>
<tr><td>Buff-bellied Hummingbird</td><td>Yellow-rumped Warbler (w.)</td></tr>
<tr><td>Golden-fronted Woodpecker</td><td>Black-throated Green Warbler (w.)</td></tr>
<tr><td>Ladder-backed Woodpecker</td><td>Wilson's Warbler (w.)</td></tr>
<tr><td>Eastern Phoebe (w.)</td><td>Great-tailed Grackle</td></tr>
<tr><td>Vermilion Flycatcher</td><td>Singing Blackbird</td></tr>
<tr><td>Couch's Kingbird</td><td>Altamira Oriole</td></tr>
<tr><td>Boat-billed Flycatcher</td><td>Hooded Oriole</td></tr>
<tr><td>Social Flycatcher</td><td>Summer Tanager (w.)</td></tr>
<tr><td>Great Kiskadee</td><td>Black-headed Saltator</td></tr>
<tr><td>Empidonax sp. (w.)</td><td>Gray Saltator</td></tr>
<tr><td>Mexican Crow</td><td>Collared Seedeater</td></tr>
<tr><td>Brown Jay</td><td></td></tr>
</table>

To find the resort-type hotel east of Valles, you would begin at the above-mentioned junction of highway 85 and 70 at the south end of Valles. From there drive about 14 km. toward Tampico on highway 70. At that point turn to the right onto a paved (but broken-up) road to the hotel (may be marked "Hotel Taninul"). The hotel is about three kilometers from the highway. As you drive on the branch road toward the hotel you can see low woodland on the right and citrus groves on the left, where many birds can be found. On moonlight nights you might hear Pauraques and **Chip-willows** along this branch road, and possibly see a **Common Potoo** on a pole or fence-post beside the road.

You might find it worthwhile to work around the open areas in front of the hotel, then the area of the golf course (may not be maintained as such). A small stream, containing sulphur water or perhaps some sewage, is out near the edge of the grassy space in front of the hotel and seems to be very attractive to birds. You could also work along the entrance road for woodland-edge birds, and perhaps find patches of woodland off to the side of the orchards or golfing area. Parrots often fly high above the ridge top which is generally west of the hotel, especially in early morning and late evening. Without getting into the jumbled rocks and dense thorny undergrowth of the hillsides, you can find most of the characteristic birds of the area, including:

Rufescent Tinamou	Ladder-backed Woodpecker
Green Heron	**Barred Antshrike**
Great Egret	Couch's Kingbird
Snowy Egret	**Boat-billed Flycatcher**
Tiger Bittern	**Social Flycatcher**
Turkey Vulture	Great Kiskadee
Black Vulture	Wied's Flycatcher (s.)
Roadside Hawk	**Mexican Crow**
American Kestrel (w.)	**Brown Jay**
Gray Hawk	**Spotted-breasted Wren**
Crested Caracara	Northern Mockingbird
Plain Chachalaca	**Clay-colored Robin**
Jacana	White-eyed Vireo
Red-billed Pigeon	Red-eyed Vireo (s.)
White-winged Dove	Red-eyed Cowbird
Inca Dove	Great-tailed Grackle
Common Ground-Dove	**Singing Blackbird**
Green Parakeet	Altamira Oriole
Red-crowned Parrot	Hooded Oriole
Red-lored Parrot	**Scrub Euphonia**
Yellow-billed Cuckoo (s.)	**Gray Saltator**
Groove-billed Ani	**Crimson-collared Grosbeak**
Common Potoo (n.)	Cardinal
Pauraque (n.)	**Blue Bunting**
Chip-willow (n.)	Collared Seedeater
Buff-bellied Hummingbird	**Blue-black Grassquit**
Lineated Woodpecker	Olive Sparrow
Golden-fronted Woodpecker	Lincoln's Sparrow (w.)

I investigated the archaeological site of Tamuín in regard to its potential for bird watching, but do not treat it at length here for several reasons. It is difficult to find, even with precise mileages; it is on fenced private property, about a half-mile from the highway over a track (through cattle range-land) that is impassable much of the year (even on foot at the worst times); it is on a steep, crumbly bluff high above the river where you don't find typical river-edge woodland; and you can see a greater number and variety of birds at the other places much closer to Valles. For those who are determined to visit the site (and succeed in getting there) because of its archaeological interest, you will find that the scrubby mesquite-grassland and scattered clumps of dry, brushy, low woodland harbor at least the following species:

Turkey Vulture	Golden-fronted Woodpecker
Gray Hawk	Eastern Phoebe (w.)
American Kestrel (w.)	Great Kiskadee
Red-billed Pigeon	**Mexican Crow**
Green Parakeet	Blue-gray Gnatcatcher (w.)

Two other places, perhaps not exceptional enough to warrant a special trip, might be worth investigating for persons already planning to drive from Valles to Río Verde (toward San Luis Potosí) on Highway 70. From a zero-point in Valles where Highway 70 west leaves Highway number 85 north at the north edge of town, you can drive about 18 km. west and pull off to the right where a dirt road branches off the highway. The second place was about 41 km. west of Valles where there was a very spacious pull-off on the left near a large tract of forest on both sides of the road. At these two places you could expect most of the birds of the NA sub-regional list for "River-edge woodland, humid forest edge...". Our combined list for very brief stops at these two places was:

Rufescent Tinamou	**Brown Jay**
Roadside Hawk	**Spotted-breasted Wren**
Green Parakeet	**Singing Blackbird**
Red-lored Parrot	Altamira Oriole
Groove-billed Ani	

Valles has sometimes been used as a base or starting-point for trips to El Salto and the El Naranjo Christmas Count Circle, but those places are about 50-60 miles from Valles (north on Highway 85, then generally west on Highway 80).

Veracruz, Veracruz - 1976 up-date, based on library studies. See FBM, 1968, p. 209.

It is still basically on Highway 180, but a new section of Highway 180D shortens the distance to Cardel and other towns northward along the coast. The population is reported to be about 214,000.

Undoubtedly some modification of habitat has occurred, and mileages indicated may no longer be exact. You should still find pools and marshes and wet pastures on the highway to Alvarado, however, as well as patches of woodland on the highways to Jalapa and Córdoba. Water birds still abound along much of the road to Alvarado and some miles beyond, and hawks and grassland birds are numerous there.

Victoria, Tamaulipas - 1976 up-date, based on field studies in June, 1975. See FBM, 1968, p. 213.

Victoria is near the center of the Northern Atlantic Lowlands Sub-region, at an elevation of about 1050 feet. It is approximately 700 km. north of Mexico City and about 310 km. south-southwest of Brownsville, Texas, on Highways, 85 and 101. The population is reported to be about 84,000. The average annual rainfall is 36 inches; 29 inches from May through October and 7 inches from November through April. Monthly mean temperatures vary from a low of 60 degrees F. in December to a high of 82 degrees F. in August.

Some of the distinctively tropical birds of river-edge woodland and partially-open brush country of the NA sub-region may be seen near Victoria. This is a city built in the traditional Mexican style, with a central plaza and a crowded business section, but with some large buildings. It is an important agricultural center, and capital of the state of Tamaulipas. The more elaborate residential developments seem to be concentrated in the western part of the city. Close to the business section they are crowded, while farther out they are more open with parks, gardens, vacant lots and overgrown fields among the houses. The surrounding countryside appears rather open and dry, the natural vegetation being some short grass and scattered, thorny, small trees and shrubs, in places forming dense thickets, and in other areas being quite open. Much of the land has been cleared for agriculture, and much of the uncleared scrubland is used for grazing cattle, horses, goats, and burros. Some distance back in the mountains to the southwest there are some tracts of oak woodland along highway number 101.

Some of the common birds of the area may be found within the city, in the parks, plazas, suburban gardens and vacant lots, as follows:

Black Vulture	Tropical Kingbird
Inca Dove	Northern Mockingbird
Common Ground-Dove	Red-eyed Cowbird
Groove-billed Ani	Great-tailed Grackle
Vermilion Flycatcher	

You can find areas north, northeast, or south of town along the main highways where you can pull off and park and walk into the countryside. Small dirt roads, trails and tracks are numerous leading past cultivated fields, overgrown fields, hedgerows, and a few patches of the natural, very scrubby vegetation. Such places can be found within two or three miles of town. The birds to be expected there are those on the preceding list and the following:

Turkey Vulture	Greater Roadrunner
Roadside Hawk	Golden-fronted Woodpecker
Crested Caracara	White-necked Raven
Plain Chachalaca	**Mexican Crow**
White-winged Dove	Olive Sparrow

For a much greater variety of birds, including a greater proportion of distinctively tropical species you can work through some river-edge woodland. There the trees are much larger and the vegetation in general is much more luxuriant than out in the open plains. The valley of the Río Corona provides an opportunity for this, along highway number 101 toward the northeast, about 20 miles from downtown Victoria. To reach a rewarding bird-study area along the Río Corona you can drive northeastward (toward Brownsville) from the junction of the Victoria bypass and highway number 101 northeast of the center of town. You would go about 28 km. (about 17.2 mi.) to a small dirt or gravel road which goes off to the left, as the highway swings toward the right. Since you must cross traffic to enter, and since the entrance is rough and easily overlooked, caution is necessary (If you miss the turn see next paragraph.) The branch road may go off at an odd angle, but once on it you will be going generally north or northeast. A short distance along the branch road you come to a fork; the right-hand road is the one to follow. The first part of the road, near the highway, is rough and rocky, while the remainder is dusty and possibly rutted in dry weather, and slippery or sticky in wet weather. It might be impassable at times - inquiry about details of directions and road conditions is advisable. If you walk along the branch road all or part of the 1.4 miles from the highway to the river you can see many of the birds on the NA sub-regional list for "Partially open country...". In the wide band of woodland near the river and in the large trees along the banks you can usually find many birds even at mid-day. If you turn left as you come near the river you reach a park-like area on the high, crumbly, sandy banks of the Río Corona. You may or may not find huts or clearings or many people in this area.

To find the Río Corona "park" when you come in *from* the northeast on highway number 101 (presumably from Brownsville) check mileage just as you enter the small town of Nuevo Padilla. You would go about 8.6 miles from there to the main-highway bridge over the Río Corona, and continue 2.7 miles past the bridge to the possibly obscure turn-off on your right, just before the main highway curves to the left.

Along the river and in the forest near its banks you would expect to find:

Great Egret	Groove-billed Ani
Snowy Egret	Greater Roadrunner
Muscovy Duck	Ringed Kingfisher
Turkey Vulture	**Blue-crowned Motmot**
Black Vulture	**Lineated Woodpecker**
Roadside Hawk	Golden-fronted Woodpecker
Gray Hawk	Yellow-bellied Sapsucker (w.)
Common Black Hawk	Rose-throated Becard
Plain Chachalaca	Eastern Phoebe (w.)
Red-billed Pigeon	Tropical Kingbird
White-winged Dove (s.)	Great Kiskadee
Inca Dove	White-necked Raven
Common Ground-Dove	**Mexican Crow**
White-fronted Dove	**Brown Jay**
Green Parakeet	Black-crested Titmouse
Red-crowned Parrot	Carolina Wren
Yellow-headed Parrot	**Spotted-breasted Wren**

Bewick's Wren   Yellow-rumped Warbler (w.)
Blue-gray Gnatcatcher (w.)   Wilson's Warbler (w.)
Ruby-crowned Kinglet (w.)   Altamira Oriole
Orange-crowned Warbler (w.)   Hooded Oriole
Tropical Parula   Olive Sparrow

Farther out on highway number 101 generally east-northeast of Nuevo Padilla the water-filled roadside ditches and flooded areas just off the highway attract many water birds. If you can arrange to go along as an observer or passenger while someone else drives you should be able to see a representation of the common and widespread water birds of this part of the world. The road is raised, however, and the shoulders so narrow that you cannot pull off the road safely, nor can you risk going excessively slowly or attempting to stop partly in the road. The birds are scattered anyhow, so that only by covering a considerable distance could you see a large sample. Species which you could expect to see in this area are:

Least Grebe   Blue-winged Teal (w.)
Pied-billed Grebe   American Wigeon (w.)
Olivaceous Cormorant   Shoveler (w.)
Anhinga   Lesser Scaup (w.)
Green Heron   Ruddy Duck (w.)
Little Blue Heron   Common Gallinule
Great Egret   American Coot
Snowy Egret   Belted Kingfisher (w.)
Cattle Egret   Tropical Kingbird
Louisiana Heron   Eastern Phoebe (w.)
Gadwall (w.)   Vermilion Flycatcher
Pintail (w.)

If you travel Highway 101 toward the southwest from Victoria you climb fairly soon into oak woodland, reaching the Northern Highlands Sub-region. At elevations of 4000 feet or more you would expect to begin seeing some of the birds of the Northern Highlands Sub-regional list for "Relatively humid woodland...". If you can find a place to pull off and walk through the oak woods you might see the following birds and others:

Mexican Trogon   Bridled Titmouse
Spotted-crowned Creeper   Painted Redstart
Mexican Jay   **Rufous-capped Warbler**

See also Christmas Counts for Río Corona, Tamaulipas, in *American Birds,* July 1981-1983.

VILLAHERMOSA, Tabasco - Special note, 1984 - information provided by Jerry and Nancy Strickling, based on field studies in December, 1980. See 1976 Suppl. to FBM, p. S119 (or 1976 up-date below), and FBM, 1968, p. 216.

Instead of the more or less random searching for side roads where one can park clear of Highway 186 southeast of Villahermosa (see below) going toward

Palenque, the birder could plan to go specifically to a marshy area about 10 km. off the main highway. To reach this area drive generally southeastward as noted above. At about K. 39 turn right on a paved road just before you reach a microwave (microondas) tower on your right. The road may be marked Jalapa, Tacotalpa, or Teapa, or some combination of these. Drive about 10 km. down this road (toward but not *to* Jalapa, etc.) watching for a marshy area. Even though this road is usually not as heavily traveled as Highway 186 be sure to park completely clear of the highway (and more, if possible) and stand or walk well off the highway.

To reach this area from Palenque drive about 70 to 75 km. westward from Catazaja (the place where the Palenque road joins Highway 186), watching for the Microondas Chichonai tower on your left. A short distance beyond that (at about K. 39) turn left toward Jalapa and drive about 10 km. to the marshy area.

In that vicinity you should see most of the birds on the second 1976 Villahermosa list, plus other waders (including possibly **Tiger Heron** or **Pinnated Bittern** or both.

Villahermosa, Tabasco - 1976 up-date, based on field studies in January, 1976.

It is on Highways 186 and 195, as well as 180. The population is reported to be about 100,000.

The park containing the colossal stone heads and other relics from La Venta is still a rewarding place for bird watching and archaeological study. Going west on highway #180 from the main part of town you should be able to see this park on your left just before you come to a conspicuous playground-park. Species to be added to the park list (1968,p.217) are:

Great Egret	Golden-fronted Woodpecker
Snowy Egret	**Barred Wren**
Cattle Egret	Wood Thrush (w.)
Ruddy Ground-Dove	Kentucky Warbler (w.)
Groove-billed Ani	Hooded Warbler (w.)
Ringed Kingfisher	Great-tailed Grackle

Along highway #186 eastward toward Palenque there are numerous water-filled ditches, wet pastures, temporary shallow ponds, and even rather extensive marshes, many within the first eight km. (five mi.) east of the Río Grijalva bridge at Villahermosa. The highway is generally raised here and the shoulders are too narrow for parking, but you might be able to park safely along the shoulder of a side road. If so you could then look over the marshes and wet pastures and expect to find:

Little Blue Heron	Black Vulture
Great Egret	White-tailed Kite
Snowy Egret	**Roadside Hawk**
Cattle Egret	Common Black Hawk
Louisiana Heron	American Kestrel (w.)
Turkey Vulture	Jacana
Yellow-headed Vulture	Black-necked Stilt

Groove-billed Ani   Tropical Kingbird
Ringed Kingfisher   Red-eyed Cowbird
Belted Kingfisher (w.)   Great-tailed Grackle
Vermilion Flycatcher   Eastern Meadowlark

XEL-HA, Quintana Roo - 1984 up-date, based on field studies in April, 1981. See 1976 Suppl. to FBM, p. S93 (or 1976 up-date below).

Xel-Há is just off (east of) Highway 307, at a point about 115 km. south of Cancún, and a little more than 9 km. south of the Akumal turn-off. It is about 13.5 km. north of the Tulum archaeological site turn-off on Highway 307. Coming from the north you would turn left into the park; coming from the south turn right. Follow the signs toward the lagoons and into the parking lot.

Since 1976 several large buildings have been built, and trails and roads and a large parking lot have been constructed within the park. Now the visitor can expect to find, almost any time, hundreds of other persons walking among the lagoons, viewing exhibits, sitting in the restaurant(s) or swimming in the coral-lined lagoons. The lagoons were still beautiful in 1981, it was still possible to see some colorful fish, and occasionally a bird would come into view. Possibly the road branching right (as you enter the park) a short distance from the gate, and within the park might lead to an interesting birding area, or you may possibly find a way to study woodland borders away from the heavily-used areas, but we did not find any such places in the short time we were there in 1981. If you do find a suitable area see the 1976 Tulum write-up for a list of birds which might be at Xel-Há.

Xel-Há, Quintana Roo - New account, 1976, based on field studies in January, 1976.

Xel-Há is in the extreme eastern portion of the Yucatan Region, approximately at sea level. It is about 400 km. or somewhat more, east of Mérida by paved road at present, via Highways 261 and 184 (through Felipe Carrillo Puerto) and Highway 307; and probably about 20 to 50 kilometers farther by way of Highways 180 and 307 through Cancún. It is about 10 to 15 kilometers north of Tulum, and about the same distance south of Akumal. There is apparently no village or settlement of more than a very few families at this locality at this writing. Weather conditions are probably much the same as at Cozumel Island (1976,p.S73).

This is a National Park, very small but well-defined. There is a high fence along the highway and a gate and check-point where an admission fee is collected. A paved road leads eastward from the check-point through rather low but humid woodland to a beautiful blue lagoon bordered by coral rock, with numerous colorful tropical fish. Most of the development in the park seems to have taken place at the lagoon up to now, with picnic areas, walkways, foot-bridges, shelters, and a parking lot near one of the coves of the lagoon. At a point a short distance from the gate as one drives toward the lagoon a paved road branches off to the right, presumably leading to some Maya ruins within the park. This branch road is potentially rewarding as a place to find birds of the humid woodland. The visitor might be able to park at the end of the road or pull off the road and park before reaching the end, and find tracks or trails leading among the trees. Birds to be expected in this area would be those listed (in the discussion of Tulum,p.S89) as having been seen in moderately tall, rather humid woodland 50 to 100 kilometers north of Tulum.

XICOTEPEC (DE JUAREZ), Puebla - 1984 up-date, by Jerry and Nancy Strickling, based on field studies in January, 1982. See 1976 Suppl. to FBM, p. S120 (or 1976 up-date below), and FBM, 1968, p. 219.

Because of new highway construction, Xicótepec is now about 200 km. driving distance from Mexico City.

Local figures indicate that the population is now about 35,000.

As you enter Xicótepec from the west (from Mexico City and Huauchinango) you should see a cemetery on your right, and a suburban motel, the Hotel Mi Ranchito, on your left (1968, p.220). To the rear (north) of the motel is an increasing number of vacation homes, occupied at times by families from Mexico City.

Just beyond (east of) the steeply climbing entrance road into the motel, a street leads to the left and swings back around among the houses in this resort development. Just beyond (east of) *that* street a bypass highway swings left from the main (business route) highway and skirts to the north of the center of town. (Drive cautiously in this congested area, and in the heavy traffic on the narrow, steep, winding roads both east and west of Xicótepec, especially when turning left across traffic. It is not safe to walk along the roadside anywhere, or to stop your car except at designated pull-outs.)

The resort area north and west of, and adjacent to, the Hotel Mi Ranchito is the one mentioned earlier (1968, p.220-221) but the main entrance to the area is now just east of the motel entrance, rather than a few hundred feet west of the motel entrance. There are still some reasonably extensive remnant patches of cloud forest, interspersed among extensive gardens, large homes, orchards, and some partly cleared fields farther to the rear. There is a stream through the area, and still some excellent habitat there as well as on the motel grounds. (Respect gates, fences, and private property in general, including the motel gardens if you're not a guest there.)

Destruction of forest, and conversion of land to agricultural use has proceeded rapidly near Xicótepec. As a result, most of the formerly accessible cloud forest habitat can no longer be found either east or west of town along highway 130. In particular the area about 3.5 miles east of the Hotel Mi Ranchito, which was featured earlier (1968, pp. 221-222) has been greatly altered and most of the birds on the earlier list cannot be expected there now. Similarly, you will find that the situation at the Rancho Santa Maura (FBM, 1968, pp. 223-224) has changed greatly, and you cannot expect to find many of the birds listed, even if you can recognize the location.

Discovery of a "new" area, the road to La Planta, may compensate partially for the loss of the above-mentioned areas as birding habitat. This road leads through some remnants of cloud forest, coffee plantations, orchards and cultivated fields, and on to a spectacular barranca and a hydroelectric plant, thence on to the village of La Union. From there it leads through cultivated fields and partially open countryside and eventually rejoins highway 130 at the town of Gilberto Camacho, about 15 miles east of Xicótepec.

To reach the La Planta road proceed westward from Xicótepec on highway 130 about 3 miles from the Hotel Mi Ranchito going *toward* Mexico City. There you should find a paved road to your left marked by a road sign pointing to La Planta.

If you turn left here (watch for heavy traffic) you proceed into partially cleared ranchlands, where you could profitably stop to look at birds near one of the several wide pull-offs which are to be found as you go along. About three miles from highway 130 you should see a forested area and then shortly a cleared area on your right where there is ample space for parking at what is apparently an excavation site for road construction material. Trails around the borders of the cleared area and along a small stream nearby provide access to the forest, where you have a good chance to see many of the birds (not marked by an asterisk) mentioned (1968,p.222) for the former cloud forest 3.5 miles east of Xicótepec.

Continuing to drive away from Highway 130 you pass through a small village. At this point it is advisable to test your brakes, and to drive in low gear as you begin descending rapidly into the barranca on a steep, winding, narrow road. Soon you will arrive at the hydroelectric plant (La Planta), and once there you can find adequate parking space close to the plant and the nearby coffee plantations. Here, as usual, check with an attendant before looking around the plant or nearby private property. When we visited, the attendant on duty was helpful and had some knowledge of the local birds. Among birds to be seen in the barranca are the **Green Parakeet, Red-lored Parrot,** and **White-collared Swift.** The surrounding coffee plantations afford favorable habitat for many of the species (not marked by an asterisk) formerly expected at Rancho Santa Maura (1968, pp. 223-224).

If you choose to proceed via La Unión to Gilberto Camacho and highway 130, you will descend further, although not as precipitously as before. The partially open, weedy fields and pastures, and croplands, in the vicinity of La Unión afford opportunities to find finches, sparrows, and other grassland birds, possibly some nesting orioles or oropendolas, and soaring or perching raptors.

Xicotepec (de Juarez), Puebla - 1976 up-date, based on library studies.

It is now only about 120 miles from Mexico City by road. We have no population figures but undoubtedly the population is greater than the 7000 of 1968.

Expect fewer patches of cloud forest and modified cloud forest near the highway. Luxuriant gardens, orchards, overgrown fields, wooded stream valleys, and park-like areas should be accessible, however, in the area of former cloud forest near the suburban motel opposite the cemetery (1968,p.220). Most of the species listed (1968,p.221) should still be there.

The area mentioned as being about 3.5 miles from the cemetery, toward the Gulf Coast, on highway 130, has almost certainly been greatly altered by now. Many of the birds marked with an asterisk (1968,p.222) and some others can no longer be found here regularly, unless you can reach favorable habitat farther down the trails or side road.

Remember the words of caution (1968,pp.221-223;1976,Introduction).

In regard to the Rancho Santa Maura, which was 37.5 miles toward the coast from the cemetery and motel in Xicótepec (1968,p.223), expect changes in mileages, land use, location of fences and gates, vegetation, and bird life. If you can find, and work through, patches of humid forest and nearby overgrown fields, or river-edge woodland and nearby woodland-edge, anywhere near here in the lowlands, you could expect many of the birds listed (1968,pp.223-224).

Feb. 1988 - Cautionary note - 1985 Supplement:

Recent press reports indicate that Africanized "killer" bees have reached southeastern Mexico in their northward spread from South America, and pose a threat of serious, even fatal, injury by mass stinging, to persons near where the bees occur. You might obtain further information from the U.S. Dept. of Agriculture or the U.S. Public Health Service.